Seasons
of
Motherhood

A Garden of Memories

Ruth A. Tucker

All Scripture references are from *The Living Bible*,
©1971, Tyndale House Publishers, Wheaton, IL 60189.
Used by permission.

Editor: Barb Williams
Designer: Andrea Boven
Cover Art: *Camille Monet and a Child in the Artist's Garden
in Argenteuil*, 1875: Anonymous gift
in memory of Mr. and Mrs. Edwin S. Webster,
Courtesy Museum of Fine Arts, Boston

Tucker, Ruth, 1945–
Seasons of motherhood / by Ruth A. Tucker.
    p.   cm.
    Includes bibliographical references.
    ISBN 1-56476-537-7
    1. Mothers. 2. Mothers—Case studies. 3. Mother and child—Case studies.
4. Motherhood. I. Title.
HQ759.T93   1996
306.874'3—dc20   95–47006
                                                          CIP

1 2 3 4 5 6 7 8 9 10 Printing/Year 00 99 98 97 96

DEDICATION

In Loving Memory

of my Grandmother

Ida Carlton

and my Mother

Jennie Carlton Stellrecht

and for my Son

Carlton Rand Tucker

CONTENTS

The noblest thoughts my soul can claim,

The holiest words my tongue can frame,

Unworthy are to praise the name

More sacred than all other,

An infant, when her love first came—

A man, I find it just the same;

Reverently I breathe her name,

The blessed name of mother.

GEORGE GRIFFITH FETTER

INTRODUCTION

A s I write these introductory lines, I'm looking out of my cottage window across a
placid bay on Lake Huron at InterVarsity's Cedar
Campus retreat in the Upper Peninsula of Michigan.
University students have come from all over the
country to take the four-week Summer Leadership
Training course, and I'm here for a week of Bible
teaching and interaction with these very bright and
dedicated young people. It's an idyllic setting, and
the challenge of making a difference in their lives
is compelling. I could not have designed a better
way to spend the last week of July. But in the midst
of this picturesque wilderness retreat, hidden
from the students and staff, is a heaviness of heart
that weighs down on me. Outwardly my life
appears to be running almost too smoothly. The
past months have been most fulfilling as I've
taught my usual seminary courses and spoken at
colleges and women's retreats. And just a short time

ago my latest book, *The Family Album*, came off the
press. In September my busy schedule starts up
again—and before then a family reunion. But
the heaviness hangs over me like a thick fog—a burden I would be without were I not a mother.

My twenty-year old son has just gone through
an employment-related crisis, brought on by his
own poor judgment and wrong choices. I know
it will pass as have other problems we've gone
through together, but I'm distraught by this turn
of events, and I so desperately want it to go away.
I'm troubled about how this will affect him in
the long run and whether or not he will allow this
to make him a better man—and a better Christian.
But why do his trials and errors and struggles of
life affect me so deeply?

My own professional and personal life is certainly not without problems. I've faced my share
of publishers' rejections and speeding tickets and

the usual assortment of daily trials that inevitably arise in maintaining a home and meeting airline schedules. But they are only bleeps on the anxiety meter in comparison to the eruptions in life that relate to my role as mother. And yet I realize that my struggles in this area are "kid's play" in comparison to what some mothers endure.

So it is with these sentiments as a backdrop that I write about motherhood. In the minds of some of my colleagues, my subject matter has no doubt deteriorated from what they would perceive as more scholarly pursuits of women's studies, church history, and missiology. But no topic has ever been so much a part of my life and my very personhood. Nor am I alone. The testimonies of mothers through the ages and the tributes to them tell me as a historian that the mother-child relationship is a powerful bond that has affected not just families but whole societies—more so than the father-child bond.

Time and again we read how a young person's life has been molded by the mother. Indeed, from the conversion experience to the career choice, the mother's influence is without equal. And it is her heart that is broken when the child goes astray. Yes, of course, the father is also affected, but distant fathers are not yet an extinct species, and the names of fathers who simply abandon their children continue to fill the pages of court documents.

I was reminded of the mother's preeminence recently when I was paging through a speakers' sourcebook. There were twenty-six entries under the heading *mother* and only one under *father*. The first one for mothers is the oft-quoted Jewish proverb, "God could not be everywhere and so He made mothers." The last one:

 The noblest thoughts my soul can claim,
The holiest words my tongue can frame,
Unworthy are to praise the name
    More sacred than all other,
An infant, when her love first came—
A man, I find it just the same;
Reverently I breathe her name,
    The blessed name of mother.
        GEORGE GRIFFITH FETTER.[1]

Like so many tributes to mother, these lines could be labeled as nothing more than syrupy sentimental drivel, but they represent a collective psyche that has been passed down from generation to generation and continues to this day. For those who say motherhood is diminishing in stature—along with baseball and apple pie—I would take exception. The outward appearance of motherhood changes as do fashions and home furnishings, but the God-given maternal instincts are as strong today as they have ever been. The mother at work watches the clock and waits for the phone to ring in midafternoon, and the mother at home watches at the window. The anxious concern is the same for both. It is simply part of our makeup as mothers.

Yet motherhood is controversial in the politically correct atmosphere of our times. On the one side are those who challenge the prominent place of the mother in domestic activities and child care, insisting that "parenting" is the proper term for modern-day families with fathers sharing equally in the responsibilities. On the other side are those who are lamenting that "motherhood went out of fashion when feminism came in." The controversy reached fever pitch when First Lady Barbara Bush was invited to speak for the graduation ceremony at Wellesley College in 1990. Some of the students protested, arguing that her role as a wife and mother did not qualify her to give the commencement address. The reaction was immediate. "The students' rejection of Barbara Bush," wrote one commentator, "was also a rejection of the concept of motherhood."[2]

Most mothers don't relate to such conflicts. We know that motherhood is still alive and well even though we often find ourselves juggling our responsibilities in the workplace and our responsibilities with our children. We may wish our employers (mostly male) took our mothering more seriously, but we never have a problem doing so ourselves.

Parenting is a good term, but it lacks the force of distinctiveness and personality. Imagine a child saying, "My parent grounded me." Of course not. "My mom grounded me"—a statement that has punch and personality. No amount of language and terminology shifts has the power to blur the differences between mother and father, and this book, without apologies, is about mothers.

I offer the book as a *Garden of Memories*—a book for and about mothers, with a garden theme opening each chapter. I have discovered that my love and efforts expended in gardening are in so many ways parallel to motherhood. The planting, the cul-

tivating, the nurturing, the pruning, the wonderful fragrances—and the disappointing failures. And beyond that— the commitment. I'm into gardening for the long haul. If I were planning to move next year, I probably wouldn't have planted so many flowering perennials and vines last year. But perhaps even more than that, my garden gives me space and time for the healing introspection I need for the mothering side of my life. And it gives me a sense of accomplishment and control that sometimes alludes me as a mother. A recent *Time* magazine article on "power gardening" offered an appropriate analogy that in many ways sums up the parallel between mothering and gardening.

For those anxious about the fate of the family, the garden at least offers the illusion of control, of nurturing something that won't run wild the minute it reaches adolescence.[3]

I'm not sure that my garden offers me the illusion of control that I don't have in mothering, but it does give me an outlet for my mothering instincts that I no longer have with my son now in young adulthood. Where once I watched and played in the sandbox and swing set and tree house with him, I now grow flowers and vines. My thirteen separate gardens in my small backyard take the energy I once expended in caring for him, while at the same time linking me with my past as I think of my mother's gardens in and around the giant oak trees in our yard in front of our blue-shingled farmhouse in northern Wisconsin. And my gardens are appropriately named. On a floral tree-slab plaque hanging from an elm are the words "Carlton Gardens," named for my grandmother, my mother, and my son.

Word association. Stream of consciousness. Seasons. Mother. Garden. Memories. They uniquely tie together. This book is titled for a reason. The words reflect change and relationships and nurture and the span of time—even as a garden grows and changes, never going back to where it was a month ago or a year ago. So it is with mothering. We cherish the memories of days gone by, while recognizing that our relationship with our children spans the seasons of life.

As a wife and mother, Gail MacDonald makes observations on the relationship between gardening and memories that I have found helpful in my own life:

 Removing the spent blossoms on petunias is essential to new blossoms. Today as I removed the old, I was reminded of how essential it is to my life to enjoy each blossom in my life, but to remember to pull it off when spent and move on to new experiences. Many live trying to keep memories of dead blossoms alive only to miss the potential of the new and present bloom.[4]

Yes, we must pick the dead blossoms of life, while at the same time passing the memories and the lessons along to others. As a mother, I have known the joys and sorrows of motherhood, and I hope the story of my own pilgrimage may somehow be a challenge to others. It flows through the narrative mingled with all the emotions that swirl through the currents of mothering. Anne Morrow Lindbergh, on the loss of her baby, says it best:

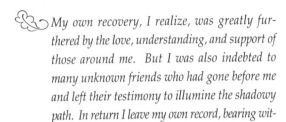 *My own recovery, I realize, was greatly furthered by the love, understanding, and support of those around me. But I was also indebted to many unknown friends who had gone before me and left their testimony to illumine the shadowy path. In return I leave my own record, bearing witness to my journey, for others who may follow.*[5]

I too am indebted to many friends who have gone before me—friends from history who had "left their testimony to illumine the shadowy path." As a historian it is my privilege to share their stories to give variety and color to this seasonal garden of motherhood.

I began these introductory paragraphs in July at a time when I was feeling the weight of a job crisis my son was undergoing. As I finish these paragraphs, many months have gone by, and the employment situation is all but forgotten. We have had happy times, including a late summer family reunion in northern Wisconsin and a quick holiday getaway to the Hyatt-Regency in downtown Chicago.

But my motherhood has once again been assaulted, and I feel the gloom as dense and heavy as the fog that has hung over the Midwest during these unusually mild January days. While thousands of stranded travelers waited impatiently in airports, I paced the floor of a hospital neurological intensive care unit—after my son had been brought in unconscious by ambulance. Head injuries, nineteen stitches inside the mouth, a broken collar bone, and a lacerated liver causing internal bleeding. But he will be all right. He's already on the mend. It could have been so much worse, and I thank God that I'm not making funeral arrangements.

Still, as a mother I agonize over a son's poor judgments and worry that there are too many hard lessons yet to be learned. Motherhood, I'm convinced is the most weighty responsibility God ever invented, and I can understand why some women choose to be childless. But this tension-filled week of worry has made me all the more grateful for the privilege of being a mother. He needs me, and I need him.

The pain and pleasures of motherhood are inexorably intertwined. They come together, and we simply must accept one with the other. With these thoughts in mind, I offer this book as encouragement and affirmation for all mothers everywhere, whatever season of life it may be. What we feel deep inside—that powerful maternal bond—is real and normal and part of God's creative and procreative design.

I also offer this book as a recognition for what mothers have done in the past and are continuing to do and recognition of the very ideal of motherhood. May this ideal never die, and may *mother* always be a word that has special significance in the family, in the church, and in society.

Mabel Barbee Lee, expressing her hopes and reasons for writing *The Gardens in My Life*, beautifully reflects my own thoughts and motivations in writing this book:

 I would write of the healing power that lies in tilling the soil and planting seeds, and bear witness to the way heartbreaking problems may be dissolved in the gentle spray of water on the parched land. I would tell of how the human spirit may be calmed in times of stress by the fragrance of garden flowers on a summer evening, or by noting new dahlia buds about to burst into bloom as one strolls along the path in the dewy morning. A garden offers privacy, I would reveal, not found elsewhere; it is a retreat where one is free to think innermost thoughts and ponderings without fear of ridicule or betrayal. And from this admixture of dreams and hopes may come answers to some of our questions, or a certain philosophy or bits of wisdom may germinate that would lighten the lonely years and lend us insight to meet them with fortitude and grace.[6]

Her love is like an island
In life's ocean, vast and wide,
A peaceful, quiet shelter
From the wind, and rain, and tide.

'Tis bound on the north by Hope,
By Patience on the west,
By tender Counsel on the south,
And on the east by Rest.

Above it like a beacon light
Shine faith, and truth, and prayer;
And through the changing scenes of life,
I find a haven there.

AUTHOR UNKNOWN

1

A Love So Fierce—and Frightening

At thirty-seven and a new bride, Margaret Ruskin had feared that she was too old to have a baby. But her prayers were answered and on February 8, 1819, during a cold, grey London winter, a healthy baby was born to the doting and very protective mother.

John Ruskin's first memories were of his mother—following behind her through her tenderly cared-for garden. She delighted in her garden, and in later years he recalled how "she tended the lilac and laburnum at the front gate."

At the back of the house she had the best pear and apple trees in the neighbourhood. The orchard was seventy years long, a whole world to the small child who followed his mother while she planted and pruned, plucked the peaches and nectarines, and in the spring gathered almond blossoms, the first flowers after the snowdrops.

It was there in that garden that he began to comprehend her fierce love that would follow him as long as she lived. He would marry and become one of the most noted writers and social critics of nineteenth-century England, but always first and foremost he was his mother's son—so much so that his wife (with whom his marriage was never consummated) was surprised to read a poem to him from his mother "in a style almost of amatory tenderness, calling John her beloved and Heart's Treasure and a variety of other terms which only, I believe, a lover would do in addressing a Sonnet to his Mistress."[1]

Reflecting on his mother in later years, Ruskin wrote:

 My mother's influence in molding my character was conspicuous. She forced me to learn daily long chapters of the Bible by heart. To that discipline

and patient, accurate resolve, I owe . . . the best part of my taste for literature.²

The powerful bond of love between John Ruskin and his mother—for good or for ill—is not an isolated anecdote in biographical literature. Stories of this nature abound, and as unhealthy as the relationship may seem, the sons—and, sometimes daughters—often attained great worldly success.

Love is impossible to quantify or to clinically analyze, but having experienced the relational bond that flows from mother to child for more than twenty years, I am convinced that there exists no stronger human love. Indeed, so fierce is this love that it too easily becomes overly protective and unhealthy for both mother and child.

I'll never forget reading a biography several years ago of Mary Baker Eddy, the founder of Christian Science. Mary's mother was quoted as having commented when Mary was a little girl, "sometimes I fear I worship Mary instead of the great Jehovah." My initial reaction was to dismiss the remark as evidence of the kind of unhealthy attachment that inevitably turns a child into some sort of religious cult leader. But on further reflection, I had to ask myself if those were not my own sentiments at times. I have wondered more than once if I could even go on living if something were to happen to my son. I know I could, but the doubt is always there.

That devotion to a child could be comparable to worship of God, I was surprised to discover, is expressed not just in the emotional sentiments of mothers themselves but also in literature and philosophical writings about motherhood. One such reflection comes from Jules Michelet, a Frenchman influenced by Rousseau, who wrote *La Femme* in 1859. Here, he views a mother's child-worship as natural to womanhood:

If the child were not God, if her relationship to him were not a form of religious worship, he would not live. He is so fragile that he would never survive did he not have in this marvelous mother someone who would worship him as if he were divine, render him sweet and desirable—who would in effect sacrifice herself for his sake.³

What do we make of this uncontrollable and unquenchable love? For many mothers it seems almost as natural as breathing itself, but that does not make it entirely good and right.

· · · · · · · · · · · · · · · ·

Sow Bear Love

As a mother, I resonate with Sue Hubbell, who ,like me, is the mother of one child, a son. She struggled with what she perceived to be her maternal instinct to be overprotective. In her book, *A Country Year*, her words speak for me and my relationship with my son Carlton.

When I was pregnant with Brian, I was pleased, curious and interested, but somehow detached and objective about the baby I was carrying. I was young, and had no notion of what he would mean to me.

After she held him for the first time, however, a powerful feeling of uncontrollable love suddenly manifested itself. That immediate intensity of emotion was part of my own experience.

> *There was fierceness to the love that was born the instant I saw him that startled and bewildered me. It was uncivilized, crude, unquestioning, unreasoning.*

Sue did not begin to fully comprehend that love until some years later when she and her family were awakened one night while camping when "an old sow bear" wandered into their campsite and became separated from her cub. In the frantic moments before the cub wandered back, the fierce protective rage of this mother bear threatened the very lives of the startled campers. From this incident, Sue made analogies to her own life:

> *In order to become an adequate mother, I had to learn to keep the old sow bear under control. Sow-bear love is a dark, hairy sort of thing. It wants to hold, to protect; it is all emotion and conservatism. Raising up a man child in the middle of twentieth-century America to be independent, strong, capable and free to use his wit, intellect and abilities required other kinds of love. Keeping the sow bear from making a nuisance of herself may be the hardest thing there is to being a mother.*[4]

An Umbilical Cord from Womb to Tomb

There truly is a bond between mother and child that is like no other bond between human beings. It is a literal physical attachment—the umbilical cord—that is severed at birth, though never entirely. But more than that it is a bond born out of pain and one that mixes pain with joy for a lifetime and ends in the sorrow at the tomb. Anne Fremantle captures this paradoxical relationship in the introduction to her edited volume of short stories, *Mothers: A Catholic Treasury of Great Stories*:

> *"Paradise," said an Eastern sage, "lies at the feet of the mothers." And hell, too. For mother and child is the unique and inevitable group. You must have a mother, and you can have only one. Other family ties are to take or to leave. They can be diverse and various as human nature itself, as saws and proverbs have testified since the world began: "It's a wise child that knows its own father," "they that are of a man's own household are his worst enemies,"—the Bible and world literature are full of such. Between mother and child, the umbilical cord, forcibly cut to permit physical life, must be also psychologically cut to permit complete maturity. But spiritually it never can be severed. Part of the curse of Eve—"I will greatly multiply thy sorrow and thy*

conception, in sorrow thou shalt bring forth thy children," it is the whole glory of Mary: "Behold, thou shalt conceive in thy womb and bring forth a son."

How poignantly our mothers cherish us, and how fully we reciprocate, or fail to. . . . For in this our journey between womb and tomb, in which every one of us "is born in other's pain, and perish in our own," the only reality is relationship, and the most universally and eternally valid relationship is that of mother.[5]

· · · · · · · · · · · · · · · · ·

Mother's Love

Her love is like an island
    In life's ocean, vast and wide,
A peaceful, quiet shelter
    From the wind, and rain, and tide.

'Tis bound on the north by Hope,
    By Patience on the west,
By tender Counsel on the south,
    And on the east by Rest.

Above it like a beacon light
    Shine faith, and truth, and prayer;
And through the changing scenes of life,
    I find a haven there.

AUTHOR UNKNOWN[6]

· · · · · · · · · · · · · · · · ·

Undying Love

The French poet Jean Richepin captured the capacity for a mother's undying love in a story of a mother and son who had lived together in harmony until an evil and heartless woman snared the son and demanded he love her exclusively. The story carries a sentimentality that few mothers could actually identify with, but the message of mother-love is inescapable. The young woman, jealous of the young man's love for his mother, demands that he demonstrate his loyalty to her:

I want the final proof of your devotion. I am afraid that you still have some affection left for your mother. I want you to go to your mother, murder her, tear out her heart, and bring it to me. Then I shall know that you love only me.

The young man, swayed by his lover's evil power over him, submitted to her ghastly request. He killed his mother, cut out her heart, and hurried back to his lover. But in his haste, he stumbled and fell and dropped his mother's heart on the ground. At that moment he was startled by a tender and familiar voice:

"Did you hurt yourself, my dear son?" asked the mother's heart.[7]

The Force of Motherhood

Mary Ann Evans, a nineteenth-century English novelist whose pen name was George Eliot, was not close to her mother who died when she was a teenager. Her deepest attachment was for her father. Yet she penned some of the most often-quoted lines on motherhood. Like many who give tributes to motherhood, she recognized the universality of mother-love, though she herself apparently did not experience or relish it.

 Mighty is the force of motherhood, it transforms all things by its vital heat; it turns timidity into fierce courage, and dreadless defiance into tremulous submission. It turns thoughtlessness into foresight, and yet stills all anxiety into calm content. It makes selfishness become self-denial, and gives even to hard vanity the glance of admiring love.[8]

A Love That Transcends All Other Affections

Washington Irving, remembered as America's first great writer, was the son of a strict Calvinist father. Deacon Irving shunned the fun and joys of life, believing from childhood that "everything that was pleasant was wicked." Washington's mother was the opposite of her husband. "A laughing woman, a loving woman, she did what she could to mitigate the sense of gloom and doom with which her husband filled the household. . . ." The boy

deeply resented his father and never wrote favorably of him. Not so his mother.

 Oh! there is an enduring tenderness in the love of a mother to her son that transcends all other affections of the heart. It is neither to be chilled by selfishness, nor daunted by danger, nor weakened by worthlessness, nor stifled by ingratitude. She will sacrifice every comfort to his convenience; she will surrender every pleasure to his enjoyment; she will glory in his fame, and exult in his prosperity— and, if misfortune overtake him, he will be the dearer to her from misfortune; and if disgrace settle upon his name, she will still love and cherish him in spite of his disgrace; and if all the world beside cast him off, she will be all the world to him.[9]

The Fierce Love for Her Child Leads a Marxist to God

Dorothy Day was one of the celebrated leaders of the working classes during the first half of this century—before and after she converted to Christianity and was baptized into the Roman Catholic Church.

Prior to her conversion, she was haunted by the slogan, "Religion is the opiate of the people," but after her baby was born her perspective was profoundly altered. She encountered a new dimension to love, and that love for her child led directly to a confident belief in the source of all love— God. She was instinctively drawn to God, even though she knew it would mean abandonment by her Marxist husband.

Our child was born in March at the end of a harsh winter. . . . When the little one was born, my joy was so great that I sat up in bed in the hospital and wrote an article for the New Masses about my child, wanting to share my joy with the world. I was glad to write this joy for a workers' magazine because it was a joy all women knew, no matter what their grief at poverty, unemployment and class war. The article so appealed to my Marxist friends that the account was reprinted all over the world in workers' papers. . . .

One of the disconcerting facts about the spiritual life is that God takes you at your word. Sooner or later one is given a chance to prove his love. . . . It was all very well to love God in His works, in the beauty of His creation which was crowned for me by the birth of my child. . . . The final object of this love and gratitude was God. No human creature could receive or contain so vast a flood of love and joy as I often felt after the birth of my child. With this came the need to worship, to adore. . . .[10]

. . . .

Is Mother Love an Illusion?

Many contemporary feminists and therapists are so perplexed by the profound expression of maternal love they observe that they seek to explain it away or call it something else. The concept of mother-love is a myth, argues Nancy Friday, the author of the best-selling book *My Mother, My Self*. In this massive study of the relationships of mothers and daughters, including her own relationship with her mother, she concludes that a unique maternal instinct to love a child that is said to characterize mothers is more an illusion than a reality. She suggests that a mother's love is often nothing more than possessiveness or anxiety.

There is much more in Friday's book than debunking the "myth" of mother-love. I commend her for her study, but on the issue of mother-love, I ask myself, why does it have to be either one or the other. Anxiety and possessiveness are part and parcel of maternal love. Any mother knows these feelings coexist with maternal love in healthy and harmful degrees. Yet, Friday's perspective serves as a challenge to mothers while posing no threat to secure motherhood, and she correctly points out that *motherhood* does not automatically correspond with *mother-love*.

 We are raised to believe that mother love is different from other kinds of love. It is not open to error, doubt, or to the ambivalence of ordinary affections. This is an illusion. . . .

I have heard daughters say that they do not love their mothers. I have never heard a mother say she does not love her daughter. Psychoanalysts have told me that a woman patient would rather consider herself "crazy" than admit that she simply does not like her daughter. She can be honest about anything else, but the myth that mothers always love their children is so controlling that even the daughter who can admit disliking her mother, when her own time comes, will deny all but positive emotions toward her children. . . . We want to believe that love is the motivation for everything mother does. Often it is not love, but . . . possessiveness [or] anxiety.[11]

A Love That Never Dies

Mother-love is a powerful force that lives long after the death of a child, as Faye Moskowitz illustrates in her book, *A Leak in the Heart*. Reflecting back on her childhood, journalist and newspaper commentator Faye tells about a lazy, warm Michigan summer day when she had climbed the steep steps up to the attic looking for something to occupy her time. While snooping through the trunks and boxes, she discovered photographs of a baby whose features were familiar but whose face she didn't recognize. When she went down to the kitchen to inquire of her mother about the little girl in the photos, she was met with an unexpected flood of emotion—an outpouring of grief that made her realize many years later how deep the love is between a mother and a child.

 I was ten years old when I first learned of my sister's existence. What puzzled me most was the depth of sorrow engendered by such a slim life span. I felt my mother's anguish was inexplicable, couldn't fathom why every visible trace of the child had been removed as though the clotting of pain was so fragile, that the merest shudder could set it to bleeding again.

    And I didn't understand for years until I had my own baby and saw in the moist bundle of flesh and bone my own freedom and feelings, bound now by inextricable knots that could only be cut but never loosened. . . . A friend wept at her mother's death and would not be consoled. "I'll never

allow myself to love anyone like that again," she said, but the two curly-headed girls who sat, stunned to silence by their mother's tears, had already made her words meaningless. . . .[12]

I felt that same grief at my mother's funeral. I had lost the one whose undying love for me never wavered—a love that was still in the future tense for me. It was not until five years after her death that I could comprehend her love for me—through the intensity of my own love for my son.

"Like a She-Lion with Her Cubs"

When more than a thousand mothers were surveyed in the 1980s by National Family Opinion, Inc., more than nine out of ten believed that a mother's love is an emotion stronger than any other. The comments these women made give flesh and blood to the survey:

 My love for my child is uppermost in my mind. It is all consuming. If I lost the love of another person it would leave a deep scar. If I lost the love of my child it would be a living hell.

    The deepest love in the world is a mother's love for her own flesh and blood. I loved my husband who is now deceased very much, but I'm glad I never had to make a choice between him and our kids.

It's totally overwhelming, like a she-lion with her cubs.

It's fiercer. More integral. The sound of a child's voice raises a heartbeat that even the greatest romance can't aspire to. It's blind and forever in a way that nothing can rival.

What they feel, I feel. It's an indescribable love. I'd rather be sick, hurt, or blind than for one of my children to be.

A mother's love for her child is different because it is all encompassing and big enough to love them through health, illness, good and bad. It can stand more abuse than other relationships, even marriage. With others you love and care, but would you give your life for them? I would for any of my children.[13]

. . . .

Risking Her Life for Her Daughter

Few mothers are ever put in the position to risk their lives for their children. One mother who did not hesitate to put her life on the line for her child has told her story in *Not Without My Daughter*, a best-selling book made into a movie.

When Betty Lover married Moody in the summer of 1977, she was convinced she had found the man of her dreams. She was in love, and she relished the flowers and gifts and notes of affection that he showered upon her. He was an Iranian who had lived most of his life in America—a well-educated professional, an anesthesiologist, Dr. Mahmoody.

In 1979, they celebrated the birth of a baby girl, Mahtob, while they enjoyed all the luxuries the high-paying physician's salary afforded. But the happiness of their early years of marriage dissipated as the Iranian revolution progressed in Moody's homeland and as problems arose in his American medical practice.

In 1982, Betty's life suddenly began to unravel. Her husband's growing excitement about a family visit to Iran terrified her—fearing that once there he would not allow them to return home. As it turned out, her suspicions proved true. In Iran, she quickly realized she was trapped with her little girl.

Through months of secret meetings and contacts back home, she arranged for an escape, but not without the terrorizing fear that she would somehow lose her darling daughter or her own life in the process. Fleeing Iran to save her daughter was the most traumatic ordeal of her life, that came to an end only after crossing the border into Turkey:

 She held me close until she fell into a deep sleep. She felt wonderful in my arms, and I tried to find a measure of comfort in her trusting sleep. My own mind still buzzed. Every part of my body throbbed in pain. I was ravenously hungry. Sleep came fitfully over the next few hours. Most of my time was spent in prayer, thanking God for bringing us this far, yet still asking for more. Please, dear God, stay with us the rest of the way, I implored. It is the only way we will make it. . . . Mahtob and I arrived home in Michigan on February 7, 1986. . . .[14]

As I conclude this first chapter, I wonder how my feminist friends are going to react to what they may perceive as my slippery slide into sentimentality. I remember the negative reaction I got some years ago while working on a gender studies team when I expressed my enthusiasm for the "mommy track." I was delighted that corporate America seemed to be waking up to the reality that many mothers wanted less than full-time careers. But some of my colleagues thought I had caved in to a scheme to keep women "barefoot and pregnant." They were arguing that the daddies should have to go on the "mommy track" too, while I was insisting that scaled-back hours in the workplace was a great bonus for women— if they could afford it. Motherhood is a controversial topic—even as is the subtopic of mother-love.

How do we analyze mother-love—in light of compelling testimonies of mothers on the one hand and, on the other hand, the challenges to the "myth" that appears in much of the literature today? From my own vantage point, it seems that certain feminists and therapists have tried too hard to discredit and debunk this profound reality of motherhood. But I readily admit that my own experience colors my perspective.

After trying for most of a year, I became pregnant in the fall of 1973. At the time I was consumed with my doctoral work in history at Northern Illinois University, and I thought very little about the implications of motherhood. My attention was focused on Marcus M. Pomeroy, a nineteenth-century journalist and political activist, the subject of my dissertation.

I was far removed from any kind of sentimental hype touting the exhilaration of childbirth or the intensity of maternal love, and in many ways the pregnancy and birth were matter-of-fact, predictable experiences.

What I did not anticipate was the powerful bond of love such as I had never felt before. Unlike love for a parent that develops apart from conscious awareness, and unlike romantic love that asks questions and demands mutuality, a mother's love for a child erupts spontaneously and never dies.

Just today I was reminded of that love as I was driving across town with my son, tuned into my favorite country music station. I turned up the dial, recognizing a song from a few years back that tells the story of a wayward son and a mother's undying love. The chorus expresses the sentiments as only a country twang could do: "Jesus and Mamma always loved me, even when the devil gained control; Jesus and Mamma always loved me, this I know."

There are obvious exceptions to every rule, and everyone knows a "Mommie Dearest" to marshal forth as proof, but no exceptions will ever quench the reality of mother-love born out by testimonies and tributes throughout the generations of motherhood.

All that is

good in my life

has come from

my mother.

Dwight L. Moody

2

Tributes to Motherhood in Poetry, Prose, and Letters

I wear for you, Mother, sweet violets of blue,
That waft me to girlhood and visions of you.
They hold in their perfume, mysterious power
To bring you close to me, our symbol this flower.

I wear for you, Mother, sweet violets of blue;
They draw me in memory to your guidance true.
I liken their fragrance to your tenderness,
Your soul strength pervasive, and your nobleness.

SERENA TRUMAN ROBINSON[1]

It may be tempting to laugh or scoff at the flowery sentimentalism so often associated with motherhood. We all know that mothers are not as holy and pure and perfect as the sugary lines often portray them to be. But these tributes of love nevertheless tell us a great deal about the beloved. Unlike the poetry and verse of romance that delivers a message of love in order to enhance courtship and lovemaking, the poetic lines to mothers are love notes of gratitude. There is no love to win and no apparent insecurity. The message is rather one of praise, recognition, and thankfulness for an unswerving love.

Men and women in every station of life have expressed tributes to their mothers, but the most often quoted are those penned by famous men. I had expected to find that these men always had close and warm relationships with their mothers, but many of them did not. Some of them lived very troubled lives exacerbated by overbearing mothers, but their mothers were nevertheless revered—at least as an ideal.

It was during the Victorian era of the late nineteenth century that the glorification of motherhood reached a peak. The tributes to mothers were part of the "cult of true womanhood" that placed women on a pedestal and almost deified them. But this perspective did not go unchallenged. One of the most outspoken feminists (and Marxists) of the day was Charlotte Perkins Gilman.

 She attacked "modern mother-worship" with gusto. After scornfully describing the mother cult—"the dying soldier on the battlefield thinks of his mother, longs for her, not for his father. The traveler and exile dreams of his mother's care, his mother's doughnuts"—she declared that "human motherhood is more pathological than any other, more morbid, defective, irregular, diseased." As a consequence, "human childhood is similarly pathological." Mothers were untrained and uninformed about their duties: "The human mother does less for her young, both absolutely and proportionately, than any other kind of mother on earth."[2]

No matter how hard they tried, Gilman and her feminist cohorts were unable to silence the tributes to motherhood. And the tributes continue today—sometimes sugary and sweet and sometimes no more than a "Hi, Mom" when the TV camera offers one moment in the limelight. Most of the mothers have been lost in obscurity, but the tributes passed down by their often-famous sons live on.

Bookshelves all over the world are crowded with biographies of men who have achieved success. Scan such lives closely and behind many you will find the profound influence of a mother. Hers, in a normal family life, is the controlling and civilizing force impressed upon the man in the period of his greatest plasticity. It is his mother who stimulates him to high ambitions who impresses upon him his most cherished ideals of personal conduct.[3]

How fortunate when a child pays tribute to a mother during her lifetime. I have been blessed with such good fortune. There are no public memorials or published accolades. But on many occasions Carlton has commented that he was telling a friend about something I had done that had made him proud or telling me that we have the best mother-son relationship of anyone he knows. The validity of his remarks are to me less important than the expression of devotion. Indeed, when he told a friend that his mom was as good a writer as C.S. Lewis, I was relieved to learn that the friend didn't have a clue as to who that celebrated author was.

In my search for tributes to mothers I have found that sons were more likely to write sentimental poetry or one-liners about their mothers—or the ideal of motherhood—while daughters tended to be more intimate and personal, often paying tribute to their mothers in letters. There were, of course, exceptions to the rule, as we will see in "Billy" Faulkner's letter to his mother and Fanny Crosby's poetic praise of motherhood. Many mothers were privileged and blessed to receive loving tributes while they were still living, but for others it came too late for them to relish—as was true of John Quincy Adams' tribute to his mother.

"My Mother Was an Angel"

More than any other woman, Abigail Adams ranks as the mother of the new nation that was born in 1788. She was the Vice President's wife in the Washington administration, the First Lady when her husband succeeded Washington, and also the President's mother, with the election of her son John Quincy. Abigail was a doting mother, and there was a powerful bond of love between mother and son—a bond that daughter-in-law Louisa found threatening during the early years of marriage. In his old age, long after his mother had died, John Quincy wrote a moving tribute to his mother—one that Louisa might have questioned on some points:

 My mother was an angel upon earth. She was a minister of blessing to all human beings within her sphere of action. Her heart was the abode of heavenly purity. She had no feelings but of kindness and beneficence, yet her mind was as firm as her temper was mild and gentle. She had known sorrow, but her sorrow was silent. . . . If there is existence and retribution beyond the grave, my mother is happy. But if virtue alone is happiness below, never was existence upon earth more blessed than hers.[4]

A Little Boy Taken "From the Arms of a Godly Mother"

By all counts Abigail Adams was the kind of super-mom who deserved accolades, but even when mothers failed their children, they were often accorded high tribute. To suggest that Mary Jane Sunday was a failure as a mother is a harsh judgment. Times were different in the nineteenth century, and perhaps children were more forgiving than they are today.

Mary Jane's son was Billy, the much-celebrated American revivalist preacher of the early decades of the twentieth century, who is remembered for his flamboyant style of preaching and his colorful language and strings of quotable one-liners. He was outspoken and brash, but underneath the egotistical exterior was a man who had endured great rejection and insecurity from his earliest childhood. His own circumstances as a little boy seem difficult to reconcile with one of his most memorable tributes to motherhood:

 I don't think there are enough devils in hell to take a young person from the arms of a godly mother.

Yet Billy Sunday himself was taken "from the arms of a godly mother" when he was only ten years old and placed in an orphanage. After his father died, his widowed mother became so impoverished that she believed that the only option left was to send her two boys away to a Soldier's Orphans Homes in Iowa. Years later, Billy vividly recalled the incident:

 When we climbed into the wagon to go to town I called out, "Good-by trees, good-by spring." I put my arms around my dog named Watch and kissed him.
The train left about one o'clock in the morn-

ing. We went to the little hotel near the depot to wait. . . .

The proprietor awakened us about twelve-thirty, saying, "The train is coming." I looked into my mother's face. Her eyes were red and her cheeks wet from weeping, her hair disheveled. While Ed and I slept she had prayed and wept. We went to the depot, and as the train pulled in she drew us to her heart, sobbing as if her heart would break.[5]

. . . .

Letters from Billy

Another Billy who had great reverence for his mother was William Faulkner, one of the great twentieth-century American novelists. He paid high tribute to his mother, Maud, in his letters. As a young man, he wrote her every week, expressing his affections and keeping her up to date on his writing progress. His style was informal and affectionate, as this letter written in 1918 illustrates:

Darling Momsey

I have so much to tell you that I don't know where to begin. Tomorrow I'm going to write you everything I know. . . . I love you more than all the world.

Billy

Faulkner's tributes to motherhood were also evident in his fiction. In *The Sound and the Fury*, Quentin, knowing the end is near, cries out in despair, "If I'd just had a mother so I could say Mother Mother."

Faulkner did have such a mother, and their love rose far above sentimentality to mutual concern and understanding. In a letter to his mother while he was a student at Yale, he wrote, "I couldn't live here at all but for your letters. I love you darling." In 1925, he wrote, "What's the trouble, moms? I know something is wrong from your last letter."[6]

. . . .

Tributes from Famous Sons

All that I am my mother made me.

JOHN QUINCY ADAMS

Men are what their mothers make them.

RALPH WALDO EMERSON

All that is good in my life has come from my mother.

DWIGHT L. MOODY

*A mother is a mother still
The holiest thing alive.*

SAMUEL TAYLOR COLERIDGE

*The angels . . . singing unto one another,
Can find among their burning, terms of love,
none so devotional as that of "mother."*

EDGAR ALLAN POE

The happiest part of my happy life has been my mother.

PHILLIPS BROOKS

*Mother, her very name stands for loving unselfish-
ness and self-abnegation, and, in any society fit
to exist is fraught with associations which render
it holy.*

THEODORE ROOSEVELT

*My mother was the making of me. She was so sure
of me, that I felt I had someone to live for, someone I must not disappoint.*

THOMAS EDISON

 *The love of a mother is never exhausted. It
never changes—it never tires—it endures through
all, in good repute, in bad repute, in the face of
the world's condemnation, a mother's love still
lives on.*

WASHINGTON IRVING

*All mothers are rich when they love their own. There
are no poor mothers, no ugly ones, no old ones. Their
love is always the most beautiful of the joys. And
when they seem most sad it needs but a kiss which
they receive or give to turn all their tears into stars
in the depth of their eyes.*

MAURICE MAETERLINCK

 *One lamp, thy mother's love, amid the stars shall
lift its pure flame, changeless and before the throne
of God burn through eternity.*

N.P. WILLIS

· ·

The Sweetest Name That Earth Can Know

Sometimes tributes paid to mothers may have
been inspired in part by the failure of fathers. I have
wondered if that might have been true for Fanny
Crosby, America's most celebrated hymn writer.
Her mother, Mercy, was abandoned by her husband,
Thomas—Fanny's stepfather—when Fanny was
a young woman. It came unexpectedly when
one day he announced that he was moving the family to Illinois to join the Mormons under the leadership of their founder, Joseph Smith. Mercy
would have no part of it, but Thomas was determined to go, with or without her. He later followed
Brigham Young to Utah, and neither Mercy nor
Fanny ever saw him again.

Fanny wrote many personal tributes to her
mother, but the greatest tribute was to motherhood—
to the name of mother, "that sweetest name that
earth can know:

 The light, the spell-word of the heart,
    Our guiding star is weal or woe,
Our talisman, our earthly chart—
    That sweetest name that earth can know.

We breathed it first with lisping tongue
    When cradled in her arms we lay;
Fond memories round that name are hung
    That will not, cannot pass away.

We breathed it then, we breathe it still,
  More dear than sister, friend or brother;
The gentle power, the magic thrill
  Awakened by the name of mother.[7]

· · · · · · · · · · · · · · · · · · ·

A Letter to a Sweetheart

Imagine going to the mailbox and reaching in and pulling out a letter addressed in familiar handwriting and then opening it up to find price-less treasure—a letter from a grown child paying loving tribute to you as a mother. I wonder at the swirl of emotions that must have overflowed on that June day in 1921, when the mother of Edna St. Vincent Millay, one of America's premier women poets, opened the letter from her twenty-nine year old daughter. What more could a mother ask for than a grateful child.

 Mother, do you know, almost all people love their mothers, but I have never met anybody in my life, I think, who loved his mother as much as I love you. I don't believe there ever was anybody who did, quite so much, and quite in so many wonderful ways. I was telling somebody yesterday that the reason I am a poet is entirely because you want-ed me to be and intended I should be, even from the very first. You brought me up in the tradition of poetry, and everything I did you encouraged. I can-not remember once in my life when you were not interested in what I was working on, or even sug-gested that I should put it aside for something else. Some parents of children that are "different" have

so much to reproach themselves with. But not you, Great Spirit. . . .

  If I didn't keep calling you Mother, anybody reading this would think I was writing to my sweetheart. And he would be quite right.[8]

· · · · · · · · · · · · · · · · · · ·

Mother

 You painted no Madonnas
  On chapel walls in Rome;
But, with a touch diviner,
  Upon the walls of home.

You wrote no lofty poems
  With rare poetic art;
But, with a finer vision,
  You put poems in my heart.

You carved no shapeless marble
  To symmetry divine;
But, with a nobler genius,
  You shaped this soul of mine.

You built no great cathedrals,
  The centuries applaud;
But, with a grace exquisite,
  Your heart was house of God.

Had I the gift of Raphael,
  Or Michelangelo,
Oh, what a rare Madonna
  My mother's life should show.

THOMAS W. FESSENDEN[9]

Valentines for Mother

Today Valentine's Day is referred to as Sweetheart's Day, and most of the cards feature romantic verse designed for a lover. But in the good old days—particularly during Victorian times—Valentines were sent to mothers—the love of any young man's or young woman's life. An 1878 Valentine featured a typical sweetheart poem, with a clear spiritual message:

Blessed Dear and Heart's Delight,
  Companion, Friend and Mother mine,
Round whom my fears and love entwine,—
    With whom I hope to stand and sing
    Where Angels for the outer ring
Round singing Saints, who clad in white,
Know no more of day or night
      Or death or any changeful thing,
      Or anything that is not love,
Human love and Love Divine,—
      Bid me to that tryst above,
        Bless you Valentine.[10]

The Holy Name of Mother

O magical word, may it never die from the lips that
    love to speak it,
Nor melt away from the truest hearts that even would
    break to keep it.

Was there ever a name that lived like thine! Will
    there ever be another?
The angels have reared in heaven a shrine to the
    holy name of Mother.

AUTHOR UNKNOWN[11]

Helen Keller's Tribute to Her Mother

Helen Keller has inspired generations of children and adults around the world through her triumph over blindness and deafness. As a little girl she was "locked in the dark and silent prison of her own body," but her mother communicated to her little girl through the language of a mother's love, and she believed in her daughter and found teachers who could set her free to communicate with the world. Because of her profound sensory challenges, Helen's relationship with her mother was so intense and deep that it was almost beyond human understanding, as Helen relates in her autobiography, published when she was twenty-two.

 How shall I write of my mother? She is so near to me that it almost seems indelicate to speak of her.

Her letters to her mother when she was away at school in Boston, express openly her depth of love—and speak of seeing her mother as certain as though she had her eyesight:

South Boston, Nov. 10, 1890

 My Dearest Mother:—My heart has been full of thoughts of you and my beautiful home ever since we parted so sadly on Wednesday night. How I wish I could see you this lovely morning, and tell you all that has happened since I left home! . . . But I cannot see you and talk to you, so I will write and tell you all that I can think of. . . . Now, sweet mother, your little girl must say good-bye.

With much love to father, Mildred, you and all the dear friends, lovingly your little daughter,

HELEN A. KELLER [12]

Mother O' Mine

 If I were hanged on the highest hill,
Mother o' mine, O mother o' mine!
I know whose love would follow me still,
Mother o' mine, O mother o' mine!

If I were drowned in the deepest sea,
Mother o' mine, O mother o' mine!
I know whose tears would come down to me,
Mother o' mine, O mother o' mine!

If I were damned of body and soul,
I know whose prayer would make me whole,
Mother o' mine, O mother o' mine!

RUDYARD KIPLING [13]

A Letter from Karen

Karen Blixen, whose autobiographical masterpiece *Out of Africa* would make her famous, paid high tribute to her mother who had been left with the responsibility for her five children after her husband committed suicide when Karen was ten years old. In 1913, when she was in her late twenties, Karen left Denmark to marry and make her home in Kenya. From there she wrote fascinating letters about life in Africa to the woman she spoke of as "My own beloved wonderful little Mother." In one of those letters she paid high tribute to this one who had given her birth:

No doubt each one of your children thinks that he or she loves you most, and so do I. It is probably not true. But each one cares for you in his or her own way, and I think that there is something in the way I love you that resembles the way Father loved you. For me you are the most beautiful and wonderful person in the world; merely the fact that you are alive makes the whole world different; where you are there is peace and harmony, shade and flowing springs, birds singing; to come to where you are is like entering "heaven." [14]

Kathy Miller's Tribute

Tributes to mothers and to the ideal of motherhood offer insights on the relationship between the child and mother—even when they are overly sentimentalized. But the most moving and revealing tributes to mothers that I have discovered in my research are not the ones that portray her as an angel with no flaws, but the ones that portray a woman of strength and devotion doing the best she can under difficult circumstances—as in the case of Kathy Miller's mother.

It was in the spring of 1977, that thirteen-year-old Kathy Miller was struck by a car in a tragic accident. The resulting injuries left her in a coma for more than ten weeks and the prognosis was grim. But Kathy beat all odds, and was able to compete in a 10,000 meter race just six months later. Kathy credits her mother for the patience and strength necessary to bring her through this terrible ordeal. In the process, she testifies that God fashioned a new mother and a new daughter.

 When I first woke up . . . Mom was the first *person I saw. Later, she was the first person I called by name. . . . She was really loving. She really tried to help me. It seemed like a long horror story, but she stuck by me through every bit of it. And during that long recovery period, there began to be big changes in Mom and big changes in me. . . . I can look back now and see the position I was in before the accident, and the kind of self-centered person I would have grown up to be. But that all got stopped. Praise God! I can truly thank Him for that accident. . . . While I was recovering, Mom was always pushing me to get out a little further, try a little harder, and she helped by encouraging me that I could do it. She wasn't critical any more; she was constantly encouraging. . . . She never forced me, just encouraged me, and waited for me to be ready within myself.*

My "old" mother didn't have patience like that. My "new" mother had all the patience in the world.[15]

When I think of tributes of mothers, I'm reminded of Proverbs 31, one of the well-known chapters in the Bible—especially the portion that is referred to as "the ideal woman." The heading on this chapter tells us that the verses consist of "sayings of King Lemuel—an oracle his mother taught him." It is here we find those glorious seven words that are music to a mother's ears:

 Her children arise and call her blessed.

Motherhood is the most intense and all-consuming obligation and opportunity that I will ever encounter in life, but I will feel more than adequately rewarded if it's ever said of me:

 Her son arises and calls her blessed.

≥© *When she was sober, she was the sweetest, most sensitive, loving, and intelligent person you could ever meet. But when she was drunk she was a holy terror. . . . I discovered I could hide the painful feelings and still make friends and love dogs and help old ladies across the street and be a good guy. I had lots of buddies, but no really close friend. I learned to be self-contained and independent. Maybe that was a gift my mother gave me.*

GENERAL H. NORMAN SCHWARZKOPF

3

Mommie Dearest

Not all mothers' gardens are full of colorful flowers and sunshine, as the 1976 documentary film *Grey Gardens* illustrates. The film tells the tragic story of Edith Beale (sister of Jacqueline Onassis) and her daughter Edith. "Little Edie" managed to free herself from her controlling mother by fleeing to New York to become a model, only to be called home to Grey Gardens in 1952 to care for the ailing "Big Edie." During the next two decades "Little Edie" rarely left her mother and the estate in East Hampton—one exception being the Kennedy Presidential Inauguration. The two Edies became enmeshed in their own world of Grey Gardens, the daughter accusing the mother of selfishness and blaming her for driving away any prospective boyfriends. Together they made headlines in a celebrated court case charging them with health code violations involving their hundreds of cats.[1]

Without nurture and loving care, children can whither away as surely as the blooming annuals and flowering shrubs in our gardens. But we've all seen lovely gardens that somehow thrive without attention. They may be a bit wild and overgrown, but they develop a hardiness that is sustained on sunshine and rain without much human intervention. So also with children. The "Mommie Dearest" stories are often as flourishing as the trumpet vine I planted over the gate that opens into my backyard. It grows whether I care for it or not, mocking me with its bright orange flowers and lure for hummingbirds.

As I have researched motherhood—particularly paging through biographies and autobiographies, the truth I have discovered that stands out above all others is that mothers are good or bad not necessarily according to their own merit but rather how they are perceived in the minds of their children.

I have the good fortune of having a son who

easily forgets the bad and accentuates the good in me—especially when he is talking to his friends or proudly telling associates at work about his mom, the writer. I know in my heart that I haven't been a bad mother, but if he were so inclined to write a "Mommie Dearest" tale, I'm sure he could dredge up enough raw material for a brief book—or at least a short story. So when I read such accounts written by children—especially when the accusations are somewhat vague, I always wonder, *Was she really a lot worse mother than I am, or is this a matter of perspective?* And the opposite is also true. Some of the most flattering tributes from the pens of children are given to abusive "bad" mothers.

There is a special bond between mother and child, and even the most mistreated child will often cover up and deny parental abuse—perhaps to internalize the deeply embedded belief that a mother is, by her very nature, a good mother and a loving mother. In *My Mother, My Self*, Nancy Friday writes:

 The most extreme example of our need to believe in the all-loving mother is found with battered children. Take a severely abused and physically mistreated child and put it with a loving foster mother. Again and again it is found that the child will prefer to go back to the original cruel mother. Stronger than the desire for cessation of the beating and abuse, stronger than life itself, the child wants to perpetuate her illusion that she had a good mother.[2]

The worst examples of mothering make the headlines. Recently I heard news reports of a woman who threw her babies over a bridge into the water below and then jumped herself—only to be rescued with one of the babies. The other one drowned. And the story of Susan Smith's drowning of her two beautiful little boys in a lake near Union, South Carolina, is not one that will be quickly erased from our memories.

Some of the abuse is not quite so apparent. A woman in Grand Rapids is on trial as I write this for negligent homicide. Her crime: falling asleep while her child crawled into a cedar chest in the next room and was smothered to death—a mother who apparently truly loved her child.

I know from personal experience that there is a fine line that exists between the compassionate love of a mother and negligence or the destructive violence—verbal or physical—that a mother is capable of wielding. I recall an incident when Carlton was not yet two years old. It was late morning and I was in bed with the most dreadful headache I've ever experienced. Three visits to three doctors had brought no relief, and I was afraid I was losing my mind. I was home alone "watching" Carlton, when I heard a strange noise out in the living room. I ventured out of bed, and there he was—somehow managing to reach up to the top of the shelf by the window and dumping out potted plants one after another on my big round beige rug. I screamed and started to lunge at him, but I restrained myself—suddenly paralyzed with a realization that I dare not go near him at that moment. Yet, as I look back I know how close I came to seriously hurting my child. And I realize that I was a negligent mother trying to care for him while I was so ill.

But, fortunately for me, Carlton doesn't remember the potted-plant experience and other incidents that might label me as a "Mommie Dearest." This was not the case with novelist Jack London, whose garden experience with his mother was forever etched in his memory:

 Young Jack had a happy relationship with his mom until a day when he was about three years old and brought her a flower picked from the yard. "I was brushed aside," he recalled, "and kicked over, by a rebellious woman, striding her egomaniacal way." Up to that moment, London said, he had believed his mother to be "the most wonderful woman in the world because she said so herself."[3]

. . . .

Mommie Dearest and a Spring Daffodil Dress

The term "Mommie Dearest" has become a part of everyday vocabulary since Christina Crawford wrote an autobiographical account of her life with her mother, Joan Crawford, by that title. The first chapter begins with the news of Joan Crawford's death in 1977—a sure sign that "Mommie" will not have an opportunity to respond to her daughter's accusations. The book ends with the opening of the will, which designated money for personal secretaries and charities, but nothing for Christina: "It is my intention to make no provision herein for my son Christopher or my daughter Christina for reasons which are well known to them." So, is *Mommie Dearest* a daughter's revenge? Perhaps so, but it is also the story of a troubled mother who abused alcohol and her children, punishing them unmercifully for minor infractions—in some instances documented in letters. For Christina, the abuse began when she was a little girl. On one occasion at age five,when she was supposed to be taking an afternoon nap, she mindlessly picked at the seam of wallpaper, "leaving a small but obvious blank spot on the wall." When her mother discovered the misdeed, she spanked Christina.

 But that was not the end of it. She was determined to teach me a lesson that no amount of spanking could accomplish. That's what she said as she marched herself into my dressing room and opened the closet door. She reached inside and withdrew my favorite dress. It wasn't the fanciest dress nor the most expensive, but it was my favorite and she knew it. It was a yellow dress with white eyelet embroidery, and it looked like a spring daffodil.

Mommie held it up ominously. . . . Mommie [took] the scissors and completely shredded my favorite yellow dress! It was hanging in tatters with just barely enough shape left to indicate it had been a dress and not just a rag. Tears sprang to my eyes and I started to cry.

Then my mother marched toward me holding the tattered dress in front of her. The sound of her voice stopped my tears. She told me that I was going to have to wear that shredded thing for one week! If anyone asked me why I was wearing a torn dress I was to reply only, "I don't like pretty things." With that pronouncement she dropped the dress at my feet and left.

Christina wore the shredded dress for a week, but even worse incidents would follow her through adolescence and her young adult years. There were some good times, but they were fleeting. In the end, at her mother's casket, Christina could say: "I love you . . . I forgive you. . . . God has set us free, Mommie dearest. Go in peace."[4]

If I have ever had any apprehensions that I might be a candidate for a "Mommie Dearest" label, my fears quickly dissipated after reading that book. It's hard to imagine such a mother, and the stories are too real to ignore. But in other instances, I wonder if the perspective on Mommie is the product of an overly exercised imagination that is enhanced by a therapist—a thought that passed through my mind as I read *The Way I See It* by Patti Davis.

· · · · · · · · · · · · · · · · ·

Estranged First Daughter

Sometimes Mommie Dearest stories have happy endings, and that seems to be true in the case of Patti Davis, who has recently written a tribute to her father and made peace with her mother.

She was the first child born to a celebrated Hollywood couple, and she was a "first daughter" of the land—when her father, Ronald Reagan, became President of the United States. She would not be the first President's child to have struggles

and problems with her parents, but she does hold the distinction of being the first to write an autobiography that is no less than a scathing attack on her parents, particularly her mother.

The dust-jacket copy puts the reader on alert: "From the moment of her birth, seven months after her parents' marriage, Patricia Ann Reagan was a source of discomfort to her mother. Pretending that Patti was born premature, Nancy embarked upon an increasingly stormy path as mother to a headstrong, defiant daughter." That "stormy path," including physical and psychological abuse, is described in detail in the book—from the daughter's point of view:

As uncomfortable as it is to talk about, and write about, abuse is part of this story. I first remember my mother hitting me when I was eight. It escalated as I got older and became a weekly, sometimes daily, event. The last time it happened was when I was in my second year of college. . . . As I got older, I became intimately familiar with what would set my mother off, and I would push those buttons, even though I knew it would end up with her hand aimed at my face. . . .

I had fantasized about my mother, too: If only she were different. . . . If only she hadn't hit me, if only she had been more loving. But no woman wants to hit her child. No woman has a baby and thinks, "Oh good, now I have someone to fight with." It's easy to lose patience with a child—any mother knows this—the line between striking your child and not is sometimes a shaky one. But in the Fifties, that wasn't discussed.[5]

It is true that issues relating to child abuse weren't much discussed in the 1950s, but they were there—sometimes hidden in diaries, as was true for Anne Frank and her mother. But again, we don't hear the mother's version of this story—only the daughter's portrayal of Mommie Dearest.

· · · · · · · · · · · · · · · · · ·

A Diary and a Mommie Dearest

One of the most celebrated and beloved and bravest girls in all history was Anne Frank. I remember touring the office building in Amsterdam and climbing the narrow staircase to the attic where she and her German–Jewish family hid from the Nazis. I was touched by her deeply sensitive spirit as I looked at old photos and read excerpts from her diary that now line the stark wooden walls that still hold the secrets never penned on paper. Her story of courage and clarity of writing is well known. Less well known is the story of her deep resentment of her mother. We do not have a diary of Mrs. Frank, but we do have *A Diary of a Young Girl* and that young girl paints a tragic portrait of her relationship with her mother.

Saturday, November 7, 1942

 *Dearest Kitty,*

Mother's nerves are very much on edge, and that doesn't bode well for me. . . . I cling to Father because my contempt of Mother is growing daily. . . . I'm the opposite of Mother, so of course we clash. I don't mean to judge her; I don't have that right. I'm simply looking at her as a mother. She's not

a mother to me—I have to mother myself. . . . I'm charting my own course, and we'll see where it leads me. I have no choice, because I can picture what a mother and a wife should be and can't seem to find anything of the sort in the woman I'm supposed to call "Mother."

I tell myself time and again to overlook Mother's bad example. I only want to see her good points, and to look inside myself for what's lacking in her. But it doesn't work. . . . Sometimes I think God is trying to test me, both now and in the future. I'll have to become a good person on my own, without anyone to serve as a model or advise me, but it'll make me stronger in the end. . . .

Friday, April 2, 1943

Dearest Kitty,

Oh my, another item has been added to my list of sins. Last night I was lying in bed, waiting for Father to tuck me in and say my prayers with me, when Mother came into the room, sat on my bed and asked very gently, "Anne, Daddy isn't ready. How about if I listen to your prayers tonight?"

"No, Momsy," I replied.

Mother got up, stood beside my bed for a moment and then slowly walked toward the door. Suddenly she turned, her face contorted with pain, and said, "I don't want to be angry with you. I can't make you love me!" A few tears slid down her cheeks as she went out the door.

I lay still, thinking how mean it was of me to reject her so cruelly, but I also knew that I was incapable of answering her any other way. I can't be a hypocrite and pray with her when I don't feel like it. It just doesn't work that way. I felt sorry for Mother—very, very sorry—because for the first time in my life I noticed she wasn't indifferent to my coldness. I saw the sorrow in her face when she talked about not being able to make me love her. It's hard to tell the truth, and yet the truth is that she's the one who's rejected me. She's the one whose tactless comments and cruel jokes about matters I don't think are funny have made me insensitive to any sign of love on her part. Just as my heart sinks every time I hear her harsh words, that's how her heart sank when she realized there was no more love between us.[6]

For whatever misconceptions she might have had regarding her mother, Anne Frank was a very thoughtful and introspective and sensitive young woman. She evaluated her mother, and her mother came up wanting. Whether her mother was the Mommie Dearest Anne seemed to portray, the very fact that she was mulling over the relationship with her imaginary friend Kitty was a healthy exercise—and, had she survived the Nazi holocaust she would have no doubt grown into an emotionally stable adult. The same could not be said for a young Hollywood star who was born three years earlier than Anne.

. . . .

The Mother of Marilyn Monroe

Most people have heard stories about Marilyn Monroe's relationships with men, but less well known is her relationship with her mother—one that may have had a much more profound influ-

ence on her life and death than the many men that came in and out of her life. The problems her mother experienced were in part inherited from her grandmother who "died in an asylum, at age fifty-one . . . with 'manic-depressive psychosis' as a contributory factor," according to her medical records. At that time Marilyn was one year old.

 Family life was virtually nonexistent. After Marilyn's birth, apparently feeling unable to cope with full-time motherhood, Gladys went back to her work as a film cutter. She provided for her baby, but left her most of the time in the care of foster parents. Gladys' older children had long since been taken away by relatives of her first husband.

Catastrophe came when Marilyn was seven and living with her mother for a while. Gladys suffered a period of deep depression, then an explosion of rage and frustration. Some reports say she attacked a friend with a knife. She was promptly committed to the very hospital in which her own mother had died.

Except for brief periods, Gladys would remain confined until after Marilyn's death. Inez Melson, Marilyn's former business manager, was eventually appointed Gladys' guardian. She spent more time with her than anyone else now alive, and considers her disturbed rather than insane.

"Marilyn's mother was overly taken up with her religion, Christian Science, and with evil," Melson says. "That was her area of disturbance. She figured she had done something wrong in her life, and was being punished for it."

In that obsession Gladys was following the pat-

tern set by her own mother. . . . Marilyn had religious zeal thrust on her during childhood by Gladys and by one of the women who cared for her, and she remained a wobbly adherent of Christian Science into adulthood. . . . Marilyn was not definitely doomed to psychiatric illness, but she was born at serious risk. . . . Manic and schizophrenic disorders frequently run in families.[7]

· · · · · · · · · · · · ·

A Millionaire Mother and Child Neglect

She was the richest woman in the world in the late nineteenth century, the only child of inherited wealth and an astute businesswoman herself. "She had a knack for getting out of the market before a panic—she was accused of causing some—and then she lent her money at 6 percent interest to strapped investors." She was Henrietta Green of New York City, the mother of two children. But with all her millions, she was unable to spend money on herself or her children. So extreme were her efforts to save money that she would have "only the bottom layer of her petticoats laundered," but far worse was her neglect of her children.

Green gained the wrath of the public when it was exposed that she went to doctors at charity medical clinics. In fact, after her fourteen-year-old son, Ned, dislocated his knee, Green first tried to cure it herself, then took him to a free clinic, where doctors said it was too late for the boy's leg to heal prop-

erly. Five years later, complications forced Ned's leg to be amputated.

Green also spent years living in tawdry boarding-houses to escape paying taxes in New York City . . . and avoided tax collectors by living under a variety of false names with her son and daughter in cold-water flats. . . . She left her son and daughter each some $60 million. Ned, whose false leg supported his six-foot four-inch, three-hundred-pound frame . . . blew most of his fortune.[8]

For Ned Green, his mother's insanity and neglect negatively affected him the rest of his life. Other children, however, are amazing survivors who thrive despite the unhealthy maternal influence, as the story of the celebrated general of the Gulf War illustrates.

· · · · · · · · · · · · ·

General Schwarzkopf's Missions against His Mother

Norman Schwarzkopf grew up in New Jersey, the son of a military man and law enforcement agent who headed the investigation of the Lindbergh baby kidnapping. It is not unusual that the son might follow his father's footsteps and become a great leader himself—long before he captured the world's attention as the commander of troops in the Gulf War. But the forming of his character came from his mother as well. Her alcoholism had a profound effect on his development as a "self-contained and independent" leader.

I used to dread coming home at night. I'd go around the side of the house, where there was a window that looked into the kitchen. I'd stand in the dark and look inside and try to judge what kind of night it was going to be. Mom had a Jekyll-and-Hyde personality. When she was sober, she was the sweetest, most sensitive, loving, and intelligent person you could ever meet. But when she was drunk she was a holy terror. . . . I didn't like confrontations, but sometimes I fought back with sabotage: when Mom was out of the house I'd search the kitchen for the bottles of bourbon and gin, pour them out behind the garage, and smash them. At times it was anger that overwhelmed me, at other times fear, but what I felt most often was complete helplessness. I simply retreated, which Mom let me do because I was the youngest and her favorite. Deep inside me was a place where I would withdraw when things were unhappy at home. I discovered I could hide the painful feelings and still make friends and love dogs and help old ladies across the street and be a good guy. I had lots of buddies, but no really close friend. I learned to be self-contained and independent. Maybe that was a gift my mother gave me.[9]

• • • • • • • • • • • • • •

"Why Did You Leave Me?"

The most heartrending "Mommie Dearest" book on the public library shelf that I have ever encountered is written not by the child but by the mother who ran away to New York and abandoned the child. In *Mama Doesn't Live Here Anymore*, Judy Sullivan writes of her "heady" experience of taking "full responsibility" for her own life, while leaving behind her husband and eleven-year-old daughter, Kathleen, in Emporia, Kansas.

I had been aware of this book, written back in the feminist heyday of the 1970s, but I had not expected it to have such an emotional impact on me. I couldn't hold back the tears as I read of this poor child, sacrificed on the altar of "Me-Generation" self-centeredness.

In some ways I could relate to the mother. She had high aspirations, and, like me, her goal had been to earn a Ph.D. in history. But that is where any sense of commonality ends. Here is a mother who could walk away from a child who would wonder aloud in a note, "Sometimes I don't think you're my mother any more," while the mother's "time and energy went," by her own testimony, "to other women." Kathleen's cry for motherly love was expressed in another note she pinned on her mother's pillow the month before she left:

Dear Mama:

> *I have a problem. I don't know who I am. I try to be kind of like the others and I try to be me. But I just turn out weird! The other day I took a good look at myself in the mirror. I then realized how sloppy and ugly I was. Please help. Love, Bean. P.S. I love you!*

In the months and years after her mother's departure, Kathleen begged her mother to come home, while she vented her anger and shared intimacies only a mother could relate to. Here are some excerpts:

Can you help me? I got the rest of my braces yesterday. And they hurt. . . . I cry myself to sleep almost every night. Why did you leave me?! Come home! COME HOME!

What are you sending me for my birthday? I know what I really want for my birthday—YOU! . . . I miss you more and more every day.

What do you want for X-mas? I want a mini-bike, Bobby Sherman records, and most of all, YOU!! Damn. Damn. I miss you. Sometimes I start thinking about you and I just start crying and I can't stop. I tell you, I MISS YOU!! My first menstrual period was five days long. School is okay. Oh, Ricky Nelson will be in town the 3rd thru the 6th. Is it against Women's Lib if I go?

Happy Mother's Day. Or is that against Women's Lib? I miss you an awful lot.[10]

"Happy Mother's Day. Or is that against Women's Lib?" Those words ring in my ears. How sad that this child confused women's equality with a selfish, self-indulgent, self-centered lifestyle that could not recognize the special place mothers have had in the hearts of their very own children and the hearts of a nation. Dear, sweet, Kathleen, my heart aches for you—the little girl you were in the book. I hope you have found happiness and I hope you have had the joy of having children of your own who can say without reservation, "Happy Mother's Day!"

It seems but yesterday

you lay new in my arms. . . .

Years slip away—

today

we are mothers

together.

RUTH BELL GRAHAM

<h1 style="text-align:center">4</h1>

Traditions of Mother's Day

Gigi Graham Tchividjian, the daughter of Ruth and Billy Graham, tells a touching story of the first Mother's Day that she shared motherhood with her own mother. The setting was the Swiss Alps, where together they enjoyed a garden of memories.

 I awoke early that Sunday morning to the sound of bells. The valley was alive with them—the tinkling of cowbells now in chorus with the tolling of church bells, calling the faithful to worship.

Opening the heavy wooden shutters and throwing open the window, I stood gazing in wonder at the beauty before me. It was one of those indescribable spring days that can only be experienced in the Alps. Bright sunshine reflecting off glorious snow-covered peaks; clean, crisp air; fields filled with wild flowers in every shade of purple, yellow, and blue. And the window boxes hanging from every window in the village (even from the barns) were a riot of color, almost gaudy in the extravagance— red and pink geraniums, yellow and orange marigolds, blue ageratum and petunias of every variety! A perfect setting for Mother's Day.

Gigi was pregnant with her second child, but it was the first time that she and her mother were together on this meaningful day as mothers. Ruth had a special Mother's Day gift for her daughter— a poem. The first and last lines spanned the years in the lives of mother and daughter:

 It seems but yesterday
you lay new in my arms. . . .
Years slip away—
today
we are mothers
together.[1]

Family traditions and special occasions are an important aspect of keeping memories alive and anticipating future good times. Mother's Day has become one of those traditions for our little family for the past several years—though it remains simple and uncomplicated. After church, Carlton and I go home and change clothes, pack a picnic lunch, put the dog in the car, and head out to Grand Valley State University to hike along the ravines jutting into and alongside the Grand River. Bordering the trail along the river bottom is a garden of wild flowers. The Virginia bluebells and buttercups are in full bloom and trillium and May flowers line the paths up to the pine forest plateau. For mothers who look forward to six-course dinners and a floral arrangement, this may not seem like the perfect Mother's Day, but for me it's become part of my garden of memories—a very special day of the year.

This past spring was the first Mother's Day in some years that we missed our little tradition. Carlton had to work, and besides it was raining. Several weeks later, on a bright Sunday morning after church, he suggested without warning, "Let's take our Mother's Day walk today." So off we went with the dog in the backseat of the car, picking up our lunch on the way.

As we started our hike down into the ravine, I asked him, "Do you know what day this is?" He gave me a puzzled expression, and I paused and reminded him that it was Father's Day. He was taken aback at first, but then concluded that it was appropriate that he make both of those days special days for me—a mother who has struggled

to do double-duty parenting a kid who needed both a father and a mother. We will always have good memories of our time together on that warm and muggy Sunday when Father's Day became Mother's Day for a mom, a young man, and a dog.

Mother's Day is a special day, but it has not always been celebrated as a day for honoring mothers. Indeed, it was originally initiated by mothers themselves and the focus was on others.

· · · · · · · · · · · · · · · · · ·

A Mother's Day with Others in Mind

The first official Mother's Day "celebration" in America was actually a workday for mothers, first organized by Anna Reeves Jarvis in 1858 to help improve sanitation for poor families in Appalachia. During the Civil War, these workdays were devoted to providing medical aid to soldiers serving both the Union and Confederate armies.

In 1872, Julia Ward Howe, a well-known philanthropist and poet (who wrote "Battle Hymn of the Republic"), organized a Mother's Day for Peace to be commemorated on June 2. Her efforts began in Boston and spread to other cities along the Eastern seaboard, where the day continued to be celebrated until the turn of the century. It was a day for mothers to band together and protest the senseless carnage of war:

 Arise then, women of this day! . . . Say firmly: "Our husbands shall not come to us, reeking with car-

nage. . . . Our sons shall not be taken from us to unlearn all that we have been able to teach them of charity, mercy and patience. We women of one country will be too tender of those of another country to allow our sons to be trained to injure theirs.

These early celebrations of Mother's Day were not designed to focus on individual mothers themselves, but rather to allow mothers to speak out in word and deed on issues they deeply cared about. According to historian Stephanie Coontz, the holiday that has become known as Mother's Day was a step backward from the earlier focus on issues that mothers cared deeply about. She makes the following observations.

In fact, the adoption of Mother's Day by the 63rd Congress on May 8, 1914 represented a reversal of everything the nineteenth-century mothers' days had stood for. The speeches proclaiming Mother's Day in 1914 linked it to celebration of home life and privacy; they repudiated women's social role beyond the household. . . . A day that had once been linked to controversial causes was reduced to an occasion for platitudes and sales pitches.[2]

· · · · · · · · · · · · · · · · · ·

Woodrow Wilson and Mother's Day

The shift from Mother's Day for Peace to the celebration we now know as Mother's Day did not occur overnight. It was in part a product of Victorian America, but the changing concept developed slowly and was not made official until President Woodrow Wilson was in the White House. Who was this man who signed the proclamation for Mother's Day, and what was his own relationship with his mother?

 A self-proclaimed "mama's boy," the twenty-eighth President of the United States dropped his first name of Thomas to use the maiden name of his "noble, strong and saintly mother" when he started on the trail that eventually led to the White House. Remembering how he "clung to her till I was a great big fellow," Wilson confessed that his "love of the best womanhood came to me and entered my heart through her apron-string." . . . No surprise then that in 1914, when Wilson affixed his signature to a resolution setting aside the second Sunday in May to be observed annually as Mother's Day, the proclamation called upon government officials and private citizens alike to display the flag "as a public expression of our love and reverence for the mothers of our country."[3]

· · · · · · · · · · · · · · · · · ·

Proclamation by Congress for Mother's Day

 Whereas the service rendered the United States by the American mother is the greatest source of the country's strength and inspiration; and

Whereas, we honor ourselves and the mothers of America when we do anything to give emphasis to the home as the fountain head of the state; and

Whereas, the American mother is doing so much for the home, for moral uplift, and religion, hence so much for good government and humanity; therefore be it RESOLVED . . . that the President of the United States is hereby authorized and requested to issue a proclamation calling upon the government officials to display the United States flag on all government buildings, and the people of the United States to display the flag at their homes or other suitable places, on the second Sunday in May, as a public expression of our love and reverence for the mothers of our country.[4]

. . . .

Five Hundred Carnations on Mother's Day

As a historian I find that the most interesting side of our heritage is not the public legislation and ceremonies, but the behind-the-scenes stories. Far more fascinating to me than the President's public proclamation is the virtually unknown woman who worked tirelessly to establish a special day for mothers only to have it backfire on her.

It was the second Sunday of May 1907. Five hundred white carnations adorned the Methodist Church in Grafton, West Virginia. The occasion was the second anniversary of the death of Mrs. Jarvis, the minister's wife. Her daughter Anna, named for her mother, planned the ceremony and decorated the church with her mother's favorite flower. It was a commemoration of her mother who had promoted "Mother's Friendship Days" in an effort

to heal the bitter wounds between the North and the South, left behind after the Civil War. The ceremony so moved Anna that she vowed to make it a national event. In the months that followed, she contacted politicians, newspaper editors, businessmen, and anyone who would listen, making an appeal for a day to honor mothers to be symbolized by white carnations.

 In 1910 West Virginia became the first state to recognize Mother's Day. A year later, amidst Jarvis's flurry of letters, nearly every state had followed. Legislators may not have been ready to grant women the vote, but Mother's Day had few enemies. . . . But Jarvis was not finished. She incorporated herself as the Mother's Day International Association and began addressing her letters to foreign leaders. Her correspondence became so voluminous that she bought the three-story brick house next door to store her letters. It was believed that by the time Jarvis died in 1948, forty-three nations had created Mother's Day observances.

But the story of Anna Jarvis, a woman who never married or became a mother herself, does not have a happy ending. She became embittered by the commercialism associated with this almost sacred day. Although she herself had started this second-Sunday-of-May celebration with five hundred carnations, she was infuriated when florists—perhaps in keeping with the law of supply and demand—raised their prices. And candy and card manufacturers also were the object of her wrath.

A printed card means nothing except that you are too lazy to write to the woman who has done more for you than anyone in the world," Jarvis snapped. "And candy! You take a box to Mother— and then eat most of it yourself. A pretty sentiment.

In the years that followed, Anna spent most of her time and money fighting against the holiday she had created. In 1925, she tried to prevent a group of war mothers in Philadelphia from selling white carnations to raise money. The sixty-one-year-old Miss Jarvis was arrested for disturbing the peace. She later became a recluse, but told a reporter before she died at age eighty-four, "that she was sorry she had ever started Mother's Day."[5]

· · · · · · · · · · · · · ·

A Mother's Last Mother's Day Card

During a recent two-day stopover in Hawaii, Carlton and I visited Pearl Harbor—which proved to be the most memorable aspect of that little vacation. We visited the *USS Arizona* memorial, where more than a thousand U.S. servicemen were killed. It made me realize once again what a heavy price has been paid for the freedom we enjoy as Americans. But sometimes recounting the deaths of hundreds of people is more difficult to put into perspective than the deaths of one or two. As we were browsing through the museum before going to the memorial, I spotted a letter from Bud Heidt to his mother. Heidt and his twin brother Wes were both

killed in action aboard the *USS Arizona* on that fateful day, December 7, 1941.

May 22, 1941
Honolulu, Hawaii

 Dear Mother,
    Did you get are [sic] mother Day card that Wesley and I sent you in time for Mother Day? We didn't know what to get you so we thought it would be better to send you some money and you could get what you wanted the most.

I wonder what their mother bought with the money they sent. I hope she got something she could keep and treasure as a token of love from her beloved sons.

· · · · · · · · · · · · · ·

Mother's Day Sorrow

Whether in poetry or letters or Sunday sermons, reflections on Mother's Day present the ideal of grateful children and a contented and fulfilled mother. But for some women the happy celebration associated with Mother's Day is the most depressing time of the year. This was true for Kaye Halverson. The title of her book says it all: *The Wedded Unmother.* Here she tells how the pain of infertility consumed her. Her feelings are not unique, and they are a reminder that the holidays that are supposed to bring cheer often only increase the pain of a broken heart.

I cried uncontrollably at almost anything: a pregnant woman walking down the street, a friend announcing her pregnancy. Baby showers became impossible for me to attend. . . . Mother's Days and holidays, formerly happy times, became difficult. . . .

One night after an elegant dinner, I cried hysterically because I felt so worthless. I wasn't a mother; I was a failure. . . .

To make matters worse, Mother's Day was approaching. I resented the church for glorifying motherhood. I hated the TV ads depicting mothers and daughters with long, flowing, golden hair running through fields and mothers powdering their babies' round little bottoms. Even shampooing hair was visualized as a partnership between mother and daughter. I was so depressed I couldn't force myself to buy a present for my mother or mother-in-law, or even send them cards. Instead I wrote a lengthy letter to Ann Landers, expressing my resentment toward Mother's Day.[6]

• • • • • • • • • • • • • • • • • • •

Two Brothers Send Mother's Day Greetings

Not all mothers can look forward to Mother's Day even when they have children—especially when the children have become so self-centered that they forget their mothers or when they have been lost to crime or indigence. Indeed, for such mothers this special day may bring more anguish than if they were childless. Thus it might have been for the fictional Mrs. Clancy.

In his short story entitled "Mothers' Day," Octavus Roy Cohen tells a tale of two brothers,

"square-shouldered, erect" Dan Clancy and "narrow-shouldered and furtive" Shamus Clancy—one a detective, the other a derelict—who are unknowingly brought together in a strange set of circumstances.

 Tonight was Saturday night—the eve of Mothers' Day—but Daniel Clancy was unaware of that fact. . . . Dan Clancy thought only of himself and not at all of women, he neither knew or cared that this was Mothers' Day eve. His thoughts were with the squint-eyed bit of human jetsam hiding out under the freight cars yonder. . . . Unerringly he catalogued Shamus Clancy as a wastrel, a drifter, a thoroughly negative and perhaps even harmless broken cog in the human machine. Dan knew that the little man might be a sneak thief: certainly no worse, for he had glimpsed the narrow-set eyes and the snarling lips and knew those were not correlatives of physical courage. . . .

But the inequality of physical odds merely amused the plain clothes man. He was the unimpeachable law; this stranger was outside the pale, alone and friendless. Of course, Dan could have picked him up willy-nilly as a vagrant and seen to it that the man received thirty or sixty or ninety days in the workhouse. But there was little pleasure in that. It amused Dan to play with his quarry as a cat plays with a mouse, when already the feline has partaken of a full meal. Perhaps desperation or hunger or the need of shelter for the frail body might drive the stranger to commit some petty offense. Time enough then to place the heavy hand of the law upon the narrow shoulders. . . .

So the detective stalked the derelict as he headed for the business district and disappeared into "a modest little shop" with a "shabby sign over the doorway" that read "Post-Card Exchange." Dan Clancy was puzzled as he peered though the outside window. Why would this drifter be browsing through the post-card racks, studying each one intently? It made no sense. But the dirty little man finally made his selection and dug into his pocket for a nickel to make the purchase. Leaving the shop he crossed the street to the telegraph office and made a transaction and then disappeared into the night while the disconcerted detective watched from a distance.

Unable to contain his curiosity, Dan Clancy entered the office, and, showing his badge, demanded to know what the "little rat" was up to. The clerk dug the card out of his desk and showed it to the detective. The clerk had wired the message on the card to a woman in Portland, and signed the drifter's name. The message read:

 Mrs. Katie Clancy
819 Arcade Street
Portland

To my Mother: My help and my inspiration, the one who has had faith in me always and who has stood by me in brightest day and darkest night. To my only sweetheart—My mother.

Your loving son—
Shamus.

The detective read the card—over and over. He gave the card back to the clerk and started out of the office, but then suddenly turned back and "seated himself at a little table, selected a telegraph blank, and nibbled reflectively at the stump of a pencil. When he was finished, he handed the clerk his telegram:

Mrs. Katie Clancy
819 Arcade Street
Portland

Lots of love to the best Mother in the world on Mothers' Day. I saw Shamus today, and he is doing fine.

Your loving son—
Daniel.[7]

Although Cohen's story is entitled "Mothers' Day," there is no mother in the story. She is anonymous with no personality—no lines devoted to character building. We have no idea what kind of a person she was or even whether she was a kind and loving mother to her two sons. But such information is not essential to the story—or perhaps even to the ideal of Mother's Day. It doesn't really matter who the mother is and how capable she was in child-rearing. Mother's Day is first and foremost a day set aside to pay homage to this anonymous woman often lost in obscurity—a woman called mother by her children.

    Ah! Little doth the young one dream,

When full of play and childish cares,

What power hath even his wildest scream,

Heard by his mother unawares!

He knows it not, he cannot guess:

Years to a mother bring distress;

But do not make her love the less.

FROM *THE AFFLICTION OF MARGARET* BY WILLIAM WORDSWORTH

5

The Guilt and Heartache of Motherhood

It came to me that I had never really lost my daughter, for she returned in ways that I had not foreseen. The destruction of that first childish patch of green led . . . to other more beautiful gardens, and the final lesson of patience. . . . There is no greater miracle, I sensed, than seeing a seed or an idea which one has planted transformed into a growing, living joy. In this way, we, ourselves, achieve our own immortality.

These are the words of Mabel Barbee Lee, reflecting back on her relationship with her daughter—a relationship that had bloomed into maturity after many early years of pain and heavy-heartedness. Mabel tells the story in her book *The Gardens of My Life.*

A single mother's struggle with child-rearing can be multiplied many times over when she is competing with a revered father who is deceased. This was true for Mabel. In 1918, the Spanish influenza descended on America, and before it ran its course, 548,000 Americans were dead, including her husband. She was left alone to raise their daughter Barbara, still in elementary school. At first she maintained a closeness with her little girl, as they gardened and traveled together. But as the years passed the relationship with her daughter deteriorated—especially after she became Dean of Women of her Alma Mater and moved with Barbara into a dormitory residence.

Soon Barbara was associating with the older girls, and Mabel was alarmed when she learned from campus security that her daughter was smoking and sneaking out at night. She realized the rebellion related directly to her own relationship with Barbara.

This alienation from my own daughter—when did it begin? Why hadn't I recognized the first symptoms and been able to overcome them? I went back over the seven years since Howe's death. She had been close to her father and needed him—I was not able to take his place.

The story has a happy ending. Decades later when Mabel was in her eighties and now the author of widely acclaimed books, her relationship with Barbara, now a widow herself, was once again close. After spending a few days together, Mabel wrote:

 I was reluctant to let her go. It was hard to think of saying good-by. It seemed as if I had waited all my life for this feeling of closeness with my daughter.[1]

The seasonal gardens of motherhood, as Mabel Barbee Lee's life illustrate, are filled with more than colorful fragrant flowers and thriving vines and shrubs. I know that well from experience. Even the most attentive care to my backyard garden doesn't prevent weeds and blight and insects from taking their toll, and these problems are multiplied if I neglect the daily care when my attention is focused on other things. So it is with motherhood. Sometimes it's routine blight and sometimes it's busyness, but the problems arise—and the result is guilt and heavyheartedness.

A mother's expression of heartache may come in many forms, but the one that most often haunts the psyche or erupts through the muffled sob is the anguished question, "Where did I go wrong?" Guilt and heartache feed on each other, and every mother has known this kind of blight in her garden. But these emotions are often only temporary, and unlike the suffering and sorrow of death or a debilitating disease, we can one day look back, as Mabel did, and smile at our struggles at making our garden grow. My greatest encouragement in mothering is listening to the stories of mothers who have passed through the difficult seasons and can now look back and say with confidence that it was all worthwhile—and much more—as I'm sure is true of Annie Dillard's mom.

. . . .

An American Childhood

An American Childhood is the title of one of Annie Dillard's perceptive and revealing books. For her book *Pilgrim at Tinker Creek* she won the Pulitzer Prize, and by all standards she has been a very successful and productive citizen—one whose faith and insights have challenged Christians and non-Christians alike. But her teenage years were difficult ones, and there were many times when her mother feared all hope for her daughter was lost. Annie Dillard ought to be a reminder for all mothers who are wringing their hands and ready to give up.

 Funny how badly I'd turned out. . . . I woke up and found myself in juvenile court. I was hanging from crutches; for a few weeks after the drag race, neither knee worked.

Surely a serious auto accident will shake a kid up. I remember clinging to that hope, as my son was lying in the intensive care unit. But not necessarily—as Annie's mother painfully discovered.

 I'd been suspended from school for smoking ciga-
rettes. . . . Late one night, my parents and I sat at
the kitchen table. . . .

"What are we going to do with you?"

Mother raised the question. Her voice trem-
bled and rose with emotion. She couldn't sit still;
she kept getting up and roaming around the
kitchen. . . . She sighed and said again, looking up
and out of the night–black window, "Dear God, what
are we going to do with you?" My heart went out
to them. We all seemed to have exhausted our
options. They asked me for fresh ideas, but I had
none. I racked my brain, but couldn't come up with
anything. The U.S. Marines didn't take sixteen-
year-old girls.[2]

Here again a mother's guilt and heartache is mixed up—with no way of discerning where one ends and the other begins. But some may wonder, maybe Annie wouldn't have gone through those difficult years if her mother had been more attentive and caring. Perhaps so, but even the best efforts result in heartache, as Ruth Graham, wife of evangelist Billy Graham, testifies. There is a lot of pressure put on the "preacher's kids," and they often have the reputation for being the worst in the congregation.

But that truism doesn't lessen the guilt and heartache for the mother.

· ·

The Graham Prodigal Sons

In the late 1960s I attended Billy Graham crusades in Houston and New York City, not even imagining that in the background—never seen preaching to masses in a stadium—was a mother whose heart was breaking. In her book *Prodigals—And Those Who Love Them*, Ruth Graham tells how her sons Franklin and Ned both got in trouble with the law and were involved in drugs and alcohol. Ruth offers advice that I have often taken to heart:

 I remember praying, "Lord, help me discipline
this boy." . . . "Love him more," He told me. And
that's exactly what Franklin needed.[3]

· ·

"Years to a Mother Bring Distress"

Ah! Little doth the young one dream,
When full of play and childish cares,
What power hath even his wildest scream,
Heard by his mother unawares!
He knows it not, he cannot guess:
Years to a mother bring distress;
But do not make her love the less.

FROM THE AFFLICTION OF MARGARET
BY WILLIAM WORDSWORTH[4]

Groaning for My Poor Children

A mother's heartbreak comes in many forms, but it is difficult to imagine a chronic aching that could hurt more than that which slave mothers endured. There was the initial stabbing pain of separation from children, but as the years and decades passed a numbing effect calmed the heaving sobs into groans of heartache. Sojourner Truth, celebrated for her sacrificial service with the Underground Railroad, captures the scene outside the slave shanty:

 I can remember when I was a little, young girl, how my old mammy would sit out of doors in the evenings and look up at the stars and groan, and I would say, "Mammy, what makes you groan so?" And she would say, "I am groaning to think of my poor children; they do not know where I be and I don't know where they be. I look up at the stars and they look up at the stars!"[5]

Does anyone understand such heartache? The black slaves knew they did not have a corner on suffering. "Nobody knows the trouble I've seen; nobody knows but Jesus," was their heart's cry. Jesus too had suffered—and so also His mother.

A Sword Piercing the Soul of a Mother

 Yea, a sword shall pierce through thy own soul also.

These were the prophetic words of the aged Simeon when he spoke to Mary, the mother of Jesus, in the temple. In this sense Mary, is a sister in suffering to all mothers, whatever their heartache may be. This was the message of an editorial printed many years ago in a publication of an Episcopal congregation in Milwaukee.

All motherhood has the sign of the cross laid upon it from its very inception; and when the mother brings her new-born child to the temple for baptism the prophetic word of the aged Simeon may pretty generally be spoken to her as it was to the mother of our Lord. . . . As the child passes through the various stages into manhood and takes his place in the world, there are many forms of that sword which may pierce the mother's soul. The uniqueness of the Virgin Mother's place was not in the vision of suffering which was presented to her. All mothers have that vision. She brought into the world a life which would bring to her a fathomless love, but which would also bring her to the foot of the cross. And this was her experience as the part of the universal experience of motherhood. She was at one with her sisters in all ages. . . . Stand with Mary at the foot of the cross. See, she makes a place for you, for yours is a place that neither she nor any other mortal on God's earth can take from you.[6]

When Mary learned she was pregnant, knowing that she would be giving birth to the Messiah, she sang a song—the Magnificat—as it has become known. It is a song of praise and thanksgiving to

God. I too sang for joy when I learned I was pregnant. But for many women, pregnancy has brought heartache—especially in generations past when birth-control measures were not readily available. This was true of one of America's best-known religious figures of the nineteenth century.

- - - - - - - - - - - - - - -

The Secret of an Unhappy Life

Hannah Whitall Smith was the author of one of the most popular devotional classics ever written, *The Christian's Secret of a Happy Life*, published in 1875 and still in print today with more than 2 million copies sold. The secret, as she identified it, was resting in God and finding victory over life's outward circumstances. This happiness eluded Hannah herself, however, especially in the area of motherhood and family trials that continued throughout her life. In 1852, she wrote in her diary:

> *I am very unhappy now. That trial of my womanhood which to me is so very bitter has come upon me again. When my little Ellie is two years old she will have a little sister or brother. And this is the end of all my hopes, my pleasing anticipations, my returning youthful joyousness. Well, it is a woman's lot and I must try to become resigned and bear it in patience and silence and not make my home unhappy because I am so. But oh, how hard it is.[7]*

Another woman whose pregnancy brought heartache was the fictional character Hester Prynne, a young woman we all read about in our youth.

- - - - - - - - - - - - - - -

The Scarlet Shame of Single Motherhood

In an era when it is commonplace for young women to have babies out of wedlock, it is easy to imagine there is no shame associated with illegitimacy, but such is not the case. There are many single women even today who are deeply distressed in facing family and friends with the humiliation of an unwanted pregnancy. The Scarlet Letter that symbolized the sin of Hester Prynne has not entirely vanished today, and Hawthorne's book by that title is as fresh today as it was when I first read it more than thirty years ago.

We first meet Hester as she is emerging from her dark dungeon cell into the bright sunlight with her three-month-old baby. The prison, which Hawthorne describes as "the black flower of civilized society" is an "ugly edifice" surrounded by overgrown "unsightly vegetation," except for a "wild rose-bush, covered, in this month of June, with its delicate gems."

In the chapters that follow we come to admire Hester who has admitted her sin and wears her Scarlet Letter as a just punishment, enduring the scorn of the townspeople while reaching out in deeds of mercy to the sick and needy. Her most anguishing ordeal occurs when the governor threatens to take away her little daughter, Pearl, who is now three years old. Hester's response is immediate and passionate:

"God gave me the child!" cried she. "He gave her in requital of all things else, which ye had taken from me. She is my happiness!—she is my torture, no the less! Pearl keeps me here in life! Pearl punishes me too! See ye not, she is the scarlet letter, only capable of being loved, and so endowed with a million-fold the power of retribution for my sin? Ye shall not take her! I will die first!"

With the support of her minister, Hester is permitted to keep her child. The minister, it turns out, is the child's father. And, unlike Hester who has endured her guilt in public and budded and bloomed, he withered away. "Her breast, with its badge of shame, was but the softer pillow for the head that needed one. She was self-ordained a Sister of Mercy." By contrast, "he was broken down by long and exquisite suffering" and "his mind was darkened and confused by the very remorse which harrowed it."

"Let the black flower blossom as it may!" This line, in reference to the minister, sums up this garden story—the garden of the soul. The minister is imprisoned in the black flower of his own soul, while Hester and her little Pearl are like the wild roses blooming amid the weeds outside the prison door.[8]

We don't know what happened to little Pearl, the fictional daughter of the fictional mother in Hawthorne's novel. Did she follow her mother into humanitarian service for others? If she did, her mother might have experienced further heartache,

as did Catherine Booth, the mother of eight children and the "Mother" of the Salvation Army.

. . . .

A Mother's Sacrifice

Catherine Booth very purposefully trained her children for ministry and they followed their parents into humanitarian service. That pleased Catherine, but it also brought her heartache. She herself had struggled with the two competing callings in her life—ministry and motherhood—and she dreaded passing that legacy on to the next generation. At the time of her daughter's wedding, she wrote of this problem that plagued her:

 Mothers will understand . . . a side of life to which my child is yet a stranger. Having experienced the weight of public work for twenty-six years, also the weight of a large family continually hanging on my heart, having striven very hard to fulfill the obligation on both sides, and having realized what a very hard struggle it has been, the mother's heart in me has shrunk in some measure from offering her up to the same kind of warfare. . . . The consecration which I made on the morning of her birth, and consummated on the day that I gave her first to public work, I have finished this morning in laying her again on this altar."[9]

From those words, it may seem as though Catherine Booth had given too much. Yet, measured in terms of those she helped—her far-extended family that included prostitutes and worse—she could never have given too much. And, as is so often true, her compassion multiplied itself. Many of those young women that were "reclaimed," went out to reclaim others and became full-time workers for the Salvation Army.

Catherine Booth's heavyheartedness for her daughter was driven by concern and worry far more than shame, and somehow that is easier to bear. She may have felt a weight of guilt, but not the same kind of guilt that results in the heartache of shame and disgrace.

．　．　．　．　．　．　．　．　．　．　．　．　．

A Son's Disgrace and a Mother's Deadly Disease

In the summer of 1974, when I was struggling with the postpartum blues and nursing my new infant, I spent endless hours in front of the TV watching the Watergate hearings. It was fascinating, and I got hooked. It was the soap opera of the seventies. But behind the scenes, away from the viewers' curious probe, subplots were unraveling, and one of those subplots involved a mother and a son heartache that led to sickness and death.

Does mental anguish contribute to physical infirmity? Anecdotal evidence would surely suggest that it does as this story of a mother and son illustrates. It was the father's fascination with the Civil War that would always be associated with the baby boy born in the fall of 1934—named Jeb Stuart for his father's favorite Confederate General. But it was his mother who would shape his personality and his intense desire to climb the ladder of success.

 He was a quiet man. He was known for his courtly southern manners, but he was usually content to let my mother do the talking. . . . He and I had an affectionate relationship without really being close. We rarely disagreed. By contrast, my mother and I often disagreed, sometimes heatedly, but we were close. She was the greatest influence on my youth.

My mother's high hopes for me triggered my youthful ambitions. . . .

His mother's high hopes were realized as her son worked his way up the corporate ladder and then became a Special Assistant to President Nixon in 1969. In 1972, he was made deputy director of the Committee to Re-Elect the President, and that is when his brilliant career began to unravel. The President was reelected, but in the process Jeb Stuart Magruder was snared in the Watergate web. His complicity in the cover-up was widely reported in the press, and in the early months of 1973 he came forward to cooperate with the Watergate prosecutors. It was a very difficult time for him and his wife and children—and for his mother.

 Early in May my mother entered the hospital. She was in her early seventies but she had always been a robust woman, and we had assumed she would outlive my father, who had a number of health problems. . . . I talked to her that week and she expressed far more concern about my problems than about her own health. However, she had cancer tests while she was in the hospital. I talked to her doctor on

*the morning of Friday, May 11, and he said that
her condition was serious, but not critical, and there
was no need for me to come to California immediately.
She died that night.*

*Her death was a great blow to me and Gail,
and it was followed in early June, just before my
Senate testimony, by Gail's father suffering three
heart attacks. . . . Gail and I had to assume that his
heart attacks, and perhaps my mother's sudden death,
were to some degree related to their anguish over
my difficulties. Certainly that thought did not make
my situation any easier to bear.*[10]

Adult children sometimes bring greater
heartache to mothers than they did as adoles-
cents. This was as true for Barbara Johnson.

. . . .

"The Bottom Rung of Sorrow"

Barbara Johnson endured more than her share
of sorrow for a lifetime. Her husband suffered brain
damage in a car accident and struggled through
years of therapy before he could resume normal
activities. In 1968 a son was killed in Vietnam, and
five years later another son lost his life in an auto
accident. These were terrible accidents that seemed
so unexplainable and beyond Barbara's control.
Only a mother who has lost a child could understand such sorrow. But there is another kind of grief
that Barbara Johnson was yet to face—a heartache
that inflicted pain like nothing she had previous-
ly endured.

 *The bottom rung of her sorrow came the day she
found homosexual magazines in her son's room and
confronted him with her knowledge.*

*"Yes, yes, I'm gay," her son, Larry, shouted
as he ran out the door and out of his family's life
for eleven months.*

For Barbara a "heavy depression settled like
a thick fog" on her life. "I felt amputated, as
though someone had cut off part of me. I was so
alone." And she wondered what she had done
wrong—especially when she read that "homo-
sexuality is caused by a domineering mother."

Through her healing, Barbara realized that she
had to stop blaming herself, and to recognize
that "Larry wasn't a tragedy but the same son who
had brought us joy and blessing through the
years." And she vowed to turn the situation into
one of reaching out to families in similar circumstances.

 *The more broken-hearted I became, the more under-
standing I was of the cry of other bleeding hearts
because I had tasted the cup of suffering.*[11]

. . . .

Would I Do It All over Again?

A few years ago Ann Landers took a nonscientif-
ic survey of her readers, asking if they would
have children if they had it to do all over again.
According to her published results, a majority of
parents—primarily mothers—said they would

not. I've never put much stock in that survey, but it is significant even if a handful of mothers expressed such feelings. How could motherhood be so heartbreaking that mothers would say no.

Antoinette, a thirty-five-year-old mother of two, speaks for many women who wonder if the negative side of mothering outweighs the positive.

 I really don't understand all this family album stuff. I just keep a few pictures of them, that's it. It's gotten so that I can't stand to see photographs of my kids when they were babies. I mean what good are memories? It's a time that doesn't exist anymore—it's gone, finished, and I just can't bear it. It makes my heart ache. Look how cute she was. She couldn't go anywhere without that filthy "blanky." And look at him standing there with his teddy bear. Whenever I see how adorable they were, I want to weep. How can anyone get any comfort or joy from remembering something that's over and done with? It's just too painful. Not that they aren't cute now. But they seem so grown–up. They're different now. All they want me to do for them is have dinner ready or drive them over to their friends' houses. *It's like I'm not really a mother anymore. I've become a cook and a chauffeur.[12]*

In a National Family Opinion survey on motherhood taken in the 1980s, some twenty percent of the mothers who responded reported that they found very little pleasure in their children. One of these mothers summed up her feelings in the following words:

They make your arms ache when they are small and your heart ache when they are grown.[13]

In some ways I resonate with everything these mothers are saying, but I know for a certainty that despite the heartache, I would do it all over again. Maybe mothers have a collective masochistic mentality. We're gluttons for punishment. We endure the guilt and heartbreak as though motherhood were a privilege. Is there something psychotic about motherhood? Some would argue there is—though perhaps not for these reasons. Indeed, the psychology of motherhood has been a hot topic since Freud and his colleagues discovered we were an intriguing topic for research.

. . . whenever the door to sublimation was open to me,

I was much happier as a wife and mother. And vice versa:

when something in my personal life interfered with my

scientific productivity, I was less happy and more

aggressive in my whole attitude toward my environment.

HELENA DEUTSCH

6

The Psychology of Motherhood

The Garden, as any psychologist knows, is feminine. The central symbol is Mother: Mother Nature, the Earth Mother, and one's own mother in that primordial unconscious time when mother, sustenance, and self were one organism—at first literally, later functionally, and finally symbolically. . . . In the American psyche, then the New World Garden is identical with the Good Mother.[1]

I like the analogy of the garden as mother. Indeed, I came to that conclusion before I read the above quote from the autobiography of Thomas Edison. But I'm a skeptic when it comes to the phrase, "as any psychologist knows." I am cautious about the field of psychology—partly because women in general and mothers in particular are the most vulnerable to the analytical knife so to speak. Women in far greater numbers than men

seek out therapy, and sometimes I wonder how much they benefit by so much analysis. I'm reminded of the subtitle of Eugenia Price's book: *Leave Yourself Alone: The Paralysis of Self-Analysis.* And sometimes self-analysis can be self-serving. We worry about our recovered memories and our inner child and our codependency, while mothers in Africa and Asia and Bosnia are worrying about the next meal for their crying hungry children. And sometimes we slight the differences—making all suffering equal.

The truth is, therapy too often focuses on ourselves while pulling our attention away from those who are hurting most. I have gone through difficult times, but I'm quick to remind myself that my problems pale in comparison to the problems of others. That is not to say that a therapist cannot be of assistance in the difficult times in life or guide us in mid-course corrections. In fact, I sought out a therapist myself during my early months as a single mother. It was difficult raising an adolescent son by myself, and I needed advice. After several sessions, I brought a very reluctant Carlton along. It was not a pleasant encounter, and he left the session much more disgruntled than when he had arrived. His half-serious, parking-lot analysis still amuses me:

 "I don't know why you're wasting your time with her! She's crazier than you are!"

The next week when I returned alone for my scheduled appointment, my therapist reviewed some of the issues that had arisen in the previous session that related to Carlton. She then said she felt that we should explore a more important issue that related to my husband. Why, she wondered, had I always referred to my husband by his first name when talking to her, but had persisted in calling him "Dad" when talking to Carlton? Was I subconsciously turning my husband into a father figure? I'm not exactly sure how I answered her, but my thoughts were, *Yes, Carlton is right, she is crazier than I am— Don't all mothers call their husbands "Dad" to their children?* She was a single woman with no children, so perhaps she could be excused, but I wasn't disappointed at the end of the session when she told me she would be taking most of the summer off. She said that I should schedule my next appointments to begin at the end of the summer so that we could get into some "dream work"—to explore my dreams so that I could better understand myself. I did not follow through, reasoning that at $75 an

hour my dreams would simply have to remain unexplored. It was the last time I saw her.

So much for my own experience as a mother with a psychologist. But what about the psychology of motherhood—from the view of the experts, the psychologists? It shouldn't surprise us that there is very little uniformity of opinion—as is true of most issues in the field of psychology. But if there has been a general theme running through the psychology of motherhood it is that of blaming the mother for the problems of her children.

· ·

"Momism"

Motherhood as an ideal and as an institution has historically remained almost off limits for criticism—especially since Victorian times. Of course, there were bad mothers in every generation—exceptions to the rule—but motherhood itself was sacred. But not even God Almighty has escaped the skeptic's scorn, and so also motherhood—particularly with twentieth century's growing interest in developmental psychology.

One of the most scathing attacks on motherhood came from Philip Wylie. In his book *Generation of Vipers* (1942), he included a chapter on the subject of "Momism," a very negative term that he coined to support his underlying thesis that basically "Mom is a jerk!" He loathed the sentimental ideal of motherhood that had such a grip on society and individuals, and was convinced that it had an irreversible and damaging effect.

I cannot think, offhand, of any civilization except ours in which an entire division of living men has been used, during wartime, or at any time to spell out the word "mom" on a drill field, or to perform any equivalent act. . . . Megaloid mom worship has got completely out of hand. Our land, subjectively mapped, would have more silver cords and apron strings crisscrossing it than railroads and telephone wires. Mom is everywhere and everything and damned near everybody, and from her depends all the rest of the U.S. Disguised as good old mom, dear old mom, sweet old mom, your loving mom, and so on, she is the bride at every funeral and the corpse at every wedding. Men live for her and die for her, dote upon her and whisper her name as they pass away, and I believe she has now achieved, in the hierarchy of miscellaneous articles, a spot near the Bible and the Flag, being reckoned part of both in a way. . . . I give you mom. I give you the destroying mother. I give you her justice— from which we have never removed the eye bandage. I give you the angel—and point to the sword in her hand. I give you . . . the black widow who is poisonous and eats her mate, and I designate at the bottom of your program the grand finale of all the soap operas: the mother of America's Cinderella.[2]

Wylie must have had a bad day when he was writing those vicious sentences, and perhaps a "Mommie Dearest" was lurking in the background. But he was correct in his assessment of the devotion accorded mothers both in the public and private sectors. That kind of blind veneration, he was convinced, was an underlying cause of many of society's ills.

Nor was he alone in that judgment. Others had drawn the same conclusions—though with milder rhetoric.

. . . .

Four Kinds of Bad Mothers

It should not surprise us that the term "Mommie Dearest" has become a cliché, and that there is no comparable "Daddy Dearest" expression. Mothers have traditionally been responsible for the primary care of their children, and mothers have traditionally been blamed for their children's problems—especially with the growing concern over juvenile delinquency.

 One thing was clear: Mother was to blame. And as the juvenile justice system grew, so did the charges against "Mom." By mid-century psychiatrist Marynia Farnham and writer Ferdinand Lundberg, warning readers that Hitler was his mother's son, could identify four kinds of bad mothers: the rejecting, the overprotective, the dominating, and the overaffectionate. All of them ruined their sons. (The experts were never much concerned with the fate of the daughters.) The overaffectionate mother produced "sissies" or "passive-homosexual males," while the rejecting, overprotective, and dominating mothers "produced the delinquents, the difficult behavior problem children" and "some substantial percentage of criminals." "Momism" had become a major social problem. . . .[3]

If "Momism" was a major social problem, then therapists were charged with ferreting out these problem mothers. The body language itself was enough to "convict" an innocent mom.

Keep an Eye on Mom

In her book *Don't Blame Mother*, Paula Caplan laments the censure hurled at mothers by therapists:

> *Since the 1960s, therapists' attitudes toward mothers have been widely influenced by Margaret Mahler's work on the importance of the child's psychological "separation and individuation" from its mother. . . . Mahler advised therapists to watch carefully when a mother entered the room used for observing the family's dynamics. They were to take note of whether she carried the child "like a part of herself"—which would then brand the mother as being unable to separate from the child— or "like an inanimate object" which would label her as the cold-and-rejecting type. Imagine being a mother observed by a therapist who used such a pigeonholing scheme in which each pigeonhole is a different form of bad mothering!*[4]

There were, to be sure, some outspoken and widely recognized experts in the field who realized the blame game had gone too far. "Momism" may catch the headlines and serve to right the wrongs of past adulation of motherhood, but it was demeaning to women, particularly homemaking mothers, who didn't have the education and degrees and recognized expertise to fight back.

Fathers and Mothers and Sigmund Freud

No individual in modern times has made a greater impact on child psychology and the roles of mothers and fathers than Sigmund Freud, and it is safe to say that he was no "friend" of women in general and mothers in particular. "Freud was unquestionably a pioneer along certain lines," writes Adrienne Rich. "But Freud was also a man, terribly limited by his culture and his gender."

> *For the male child, Freud believed the Oedipus complex to consist of the process whereby a little boy first experiences strong sexual feelings for his mother, then learns to detach and differentiate himself from her, to identify as a male with his father instead of perceiving him as a rival, and finally to go on to a point where his erotic instincts can be turned toward a woman other than his mother. . . .*
>
> *The fundamental assumption here is that the two-person mother-child relationship is by nature regressive, circular, unproductive, and that culture depends on the son-father relationship. All that the mother can do for the child is perpetuate a dependency which prevents further development. Through the resolution of the Oedipus complex, the boy makes his way into the male world, the world of the patriarchal law and order. . . .*
>
> *Freud also held that [for] the little girl . . . to become a woman, she must substitute pregnancy and a baby for the missing male organ.*[5]

Another Perspective on Freud

It is difficult to imagine how Sigmund Freud gained such respectability and popularity considering his low view of women and motherhood—and amazing as it may seem, women have been among his most committed followers. In fact, my sister named her cat Sigmund—after him. But he was no friend to mothers.

 [Sigmund Freud's] unique contribution was to encase the father-son conflict in the amber of scientific concept, by elaborating the notion of an Oedipus complex. In his elaboration, Freud made of the Oedipus complex a universal, eternal generalization. All fathers and all sons, presumably, had to encounter one another in this conflict, irrespective of the historical period or society in which they found themselves. The intensity and the resolution might be different, but the basic conflict was the same. . . . Mothers, it would almost appear, are merely objects of libidinal strife between father and sons, instead of being formative influences at least equal in importance to fathers, with a character and individuality in their own right.[6]

Sigmund Freud's Mother

 A man who has been the indisputable favorite of his mother keeps for life the feeling of a conqueror, that confidence of success that often inspires real success.

SIGMUND FREUD, LETTER[7]

This commentary on the mother-son relationship came from Freud's own experience. He was confident of his own success, and he was convinced he was his mother's favorite. "This self-confidence, which was one of Freud's prominent characteristics," writes Ernest Jones, "was only rarely impaired, and he was doubtless right in tracing it to the security of his mother's love. It is worth mentioning that, as one would expect, he was fed at the breast."

His relationship with his father was quite different. When he was a child, his father once rebuked him by saying, "That boy will never amount to anything." Later Freud reflected on that incident:

 This must have been a terrible affront to my ambition, for allusions to this scene occur again and again in my dreams, and are constantly coupled with enumerations of my accomplishments and successes, as if I wanted to say: "You see, I have amounted to something after all."

Unlike his father, Freud's mother was described as having a "lively personality" that did not diminish in old age.

 When she was ninety she declined the gift of a beautiful shawl, saying it would "make her look too old."

When she was ninety-five, six weeks before she died, her photograph appeared in the newspaper; her comment was: "A bad reproduction; it makes me look a hundred." It was strange to a young visitor to hear her refer to the great Master as "mein goldener Sigi" and evidently there was throughout a close attachment between the two.[8]

. . . .

A Freudian Historical Perspective

Howard R. Wolf attempted to bring a historical and literary perspective to Freudian psychology. He argued that eighteenth- and early nineteenth-century literature portrayed sons as submissive to their fathers in their Oedipal conflict, but as the nineteenth century progressed, sons rebelled against their fathers and defeated them.

 But by the beginning of the twentieth century, according to Wolf, the father-figure was fading away, and the son's relations were predominantly with the mother. The father was no longer perceived particularly as an authoritarian mentor or fierce competitor. The son had won in the fight for the mother, but the victory brought its own anxieties: an overinvolvement with the mother, a fear of oversubmission to her, and a need to reject her too, in order to maintain autonomy, identity, and self. The woman now threatened totally to absorb the son—a partly desired "return to the generous bosom where I and Thou are indistinguishable."[9]

Closely connected with the study of the psychology of motherhood is the inquiry into the child's attitude toward the mother. Why is the child overly dependent on the mother, or intimidated by the mother—or, as in the case of John Stuart Mill, seemingly oblivious to her very existence?

. . . .

The Obliterated Mother

Good mothers, bad mothers, dead mothers, deranged mothers, deserting mothers—they all have an impact on their children. But what about the mother who is seemingly obliterated by the child—as though she never existed. It has been said that there are many men who don't know they are fathers, or if they do know, don't know how many children they have fathered. Indeed, the case could be made that any man who has ever had sexual intercourse with a woman with whom the relationship soon after ended, could be a father of a child and not know it. Not so with mothers. It's hard to imagine how it would be possible for a woman to be a mother and not know it. But that doesn't mean that she will be acknowledged by her children—even when she had the primary responsibility in raising them. She can be obliterated from her child's memoirs, with no credit given her in either a positive or negative way for her influence in the child's life. So it was with John Stuart Mill, the most noted nineteenth-century English economist and social scientist whose impact is still felt today.

"I was born in London on the 20th of May, 1806,"
John Stuart Mill begins his Autobiography,
"and was the eldest son of James Mill, the author
of the History of British India." Most readers, and
this includes most scholars, have not noticed what
an extraordinary statement this is. It invokes a new
version of an immaculate conception, in which
the mother is entirely missing; indeed, John Stuart
Mill never mentions her throughout the published
version of his work. Instead, we have "book and boy"
both produced by James Mill, seemingly acting alone.
The rest of the Autobiography *appears to bear out*
this conception. It is as much about James Mill, the
father, as it is about the son. Taken together, the
relations of the two make up one of the great father
and son stories of the nineteenth century. . . .

Who was this forgotten mother in Mill's autobiography? She was Harriet Burrow who married
the thirty-one-year-old James Mill when she was
twenty-one. His "strong affectionate outpour-
ings" for her are documented in a letter he wrote
prior to their marriage, and during the course of
their marriage they had eight children. But according to Mill's biographer, "One year after the birth
of John, the father had fallen out of love with his
wife, who he came to regard as a stupid woman.
. . . The charge of stupidity hardly seems fitting to
one who reads Harriet Mill's letters, which are leg-
ible, literate, and sensible."

John's sister defended her mother, arguing that
it was "no 'fault' of my poor mother that she was
not the intellectual equal of her husband. But, the

disdain with which he now began to treat her
shocked all his friends," and would have a lifelong
impact on the son who likewise viewed her with
disdain. "John Stuart Mill's contemporaries were
shocked at his callous treatment of his mother."[10]

. . . .

Psychology for Pregnant Mothers

How does the mental and emotional well-being of
a pregnant mother affect her unborn child? That
question produced some unusual answers in generations past. In his book *Sex in Education*, published
in 1873, Dr. Edward Clarke argued that women who
studied or thought too deeply during pregnancy
drained energy from the reproductive organs and
risked the likelihood of an unhealthy birth:

 The psychosocial rule that begins to take form, then,
is this: the more educated the woman is, the
greater chance there is of sexual disorder, more or
less severe. The greater the disordered sexuality
in a given group of women, the fewer children do
they have.

Such beliefs were popularized by Margaret
Ribble in her book *The Rights of Infants*, published
in 1943. She urged the pregnant mother to refrain
from "mental activity" so that she would not give
birth to a "nervous infant." Testimonials from
women supported Ribble's theory. One woman
confessed:

I cannot deny that during my pregnancy I did an inordinate amount of reading and thinking and that my mental activity could have resulted in the present feeding problem. My son who rejected my milk was somehow aware that during my pregnancy my interest was diverted; thus depriving him of unrestricted attention.[11]

The Psychology of Passive Pregnancy

Helena Deutsch, a student of Sigmund Freud, and a noted psychoanalyst and interpreter of female psychology, argued that a woman's life "is fully active and rooted in reality only when she becomes a mother. Until then everything that is feminine in the woman, physiology and psychology, is passive, receptive."

In childbirth the woman was to be passive—the same passivity that she should display in sexual intercourse. Any woman who wanted "her delivery to be an active accomplishment on her part," according to Deutsch, had turned her femininity into masculinity that would result in birth complications and interfere with her ability to properly mother the child.[12]

A Psychoanalyst's Struggle with Motherhood

Helena Deutsch was not only Freud's student but also his patient. As patient, she opened herself up to her teacher and mentor, but "during her analysis with Freud, she never mentioned her painful conflicts as a mother." We learn of this "shocking and enlightening" confession in her autobiography *Confrontations with Myself*.

She was a very active working woman whose personal life countered her claim that a woman is characterized by passivity except in motherhood. She hired a nurse to care for her child, but she writes, "I always had the painful suspicion that I was depriving both my son, Martin, and myself of a rich source of happiness." Why then didn't she share this anguish with her famous therapist?

Freud may have unconsciously colluded with Deutsch's silence about her conflict as a mother. Deutsch may have sensed that Freud did not want to know that his gifted pupil had relinquished her role as a mother, choosing instead to succeed in a man's world—as a distinguished psychoanalyst and eventually as a proponent of his ideas on the psychology of women. . . . Had she been more open about the complex feelings her child aroused, Freud might have examined the psychology of women in a different light, exploring the early mother-child relationship with more interest in the mother's side of the dyad. Instead, his theories ignore the mother's experience and the emotional realities of nurturing. . . .

As a career woman, Helena Deutsch was far more than a noted researcher and she struggled with the anguish so many working mothers face:

. . . whenever the door to sublimation was open to me, I was much happier as a wife and mother. And vice versa: when something in my personal life interfered with my scientific productivity, I was less happy and more aggressive in my whole attitude toward my environment.[13]

. . . .

Maternal Instinct

Much of the discussion in recent years on motherhood has in one way or another touched on the issue of the maternal instinct fused with maternal love— once thought to be sacrosanct, a given that no one would think of challenging. This was the view of Rousseau and his fellow Frenchman Jules Michelet who wrote: "The maternal instinct dominates everything else. . . for, from the cradle onward, woman is mother, made with motherhood." Anyone who challenged this perspective was greeted with skepticism, as is related in the preface of Elisabeth Badinter's *Mother Love: Myth or Reality:*

 "You must admit it's a little scandalous. . . . You're questioning the existence of maternal love!" The gentleman interviewing Elisabeth Badinter in the French periodical Le Nouvel

Observateur is clearly alarmed, and focuses with characteristic media savagery on a sensationalistic misinterpretation of her book.

"I'm not questioning maternal love," the author replies. "I'm questioning maternal instinct.*"*

But her retort is not a palliative. In matters of motherhood, the severance of love from instinct seems to threaten one of the most sacred premises of Western culture.[14]

How then do we evaluate the impact of psychology on motherhood? On the positive side, it has challenged the sentimentality and mythology connected with motherhood. But negatively, mothers became an easy target, and were too quickly blamed for their children's problems. So in correcting the myth and misconceptions, the pendulum swung too far the other way—though there are signs that it has started to swing back toward the center.

The debate over the psychology of motherhood continues. The mental and emotional pathology of the mother is analyzed and evaluated and diagnosed by the experts. But the vitality of motherhood endures as it has through the generations. It has little time for analysis. It's too busy being and doing.

❧ *There is perhaps no such moment of exquisite joy,*

of deep unutterable thanksgiving taking the place

of pain and sorrow as when a woman knows

herself to be the living mother of a living child.

ANDREW MURRAY

7

The Changing Traditions of Pregnancy and Childbirth

*T*hough motherhood is the most important of all the professions—requiring more knowledge than any other department in human affairs—yet there is not sufficient attention given to the preparation for this office. If we buy a plant of a horticulturist we ask him many questions as to its needs, whether it thrives best in sunshine or in shade, whether it needs much or little water, what degrees of heat or cold; but when we hold in our arms for the first time, a being of infinite possibilities, in whose wisdom may rest the destiny of a nation, we take it for granted that the laws governing its life, health, and happiness are intuitively understood, that there is nothing new to be learned in regard to it.[1]

These are the words of Elizabeth Cady Stanton, the well-known feminist and social reformer of the late nineteenth century. Two years ago I visited her restored home in Seneca Falls, New York, and was fascinated by her gardens and her home furnishings and nursery as well as her diverse views on motherhood and child-rearing. She was a controversial woman on many issues, but few would disagree with her concern that women have too little preparation and training for childbirth and motherhood. Yet, she herself claimed that childbirth was routine, and she scolded women for turning it into a painful ordeal.

. . . .

Beyond the Curse

Pain in childbirth was considered by many a just penalty all women should pay to expiate the sin of Eve. Not so, according to Elizabeth Cady Stanton. She was convinced that women have a choice of whether or not to suffer. I have to wonder, though, if her insistence that the pain women endured was their own fault may have inflicted more guilt on women than was theirs vicariously through Eve.

 If you suffer, it is not because you are cursed of God, but because you violate his laws. What an incubus it would take from woman could she be educated to know that the pains of maternity are no curse upon her kind. We know that among Indians the squaws do not suffer in childbirth. They will step aside from the ranks even on the march, and return in a short time bearing with them the new-born child. What an absurdity, then, to suppose that only enlightened Christian women are cursed.

But one word of fact is worth a volume of philosophy; let me give you some of my own experience. I am the mother of seven children. My girlhood was spent mostly in the open air. I early imbibed the idea that a girl is just as good as a boy, and I carried it out. I would walk five miles before breakfast, or ride ten on horseback. . . . I wore my clothing sensibly. . . . I never compressed my body. . . . When my first four children were born, I suffered very little. I then made up my mind that it was totally unnecessary for me to suffer at all; so I dressed lightly, walked every day. . . and took proper care of myself. The night before the birth . . . I walked three miles. The child was born without a particle of pain. I bathed it and dressed it myself.[2]

Pain, Ecstasy, and Changing Traditions

I am in awe of Mrs. Stanton and her birthing abilities—especially having seen her little two-story house, lacking all the modern conveniences that I enjoy. But she was missing the mark in not seeing herself as an anomaly—not just in the nineteenth century, but for all times. Women have pain in child-bearing. That fact is as true today as it was in ancient times.

Indeed, with few exceptions, two aspects of childbirth have remained constant since Eve gave birth to Cain: the pain and the ecstasy. But every other tradition of childbirth, it seems, has radically changed over the centuries since that first baby was born.

I'm reminded of the pain and ecstasy of childbirth this morning as I sit in my air-conditioned guest bedroom, not venturing into the sweltering heat of the rest of the house or my backyard garden. It was twenty-one years ago today on July 13 that the temperatures in the Midwest also soared into the high nineties. The thermometer in Woodstock, Illinois, topped out at ninety-eight degrees that Saturday afternoon as I rested in a lounge chair in our musty, unfinished basement reading a book and timing contractions.

The contractions had started early that morning when I was twelve days past my due date, so it was not unreasonable to assume that this might be the big day. But I didn't want to rush it. We had no health insurance, and I had the dread fear of being admitted to the hospital only to be sent home on charges of false labor. So I patiently watched the clock as the contractions grew stronger and closer together—waiting until midafternoon to call my doctor.

I had grown very fond of Dr. Kang, so it was a devastating blow when she informed me she would not be available that Saturday night due to a prior engagement hosted by her husband's employer. But it was probably only false labor, she insisted, assuring me she'd be available in the morning. I hung up the phone and could hardly hold back the tears. How could a social engagement keep her away from delivering my baby? After twenty-one years, I'm still wondering.

By early evening my contractions had convinced me my baby wouldn't be waiting for a convenient time in my doctor's schedule. He was on his way, and so were we—to the hospital. We lived only a mile away from the Memorial Hospital in Woodstock, so transportation should not have been an issue, but it was. My husband and I were avid bikers and we didn't let my pregnancy stop us. So it was on a dare from a friend that we rode our bikes to the hospital, despite my last minute protests.

My contractions were now hard and fast, but fearing that I still might be in false labor, I stayed in the waiting room, eyed by a nervous receptionist, for a half hour before I agreed to be admitted. After an hour in the labor room, I was wheeled into delivery, and a strange doctor, who hardly had time to greet me, delivered Carlton, weighing in at nine pounds, twelve ounces.

How times have changed in twenty-one years. In 1974, our local hospital only reluctantly permitted husbands in the delivery room. Today it's different—as Carlton discovered some months ago when he was spending the night with his best buddy at a friend's house. During the night the friend's sister—an unmarried nineteen-year-old—went into labor more than a week early. So the boys were roused from their sleep to make the forty-minute drive to Butterworth Hospital. By this time the morning dawn had turned into daylight and, with nothing else to do—and perhaps as a reward for their services—they were invited to stay on and witness the birth.

Carlton was sobered by the intense pain the young mother endured, but exhilarated by the incredible experience of being present at the moment of birth and the baby's first healthy cry of life.

As for me, I'm still trying to come to grips with how quickly traditions have changed even in my lifetime. I'm tempted to wonder where this world is going when two boys, barely out of their teens, stand in for an absent father during the birth of his baby. But amidst all that was wrong in this particular situation, the miracle of childbirth triumphed with a healthy baby boy. Carlton witnessed a miracle and will hopefully be a better man and better father because of it.

Traditions of childbirth have changed dramatically over the decades and centuries, and one of the most interesting aspects of my research on motherhood was discovering how beliefs and practices relating to childbirth have developed through the years.

Caesarean Section

Is there any truth to the legend that Julius Caesar was taken from his mother's womb through a surgical procedure, thus leaving forever his stamp on the cut in the mother's abdomen known as "Caesarean section"?

Medical historians now believe that the first instance of a baby taken from a living mother's uterus by surgical means did not occur until around A.D. 1500. Although it was a common practice in early Roman times to remove babies by cutting through the abdominal and uterine walls of dead mothers, Caesar's mother, Aurelia, lived on for many years after his birth and so obviously did not undergo such an operation.

The theory is now that the term "Caesarean section" came into being because of an old Roman law making it mandatory for women dying in advanced pregnancy to have their babies removed by surgical means. The lex Caesarea, *as it was called, gave rise to the custom of referring to all surgically assisted childbirths as being "Caesarean."*[3]

Today new mothers are usually up and about in a day or two, and we cannot imagine being confined for a week as our mothers and grandmothers were—or even longer as was common a century ago. Carlton was born at 9:48 P.M., and I was dismissed from the hospital the next evening. This was the 1970s and I was making a valiant attempt to be a thoroughly modern woman and take childbirth in stride—to pretend it was just a routine part of my busy life.

Before the advent of modern medicine, however, childbirth was anything but routine. It is true that there are stories of pioneer women giving birth while working out in the woods, and at the end of the day—hardly missing a beat—bringing home a baby and a load of firewood. But for most women childbirth was a life-threatening ordeal. The thrill of nursing a newborn carried the very real risk of death.

A Dangerous Venture

Poorly trained and ill-equipped midwives contributed to the high mortality rate in childbirth. Most midwives learned by trial and error, and even when licensing was required there were few people capable of adequately checking the skills of the applicant. Horror stories of ignorant knife-wielding midwives abound. A 1662 English oath required of midwives leaves little to the imagination. Among other things, the midwife promised:

I will not destroy the child born of any woman, nor cut, nor pull off the head thereof, or otherwise dismember or hurt the same, or suffer it to be so hurt or dismembered.

The most significant obstetrical advance of the seventeenth century was the invention of forceps, but the inventor, Peter Chamberlen, and his heirs kept this life-saving invention secret—all on account of professional jealously and competition. It was not until the eighteenth century that forceps were reinvented and widely used in difficult childbirths.[4]

. . . .

Superstition and Childbirth

 Swing a silver needle over the mother to tell if it's a boy or girl.
Swing a golden ring over the mother to tell if it's a boy or girl.
If it spins, it'll be a girl.
If it swings, it'll be a boy.

If you carry the baby low, it'll be a boy.
If you carry the baby high, it'll be a girl.
If you're pointed it's a girl.
If you're round or broad it's a boy.[5]

. . . .

Magic and Childbirth

Although Cotton Mather encouraged the use of the lodestone as a medicine for women in childbirth, he and his fellow Protestants denounced the use of magic that was associated with medieval Catholicism.

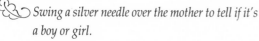 *Before the Protestant Reformation midwives regularly used magic to call spiritual powers to aid the birth. The midwife might employ special charms, potions, incantations, and even girdles of Mary*

Magdalene or of Our Lady. Protestant reformers and churches disparaged these magical means as both useless and impious. . . . . Protestants wanted birth to be a religious occasion, a time for salvation; expectant women were not to avoid this by seeking to avert bad luck or misfortune through magical practices.[6]

. . . .

The Birth of Thirty Monsters

One of my "friends" that I've come to know through my study of American church history is Anne Hutchinson. She was the infamous Massachusetts Bay "heretic" brought before the court and banished from the colony in 1638, because she challenged the legalistic "covenant of works" in favor of her own version of a "covenant of grace." She drew scores of followers in and around Boston—so many that they became known as the "Hutchinsonians." But Anne was first and foremost a homemaker. She was the wife of William Hutchinson and the mother of fifteen children. Her contacts with other women began through her midwifery skills and when she invited small groups of women to her home to exchange practical household tips and child-care advice. Her minister, John Cotton, initially praised her work:

 Shee did much good in our Town, in womans meeting at Childbirth-Travells, wherein shee was not onley skillful and helpfull, but readily fell into good discourse with the women about their spir-

*itual estates . . . By which means many of the women
(and their husbands) were . . . brought to enquire
more seriously after the Lord Jesus Christ.*

As more and more people began overflowing her house to hear her commentaries on the Sunday sermons, however, she became the target of bitter attacks by the church fathers who were threatened by her popularity. A court battle ensued, and not surprisingly, the religious establishment won. She was banished to Rhode Island, where word came from her detractors that due to God's judgment she had suffered a miscarriage—but more than that. God was humiliating and crushing her at the core of the very motherliness that had originally drawn her followers.

 Rev. Thomas Weld of Roxbury, brother of Anne's jailer, reported that Anne had brought forth "thirty monstrous births or thereabouts, at once, some of them bigger, some lesser, some of one shape, some of another; few of any perfect shape, none at all of them (as far as I could ever learn) of human shape."

There is no "happily ever after" ending to the story of Anne Hutchinson. She was widowed in 1642, and the following year, while living on Long Island, far away from her adversaries in Boston, she and her children were attacked and killed by a band of Indians.[7]

The Joy of Childbirth

 There is perhaps no such moment of exquisite joy, of deep unutterable thanksgiving taking the place of pain and sorrow as when a woman knows herself to be the living mother of a living child.

ANDREW MURRAY[8]

Warnings to New Mothers

Women of the Victorian era were often perceived to be weak and frail and ever dependent on the protection and advice of men—even be more so during and after pregnancies. Popular advice books warned women to avoid any form of exercise or strain. In *The Physical Life of Women*, G.H. Napheys warned new mothers not only to stay in bed but also to remain "rigidly in the recumbent position for the first few days, not raising her shoulders from the pillow for any purpose." Moving the arms and body to change her birthing gowns was considered too strenuous until the fourth day, but even then she was instructed not to lift her head off the pillow. By the second week she was permitted to sit up, and after two weeks of bed confinement the new mother was encouraged to get out of bed for short periods each day. Such restrictions were heeded by women who could afford household help.

For working-class and pioneer women, child-birth granted no such luxuries.[9]

Saved from Therapeutic Abortion

Abortions were not numbered in the millions in 1918, as they are today, but therapeutic abortions were occasionally performed by doctors in order to save the life of the mother. This procedure might have ended the life of Madeleine L'Engle, an internationally known speaker and best-selling author of many books, including *The Crosswicks Journal* series. She tells her story in the second book of that series, *The Summer of the Great-Grandmother:*

> *I was a much longed-for baby. It wasn't for want of trying that my parents were childless for so long. But Mother could not hold a baby past three months. "All I needed to get pregnant," she once remarked, "was for your father to hang his pajamas over the bedpost." She had miscarriages all over the world—Paris, Berlin, Cairo, and—I think—one in China. Sometime toward the end of . . . World War I, Father came home on leave from Plattsburg, and I was conceived. Because Father was sent immediately overseas, Mother was able to spend most of the nine months in bed. Even so, I am a witness to her determination. The first doctor she went to told her that she could not possibly carry a baby to term, and that if she did not have a therapeutic abortion, both she and the baby would die. Then she went to a Roman Catholic doctor: that was in 1918. So I am here to tell the story.[10]*

Vicarious Motherhood

During the late eighteenth and early nineteenth century, Martha Ballard kept a diary of her life and work as a midwife in the region in and around Augusta, Maine. Laurel Thatcher Ulrich tells her fascinating story in *A Midwife's Tale* and speculates as to why she followed this "calling."

> *What took Martha Ballard out of bed in the cold of night? Why was she willing to risk frozen feet and broken bones to practice her trade? Certainly midwifery paid well, at least by standards usually assigned women's work. Martha cared about her "rewards," and she kept her midwifery accounts carefully. Yet money alone cannot account for her commitment. Nor is it enough to say that serving others was her way of serving God. She interpreted her work, as all of her life in religious terms: God rescued her from the spring flood, sustained her through difficult deliveries, preserved the lives of mothers and children, and gave her the strength to continue her work. (Even such a prosaic end-of-the-year summary as "I have Lost 42 nights sleep the year past" was a kind of spiritual accounting.) Yet religious faith is also an inadequate explanation. Midwifery was a form of service and a source of material rewards, but even more than that it was an inner calling, an assertion of being. Martha Ballard's specialty brought together the gentle and giving side of her nature with her capacity for risk and her need for autonomy.*

The fathers who fetched her in the black of night leaned on her skill, offering her the command of their horses and bedchambers, bestowing lumber credits and teapots for her service. The women who circled around her at the height of travail respected her caring and sustained her strength. The women who reached for her in the anguish of travail extended her motherhood in their own. Martha Ballard needed her patients as much as they needed her.[11]

. . . .

A Mother's Concern for the Unborn

When I was pregnant with Carlton, we lived across the street from a "thalidomide baby"—as the little boy was sometimes referred to. His mother—an immigrant from Germany—had taken the drug when she was pregnant. I was very careful about taking any medication, and often wondered how I would feel if the baby I was carrying was harmed in some way by my ignorance or lack of caution. How could I live with myself? Yet, despite his deformity of having no arms—just hands sticking out of stumps on his shoulders— the boy was a great athlete and seemed as happy as any of the other kids in the neighborhood. I felt sorry for the mother, and have only recently discovered that were it not for another mother, "thalidomide babies" might be commonplace in America today.

Frances Kelsey was a working mother, married to a physician. Although she already held a Ph.D. in pharmacology from the University of Chicago, she felt she needed more training, so she went on to medical school, during which time she gave birth to two children. With this training Dr. Kelsey was hired by the Food and Drug Administration in 1960, and her first assignment was routine—or so she thought. She was to review the application to market thalidomide. "It was deemed to be a simple application," she later recalled, "and since I had just reported to work, it was assigned to me."

Thalidomide was known as "Europe's favorite sleeping pill," and was being marketed in Europe and elsewhere. The American company eager to profit from the drug anticipated a speedy approval especially coming up against a woman working on her first case. But Dr. Kelsey was not easily intimidated by powerful corporation executives. "A tall, severe-looking woman in sensible tweeds and low oxfords," she demanded that her questions be answered. She had read a report that the drug caused numbness and twitching and cramps in some users. The findings prompted Kelsey to inquire whether thalidomide might adversely affect an unborn baby when the medication was taken by the pregnant mother. Such a concern would be natural today, but at the time Dr. Kelsey was regarded eccentric by some of her colleagues. The drug company fought the delays and appealed to the head of the FDA—until November of 1961, when shocking evidence was coming to light that thalidomide was the cause of terrible defects in thousands—"babies with no arms and flipper-like hands attached to their shoulders, others with no legs or deformed internal organs."

Most Americans were oblivious to the thalidomide controversy at the FDA until the toll from Europe became clear. Then, in 1962, Kennedy presented Kelsey with the President's Award for Distinguished Federal Civilian Service, the highest honor for a U.S. Government employee. Kelsey received a flood of mail from American mothers thanking her, some enclosing pictures of their healthy newborn babies.

As a result of the thalidomide episode, the FDA was given new powers to limit the testing of new drugs. Kelsey was put in charge of a new department to monitor the research that pharmaceutical companies produce to support their applications. It is a job she was still performing in 1990, at the age of seventy-six.[12]

. . . .

The Great Childbirth Heist

So, what can we conclude about the changing traditions of childbirth? Should we hark back to an earlier age when women were in charge of the birthing rituals and routines of life? Childbirth no longer belongs to women. It is no longer their exclusive domain, and they no longer are confident about giving birth without an attending physi-

cian. Men have stolen this womanly activity from them, so says Suzanne Arms in her book *The Immaculate Deception:*

 The history of childbirth can be viewed as a gradual attempt by man to extricate the process of birth from woman and call it his own. . . . Man placed woman on her back in labour, then devised metal tools to pull her baby out, then knocked her senseless with anaesthesia. And it was man who, throughout history, did it all in the name of "saving woman from her own body.[13]

Suzanne Arms is wrong. Childbirth has not been taken away from women. There are more female physicians and nurse midwives today than ever before, and childbirth is safer than it has ever been. But as mothers perhaps we have lost some of the womanly comaraderie by not sharing this time with sisters and close friends, and we have run roughshod over the childbirth process by rushing back to work—perhaps due to no fault of our own—only weeks after our little one has arrived. It's sad when childbirth and recovery become synonymous with *maternity leave.*

It pleased God to keep me a long time

without a child, which was a great grief

to me, and cost me many prayers

and tears before I obtaind one,

and after him gave me many more.

⁓ ANNE BRADSTREET

8

Childless Mothers

"The Heart of a Rose"
(To My Son)

When I gaze into the heart of a rose,
I think, little boy, of you.
Pure, sweet as a flower
Kissed by the evening dew.

Your hair was like golden petals
Lips American beauty red
Cheeks as pure as dawn, dear,
I can not call you dead.

You live little son in a garden,
Tended by God's loving care,
A fragrant little rose bud
Unfolding your beauty There.

ETHEL T. WOOD[1]

There are countless images that come to mind when I think of childless mothers. Some are of women desperately longing to become pregnant and give birth; others mourning the loss of the child or children they once had.

One of the most painful of these stories is forever etched in my memory through my reading and travel. Several years ago while vacationing out west with my family, we visited the Whitman Mission, a national historic site near Walla Walla, Washington. I had written about the ministry of Marcus and Narcissa Whitman in my history of missions text, and was now making a pilgrimage to the mission settlement they founded. There is much about their story that is gripping—most notably the Indian massacre that ended their lives. But the story that touched my heart the most was that of a grief-stricken childless mother. I write of that tragedy in *From Jerusalem to Irian Jaya:*

It was a late June Sunday afternoon at Waiilatpu. It was not just Sunday, but the Sabbath—a day of rest from the week's heavy labor. Marcus and Narcissa were engrossed in reading and little Alice was playing close by—or so they thought. When they suddenly realized she was missing, it was too late. The precious little two-year-old had wandered off and drowned in a nearby stream. . . . A year later a package arrived from back east with the little shoes and dresses Narcissa requested from her mother.[2]

I'll never forget walking along that stream where the wild flowers bloomed and thinking back on the deep sorrow that arched over that isolated mission station in the summer of 1839. How did Narcissa survive such a painful tragedy? "A weaker woman could not have endured," I write, "but Narcissa's faith carried her through."

There are other kinds of childless mothers, and among them are those who grieve for children never born—whose heart aches for the little one they will never hold in their arms. Since biblical times, this has been one of the great sorrows of womanhood—described with such seeming finality by that haunting hollow word *barren*. Sarah was barren and so were Rachel and Hannah—all of whom later gave birth. But for many women, there is no such happy ending. Barren means barren.

The Wedded UnMother

The term "unwedded mother" is not viewed as politically correct by some who would suggest that it is a label that is offensive to women who have a baby without a husband. But the term and the circumstances themselves can be even more dispiriting to a married woman struggling with infertility. It just isn't fair that young women—often teenagers—have babies without the benefits of a supportive marriage, when married women can't conceive. In *The Unwedded Mother*, Kaye Halverson writes of the pain and depression she experienced as the months turned into years with all hopes of having a baby diminishing.

 The crowning blow came when my youngest sister became pregnant. I hit an all-time low. I would not be the one to give my parents their first grandchild. Although they had never asked us to do this, we had wanted to. And now I was jealous of my sister. We had become very close since her marriage, but I couldn't bear this. I didn't want to ruin her happiness by letting her know my feelings. I had to become closed, cool, and uncommunicative, or fall apart.

But failure to communicate only made matters worse. Kaye needed to know that those dearest to her really cared. Her mother knew her pain but did not want to exacerbate the problem by bringing up the subject and rubbing salt into the wounds, but her silence only made the situation worse.

Kaye wrote to her mother after her little niece was born—crying out for help:

> *Mom, I needed you so much the night you stayed over with me alone before going to see Ruth's new baby. I needed some words like "I know how this must be affect you." I wanted so badly to go into your room and let everything out, but my stubborn pride prevented me. I cried myself to sleep, softly for fear you'd hear my grief. I felt that since you were the mother, older and wiser, you should understand me better than I could understand myself. I probably needed you even more than Ruth did that week.*

Kaye's story ends on a positive note. Soon after her ten-year college reunion, she received a phone call from a social worker informing her that they had a baby girl waiting to be adopted. The long years of struggling with infertility and adoption had come to an end.

> *God had his hand in the timing of our becoming parents. He led us in special ways we never foresaw. How much pain we could have spared ourselves had we simply put our trust in him.[3]*

A Woman's Desperate Plea for a Baby

> *I am in pain*
> *Someone just died.*
> *Who you say?*
> *Someone who never was.*
>
> *I am infertile*
> *My period just came*
> *I hurt so much.*
>
> *My own body*
> *Keeps reminding me*
> *That I am incomplete,*
> *I don't function properly.*
>
> *Why? Why? Why?*
> *Oh, my baby,*
> *Why can't you be?*

AUTHOR UNKNOWN[4]

Motherhood Deferred

When we think of an infertile woman longing to be a mother, we may not picture a highly successful middle-aged journalist and radio commentator. But "barren" women come in all forms, and Anne Taylor Fleming was one such childless mother. She tells her story in *Motherhood Deferred*. As a college student and later as a columnist for *The New York*

Times, she was part of the women's movement that did not concern itself with babies. She had been schooled in the philosophy of feminism and its "message that motherhood was a desexualizing trap."

The world was coming deliciously unglued and I was part and parcel of it there on my wooded campus. Armed with my contraceptives and my fledgling feminism, I was on the cusp of a fabulous journey. My sisters and I were . . . the best and the brightest. The luckiest young women on earth. Everything was before us. With our birth control pills and the exhortations of the feminist foremothers to urge us on, what could stop us? Who could? We were the golden girls of the brave new world, ready, willing and able to lay our contraceptively endowed bodies across the chasm between the feminine mystique and the world the feminist envisioned. Strong, smart, educated, we were the beneficiaries of the unique historical timing when the doors were opening, the old male-female roles were falling and the world was ours to conquer, to be part of, to matter in, the world of men, of lawyers and doctors, astronauts and poets. I wanted in that world. I wanted to matter. I wanted to be somebody.

Later, after she married, she writes that when her husband talked about having a baby, she "would freeze in terror." But these feelings faded as she moved through her thirties, but by then it was too late. She went to one specialist after another and did everything clinically possible to become pregnant but to no avail.

So after all those years of sex without procreation, here I lie, engaged in this procreation without sex. It's a stunning reversal, a cosmic joke. . . . A thousand whys dance through my brain, a thousand questions, threads that wind around each other containing the secret to my babylessness. How could something so primal as this longing to procreate have been so long repressed, so long buried? . . . Had I been led astray, had we, by bruised and bitter women who had warned us away from something magic, important, noble even? Had we, in the name of liberation, simply ended up aping the cultural dismissal of women, femaleness, motherhood, our mothers?[5]

⋅ ⋅ ⋅ ⋅ ⋅ ⋅ ⋅ ⋅ ⋅ ⋅ ⋅ ⋅ ⋅ ⋅ ⋅ ⋅ ⋅ ⋅ ⋅

Miscarriages and Missed Adoptions

all my life,
only one thing really mattered
to me. . . .

all my life, i just wanted to be a
mother. every year i received only
one Christmas gift that truly
counted: a doll. not a barbie or a
fashion doll, but a baby doll. . . . i was twelve
when I finally
decided to tuck my dolls away and grow up. but my
dream of motherhood burned on as fervently as ever.

These are the opening lines of the first chapter of *And with the Gift Came Laughter* by Ann Kiemel Anderson, who is perhaps best known for her books that relate to her struggles and victories as a single woman. At thirty-five, Ann married Will Anderson, expecting that her dream of motherhood would now become a reality. It did. But before that would happen, she would endure the utter anguish of childlessness.

 after miscarrying baby after baby . . . after will's determination not to adopt the first newborn offered us (which nearly finished me) . . . after will's agreeing to the next baby offered to us, and our flying to the east coast to pick up the baby . . . after the mother changed her mind, and we flew home with the diaper bag still on my arm and dark waters of sorrow washing over me . . . after all this, i walked into the empty nursery to hang up the diaper bag and found will—6'3"—kneeling by the crib. it shocked and almost frightened me to find him there, for i had been so lost in my own sorrow—so isolated in my self-absorption—that i hardly had observed his level of grief. quickly i knelt beside him, and he began to pray: "Father God, i don't know why things like this happen. i do know you love us. we go through life only once; i don't want to take second best. so, if you aren't finished with us . . . if there are still lessons to learn . . . keep pouring on the heat. don't let up. don't let us look back, knowing you didn't teach us all we needed to learn.

hearing his prayer, i shuddered. at first i felt anger. how could he pray that way? how dare he tell God to give us more sorrow if he needed to? . . . but very quickly, in the utter silence of that little nursery,

i knew in my heart that will's prayer was truth. i said "yes" to it as i clung to his big, strong hand. i walked out of that room a freed woman.[6]

. . . .

Childless Mother at Twenty-One

Today a mother who has not been able to bear a child by age twenty-one would not typically be viewed as a "barren" woman. Not so in Colonial New England—at least with famed poet Anne Bradstreet. In a private journal entry of 1633 or 1634, she wrote:

 It pleased God to keep me a long time without a child, which was a great grief to me, and cost me many prayers and tears before I obtain one, and after him gave me many more.

"She could not have been more than twenty-one years old when Samuel was born," writes her biographer, "but five or six years of marriage without motherhood had distressed and alarmed her." In 1647, when her firstborn son was about to sail for England, she wrote a prayer in verse:

Thou mighty God of Sea and Land,
I here resigne into thy hand
The Son of Prayers of Vowes, of teares,
The child I stay'd for many yeares.
Thou heard'st me then and gav'st him me;
Hear me again, I give him Thee.[7]

. . . .

A Tribute to a Childless Woman

Frances Willard, founder and director of the Woman's Christian Temperance Union, was a single woman who missed the joy of having children of her own, but through her sacrifice she was a mother to many:

"Sacrifice is the foundation of all real success" and it was a crucial moment in Miss Willard's life when she relinquished . . . that which women hold the dearest—the sacred, sheltered life of home. For her no children wait around the Christmas hearth, but she has lost that life only to find it again ten thousand fold. She has understood the mystery of the wider circle of love and loyalty, and the world is her home as truly as John Wesley said it was his parish. She has understood the divine motherhood that claims the orphaned hearts of humanity for her heritage, and a chorus of children's voices around the world hail her as mother, for organized mother-love is the best definition of the Woman's Christian Temperance Union.[8]

. . . .

Coming to Terms with Sorrow

How could a mother ever move beyond the sorrow of losing her husband and all four of her children in a matter of weeks? It's hard to even contemplate such sorrow, but Mary Jones was not alone in her grief in the spring of 1867. The rains were heavy that year, and the puddles and drainage ditches around Memphis provided perfect breeding pools for the worst infestation of mosquitoes in many years. The plague—Yellow Fever—ravaged the town, and those with relatives out of town or rich enough to live elsewhere fled the area.

But the plague continued. "The dead surrounded us," Mary later wrote. "All about my house I could hear weeping and the cries of delirium." Every morning, just before dawn, the grating sounds of the death wagon could be heard, touring the streets to collect the bodies. "Bring out your dead," called the drivers, hooded and masked, as the horses clattered down the silent streets.

Catherine, five years old was the first of Mary's children to die. Then Terence, two, and Elizabeth, three, were dead. The next week, the first week in October, Mary stood in her doorway and looked at the dawn, her last child, barely a year old, dead in her arms. "One by one my four little children sickened and died," she wrote. "I washed their little bodies and got them ready for burial."

George [Mary's husband] was stricken and died in the week that followed. . . . At first Mary prayed that she too would be taken. But something, perhaps the very grief she was experiencing and the suffering her own family had gone through, impelled her to go and try to help the others. A few days after burying her husband, Mary got a permit to enter quarantined homes and nurse the victims. In one cottage, she found a woman with a baby in her arms. The woman was walking the floor and singing a lullaby. She neither saw nor heard Mary as she let herself into the room. The baby had been dead for hours. In another house, a woman was sitting in a rocking chair, dead, with a dead child on her lap. On the floor beside the chair, a second child lay dying.

The plague left Memphis as quickly as it came—with the cold weather of late autumn. Mary was now alone with no mothers and babies to try to nurse back to health. She moved to Chicago to work as a seamstress, and there, four years later, she suddenly found herself in the midst of another great catastrophe—the Chicago fire. She escaped with only a bag of food. Everything else that she could call her own was gone.

In the wake of the fire, still grieving for her husband and children, Mary was confronted again and again with the vulnerability of poor working families. Her husband had been a union organizer, and she vowed that she would make that mission her own. For the next fifty years and more she traveled around the country from factories and train yards to coal fields and logging camps preaching the necessity of organizing. As a powerful and effective union organizer, she was a "mother" and heroine to oppressed workers, but regarded as "the most dangerous woman in America" by wealthy industrialists. She died in 1830 at the age of one hundred—always to be remembered simply as "Mother Jones."[9]

The Mourning Mother

Dost thou weep, mourning mother,
    For thy blind boy in the grave?
That no more with each other,
    Sweet counsel ye can have?—
That he, left dark by nature,
    Can never more be led
By thee, maternal creature,
    Along smooth paths instead?
That thou canst no more show him
    The sunshine, by the heat:
The river's silver flowing,
    By murmurs at his feet?
The foliage by its coolness;
    The roses, by their smell;
And all creation's fulness,
    By Love's invisible? . . .
Look up, O mourning mother,
    Thy blind boy walks in light!
Ye wait for one another,
    Before God's infinite.
But thou art now the darkest,
    Thou mother left below—
Thou, the sole blind,—thou markest,
    Content that it be so,—
Until ye two have meeting
    Where Heaven's pearl gate is,
And he shall lead thy feet in,
    As once thou leddest his.
Wait on, thou mourning mother.

ELIZABETH BARRETT BROWNING[10]

One of the most difficult choices a mother could ever confront is the decision to give up a child. I've read the stories of women who have given up their babies and the hurt is always there—even though they knew what they had done was best for both them and the child. The decision to give up a baby may mean that a young girl can stay off welfare and go to college, while giving an infertile couple the joy of having their own child. The choice of one young mother a hundred years ago to give up her baby had an effect on me and my son's education. Carlton started his public school education in Montessori kindergarten—an unstructured program that forced him to concentrate and be more self-motivated than he otherwise would have been. I didn't realize it until recently that this program probably would never have been developed had it not been for the difficult decision of one young woman to go through life as a childless mother.

. . . .

The "Mother" of Montessori

She was the first woman to graduate from the University of Rome medical school and she quickly distinguished herself in the field of childhood diseases and mental deficiencies. But when she realized she was pregnant, the thirty-year-old Maria Montessori had little choice but to go into hiding and have the baby without creating a public scandal. She was single and had fallen in love with Dr.

Montesano, a colleague at the Orthophrenic School where she worked. Marriage was not in the picture for the two of them, and not long after the birth of their child, he married another woman. Maria gave up her baby to be raised by friends, and the scandal was hidden from the public. She could not go back to the school where she had worked, so she went on to other educational endeavors, which eventually included her development of the Montessori method, now used worldwide.

 The child whose name in the world would be his mother's—Mario Montessori—has shadowy memories of visits from time to time from a "beautiful lady" who was never identified. . . . No one can know what the experience of her tragic affair or its aftermath cost her. We only know that she decided to leave the institution where she worked beside the father of her child, now another woman's husband, and refocus her interests and energies. It was, as it turned out, a momentous decision, for her and for the world.[11]

. . . .

My Arms Are Empty

 I know—yet my arms are empty,
That fondly folded seven,
And the mother heart within me
Is almost starved for heaven.

MARGARET ELIZABETH SANGSTER
(FROM "ARE THE CHILDREN AT HOME")[12]

A First Lady's Frustration with Infertility

Jackie Kennedy, remembered as the most glamorous First Lady in modern times, focused her attention on beautifying the White House while her husband served as President. But more than that, in the mind's eye of Americans, she is remembered for instinctively lunging to protect the President on that dreadful day in Dallas, November 22, 1963, and for her courage and poise in the days that followed as the nation mourned. But the man who was killed by the assassin's bullet was far more than a President to her. He was the man she had married for better or for worse—and he was the father of her children. We now know that theirs was not a blissful union, and there were times— especially early on in the marriage when the relationship was very shaky—in part because Jackie was childless. In *A Woman Named Jackie,* C. David Heymann tells the story:

 Despite Kennedy's outward calm, his marriage had reached a turning point. A hospital spokesman attributed the stillbirth (her second unsuccessful pregnancy in as many years) to "nervous tension and exhaustion following the Democratic convention." . . . The situation was exacerbated by several factors, not the least of which were two other Kennedy family births. . . . These joyful births in the wake

of Jackie's tragic loss only served to heighten her personal sense of failure and despair. . . . The breach between Jack and Jackie widened. Rumors of an impending divorce began to circulate and eventually reached the gossip columns.

The marriage did not end in divorce largely because of Jackie's third pregnancy that came to term with the birth of a healthy baby girl.

 Baby Caroline was three weeks old when Jackie draped her in the same soft robe she had worn at her own christening and, with the beaming father in attendance, took her to St. Patrick's Cathedral to be baptized by Cardinal Cushing of Boston. For her parents, Caroline's birth represented something of a triumph. Jackie was ecstatic, and . . . the mood of their marriage took a distinctly upward swing.[13]

Whether she is Sarah, the wife of a Patriarch, or Jackie, the wife of a President, there is no soft or gentle way to describe the circumstances. The word is barren—or infertile or childless. However we say it, the anguish is the same. And even more painful is childlessness after having given birth—to no less than four as was true of Mother Jones. But maybe not. Does the proverb, "'Tis better to have loved and lost than never loved at all"—referring to romantic love—also apply to mothers? A mother's love is surely no less than a romantic lover's.

Dear God!

How can you walk serenely

Through the starry meadows of eternity,

Swinging your moonlit lantern,

Calling the long night watches:

"All's well! All's well!"

When my heart's only heaven

Is black with grief . . .

My life's great lamp is broken and dark,

And I falter . . . unmothered!

MEREDITH GRAY

9

Motherless Children

One of my favorite books as a child was a book my mother loved and passed on to me, *The Secret Garden*. Indeed, so fixed in my imagination is that story of two children on the desolate moors of Yorkshire that I cannot bring myself to see the movie. I know that no film could ever capture the setting as my own imagination has. The story fascinated me and, though I was anything but motherless, I identified with those motherless children who found new life in an old garden.

In Frances Hodgson Burnett's novel, the secret garden is symbolic of a mother's devotion and care that will eventually heal her son both physically and emotionally. Sickly, sallow Colin is a bed-ridden child—a "deformed and crippled creature." His mother's death in childbirth so devastated his father, Archibald Craven, that he locked up her walled garden on his great estate Misselthwaite, buried the key, and turned his back on his son,

despising him for being the cause of his wife's death—as the son confessed.

 My mother died when I was born and it makes him wretched to look at me. He thinks I don't know, but I've heard people talking. He almost hates me.

When the embittered orphan Mary enters the picture, Colin grudgingly finds a companion, and through her persistent spirit of adventure, the key is found and the garden becomes their secret paradise. As the garden comes to life, so do they; and they also come to realize that the presence of Colin's mother has never left the garden.

The climax to the story comes when Archibald Craven returns to Misselthwaite:

 He had not meant to be a bad father, but he had not felt like a father at all. He had supplied doctors and

nurses and luxuries, but he had shrunk from the mere thought of the boy and had buried himself in his own misery.

But when he hears the sounds of joyful laughter in the closed garden, he discovers their secret, and he too is healed. And what of the garden?

 The place was a wilderness of autumn gold and purple and violet blue and flaming scarlet and on every side were sheaves of late lilies standing together—lilies which were white or white and ruby. He remembered well when the first of them had been planted that just at this season of the year their late glories should reveal themselves. Late roses climbed and hung and clustered and the sunshine deepening the hue of the yellowing trees made one feel that one stood in an embowered temple of gold. The newcomer stood silent just as the children had done when they came into its greyness.[1]

I recently reread *The Secret Garden*, and now as a motherless (adult) child found special meaning in the mother's lingering presence in the garden, and a sense of gratefulness that my mother passed the book on to me.

The death of a mother is a terrible thing. It is no less than a searing of the soul. It is true that the razor sharp severing of the umbilical psyche numbs over the course of time, but the loss is always there.

· · · · · · · · · · · · · · · · · ·

Mothers

What a wonderful thing
is a mother!
Other folks can love you,
But only your mother
understands;
She works for you—
looks after you—
Loves you, forgives you—
anything you may do;
And then the only thing
bad she ever does do—
Is to die and leave you.

—BARONESS VON HUTTON[2]

Last night I got a phone call from David, the husband of my very dear friend Margaret who died of breast cancer just ten months ago. Jenny, their daughter, is getting married this weekend, and he realized that my name had been overlooked when he was compiling the invitation list. His recent calls, during my trip to Singapore, had gone unanswered, and now he was making one last attempt to contact me before the big day.

The garden wedding is tomorrow in Cumberland, Wisconsin, and I won't be there. But amid the festivities, my presence will go unnoticed. Everyone's attention will be focused on the beautiful bride—and the missing mother.

Margaret was one of the most vibrant and radiant individuals I have ever known. She drew people to her like a magnet. No one will attend that wedding without an overwhelming feeling that someone is missing. But for the motherless Jenny there will be an even more profound sense of loss. This is her biggest day—missed by her mother. And the loss is so recent. It was only last October that she and her college friends were collecting brilliant maple leaf boughs to fill the funeral home with the colors and fragrance her mother so loved.

Margaret knew she was fighting a battle of life and death ever since the doctors at Mayo Clinic told her she had only a five percent chance of surviving five years. She vowed she would beat the odds, but she didn't. We talked about death on several occasions, and she wasn't afraid. Her faith was strong, and she knew God was ultimately in control. But there was that gnawing dread of leaving behind motherless children. She had confidence in David, but she knew how desperately Jenny, Davey, and little Christopher needed a mother too.

I have not faced death as an impending reality, but I have in my own way experienced the fear of leaving behind a motherless child. My fear of dying—especially during one unusually turbulent commuter airline flight—was not fear of death itself, but fear of leaving behind Carlton without a mother.

But when and if I do die while Carlton is still alive, I hope he will sense my presence even as I truly hope that Jenny feels her mother's love and presence in the garden tomorrow on this very special day of her life.

When I think of Jenny and her wedding day, I am reminded of a sweet and sentimental garden story of a motherless daughter and her wedding night—a fictional tale, entitled "The Mother," by Katherine Holland Brown.

. . . .

Dorigen's White Rose Wedding Bouquet

As the story opens, we meet Dorigen, a poor "neglected foster-child" who is swept off her feet by Flavius, "a young patrician of vast wealth."

 The night before her bridal, she crept out of the house, and wandered away, down the deep, lonely garden. It was late October; the blue fever-mists hung thick over the wide sweep of the Campagna. The garden, in its autumn mimicry of death, was still darkly green. . . . She paused by a tall white rose bush. . . . Every spring it was a drift of beauty. But now it bore not one solitary bud. It was a mass of dark, shining green.

"I wish I could have a white rose for my bridal," thought Dorigen. Then she laughed at her own foolishness. She, to wish for a rose! She who had all the world!

She had all the world, but there was a heaviness in her heart. She had a wealthy and charming lover, but she had no family of her own.

"Oh, if only I had my mother! If just she would come back, only for one hour—one minute!"

Useless to try to vision that sweet girl-mother. Dorigen had been too tiny when war tore them asunder. But engraved deep on her baby consciousness was the tenderness, the endless tenderness, the strong young arms that had snatched and enfolded, the deep young breast that cradled her, the warm, eager lips that showered waking kisses on her drowsy little face. . . .

Suddenly Flavius appeared in the darkness, and held his soon-to-be bride in his arms. As they talked, she told him of her wistful dream of having a white rose for her wedding—and her wish to be with her mother again.

 Your mother? Beloved—your mother died. . . . She is dead. The dead, my child, are gone from us. Forever.

But Dorigen reminded him of the apostle who spoke with authority and said that "In Christ shall all be made alive." But Flavius scoffed:

 She is gone forever. She cannot come again. Sooner could this rose tree, autumn chilled, burst into bloom. Surely you have never seen roses bloom in October? . . . No more, then, can the dead awaken. Autumn is autumn. Death is death. . . .

Flavius bid Dorigen a good night, and left her alone with her thoughts in the garden. As she silently looked into the darkness, Dorigen began to realize that she was no longer sitting on the marble bench, but was being held by "young, strong arms," that "enfolded her warm and deep." And "against her cheek lay another cheek, velvet-soft."

 "I knew you'd come," she sighed, at last. There was no answer . . . but pulse on pulse, she felt the mother-tenderness beat through her own flesh. . . . Soft as a petal, the mother's cheek pressed hers. Clearly as words, she knew, it was a promise, a covenant.

"And you will go on watching, shielding, all my days?"

Then, and not till then, the face above her bent and spoke.

"Child, your mother is your mother forever. My love is yours forever, and my shielding. You will know that I speak truth, my darling, when they put your first child into your arms."

When Dorigen opened her eyes, Flavius was bending over her, and every branch of the rose bush was "wreathed in roses, whiter than frost, than pearl; and every twig was radiant, a miracle of bloom."[3]

. . . .

The Motherless vs. the Mothered

How do motherless children fare in comparison to children with mothers? I know of no such study that has ever been done, but the stories of motherless children offer hints of the effects of motherlessness.

In *The Mother Book*, Liz Smith maintains that there are common traits among motherless children—especially artistic qualities. "I notice that many great poets emerge from motherless childhoods."

 They are either early orphans or their mothers are not mentioned at all. It is not so amazing that many of these same artists turned out to be hounded by depression, drugs, and insanity, but did being motherless also drive them to creativity?[4]

Motherless

 Dear God!
How can you walk serenely
Through the starry meadows of eternity,
Swinging your moonlit lantern,
Calling the long night watches:
"All's well! All's well!"
When my heart's only heaven
Is black with grief . . .
My life's great lamp is broken and dark,
And I falter . . . unmothered!

MEREDITH GRAY[5]

Is there a connection between motherlessness and creativity? Perhaps so—especially as we read the stories of such creative geniuses as Leo Tolstoy, George MacDonald, C.S. Lewis, Art Buchwald—and maybe even Madonna.

A Fictional Russian Mother

The great Russian novelist, Leo Tolstoy, created in fiction the mother he never had in real life. In *Childhood* (1852), the ten-year-old who tells the story lives on a country estate with mother, father, brothers, and sisters—enjoying games and picnics as part of the "happy, happy, never-to-be-recalled days of childhood." But sweetest of all are the moments with his mother, looking into her "lovely" face, feeling her "gentle" hands, and listening to her "dear familiar" voice. The boy cannot help expressing his devotion: "Oh dear dear Mamma, I do love you so!"

 This is the novelist, in his twenties, giving his younger self the mother he had in reality lost before his second birthday. . . . After a time, she became a mythical being to whom he had recourse in periods of distress and upon whom he relied for supernatural assistance. Throughout his long life he continued to yearn—"Maman, hold me, baby me!"—for what he had so briefly lost.[6]

Of his deceased mother Tolstoy wrote:

 Such was the figure of my mother in my imagination. She appeared to me a creature so elevated, pure and spiritual that often in the middle period of my life, during my struggle with overwhelming tempta-

tions, I prayed to her soul, begging her to aid me, and this prayer always helped me much.[7]

The Mother Figure in the Myth of George MacDonald

George MacDonald was one of the great fiction writers of the nineteenth century, who is known to many as the man who most profoundly influenced C.S. Lewis. His fantasies have intrigued children and adults—and are filled with allusions to his own struggles in life, including the loss of his mother when he was a child. His memories of her had faded, but not her presence—especially in *Lilith*, a piece that took him five years to write.

> *Lilith is MacDonald's masterpiece. It was also his "dark night of the soul," exposing the terrible struggle between light and shade that had battled his consciousness since his earliest days. . . . He had long grappled with the loss of his own mother, taken from him when he was eight. In his writing there is a long parade of twisted mothers, summed up in Lilith. . . .*[8]

Freud reasoned that a child who had lost a mother often equated her death with abandonment, and then later projected feelings of anger on other female figures—sometimes evil women created as fictional characters. This Freudian analysis may be a key to understanding MacDonald and his writings.

A Nightmare Turned True

He heard footsteps in the hall, and then the creaking of his bedroom door as it opened slowly. It was late, and it seemed as though he'd been in bed for hours. But he was unable to sleep. He was tense, and every sound of the wind against the window pane and every rattling shingle jarred his senses. Now he was wide awake and shivered in the darkness, dreading what message this phantom of the night might bring.

The silhouetted frame in the doorway was that of his father who suddenly seemed larger than life to the terrified ten-year-old boy trembling beneath the covers. The shadowy figure now moved toward him across the room and bent over to see if he was still awake. There was a long pause—an almost deadening silence—and then his father spoke. His deep voice cracked and faltered, but the message was unmistakable—forever frozen in time and space in the deepest recesses of the boy's memory. There was no way to soften the dreaded news. His mother was dead. It shouldn't have surprised him. She had cancer and her condition had been getting progressively worse. But it hurt so terribly bad. Nothing, it seemed, could ease the pain of that night and the awful aching he felt in the weeks and months that followed.

That young boy was Clive Staples Lewis, remembered today as C.S. Lewis, author of *The Chronicles of Narnia, The Screwtape Letters, Mere Christianity,* and many other writings. But to his family and friends he was known simply as Jack. Life had been carefree and happy for him as he was growing up in Belfast, Ireland, in the first decade of this century. He lived in a house on the outskirts of town with his parents and his older brother Warren, and every day the boys were out in the fields and woodlands looking for new adventures. The only troubling aspect of his early years were his recurrent nightmares, but the worst nightmare of all was the night his mother died.

Jack and his brother had gone to church on Sundays with their parents and were taught to say their prayers every night. They took their faith for granted and never questioned their belief in God. In fact, Jack's faith increased during his mother's illness. He prayed fervently for her recovery, and he believed God would heal her. If there was really a God, and God answered prayers like he was taught to believe, why wouldn't God answer his prayer for his mother?

These questions haunted him in the years that followed his mother's death while he was away at prep school, and it was not until he was a grown man that he truly found God.[9]

· · · · · · · · · · · · · · · · · ·

Losing a Mother to Mental Illness

Art Buchwald, the well-known, prize-winning syndicated columnist and humorist, grew up without a mother. He was a motherless child. She was not dead in a physical sense, but she did not exist in his world, as he writes in his memoir, *Leaving Home.* Chapter one begins:

 Shortly after I was born, my mother was taken away from me or I was taken away from my mother. This was done because she was mentally ill. She suffered from severe chronic depression, which required that she be committed to a private sanitarium. She never recovered, and eventually, when my father ran out of money, she was placed in a state hospital in upper New York for thirty-five years—the rest of her life. . . . I never saw my mother, although she lived until I was in my thirties. When I was a child, they would not let me visit her. When I grew up, I didn't want to. I preferred the mother I had invented to the one I would find in the hospital. The denial has been a very heavy burden to carry around all these years, and to this day I still haven't figured it all out.

Early in life I had to explain her absence to strangers, as did my sisters. The easiest thing was to say she died giving birth to me. I don't know how many times I told this lie, but apparently every time I did I committed a form of matricide. She was dead as far as friends and strangers were concerned, but she was very much alive to me—sequestered away in a distant place I had never seen. The story was credible—but for most of my life I have lived in fear that someone would unearth my dirty secret and I would be severely punished for not having disclosed it.

When I grew up and I was in analysis in Washington, D.C., with Dr. Robert Morse, dis-

cussions about my mother took up quite a bit of our time. One of the reasons for this was that she turned up in so many dreams—watching me, following me, but never saying anything. I might escape her in the daytime but not when I slept.[10]

. . . .

A Motherless Madonna

Today she is identified around the world as America's most outrageous female performer—known only as Madonna. She is shameful and shocking and scandalous and sacrilegious—and yet there are moments when even a skeptic could wonder if deep down she might feel a tinge of regret and remorse for her offensive behavior. No one but Madonna herself is to blame for the choices she has made in her career and personal life, but the painful loss she suffered as a little girl sheds light on her situation. "Nonni," as she was affectionately called, realized something was wrong one day when her mother was too sick to play with her.

 As their mother's illness progressed, all the children grew increasingly impatient and confused. "We really tortured her when she was sick, because we wanted her to play with us," Madonna said. "I think little kids do that to people who are really good to them." One afternoon, as her mother sat on the couch, Little Nonni climbed on her back and demanded that they play together. Too tired to move, her mother began to sob. Little Nonni responded by pounding on her mother's back and shouting,

"Why are you doing this? Stop being this way, please, please stop, please stop. Be who you used to be. Play with me!"

It was then that Little Nonni realized her mother was crying and wrapped her arms around her. "I remember feeling stronger than she was," said Madonna. "I was so little, and yet I felt like she was the child. I stopped tormenting her after that. I think that made me grow up fast."

The diagnosis was breast cancer and she did not live to celebrate Little Nonni's sixth birthday. She died December 1, 1963, and the daughter would never be the same.

 My mother's death left me with a certain kind of loneliness, an incredible longing for something. If I hadn't had that emptiness, I wouldn't have been so driven.[11]

. . . .

Mothering Best by Dying

Letty Cottin Pogrebin is a founding editor of *Ms* magazine, a leading Jewish feminist, and the author of several books on gender and family issues. In her book, *Deborah, Golda, and Me: Being Female and Jewish in America,* she writes about the death of her mother when she was a teenager and how that loss affected her as a young woman seeking to come to terms with her own identity. In a chapter entitled, "Mother, I Hardly Knew You," she offers mixed emotions about her mother's passing.

I feel about mothers the way I feel about dimples: because I do not have one myself, I notice everyone who does.

Most people who have a dimple or two take them for granted, unaware of how these endearing parentheses punctuate a smile. While I spent months of my childhood going to bed with a button taped into each cheek trying to imprint nature, my dimpled friends fell asleep unappreciative of their genetic gifts. They did not notice what they had always had.

Most people who have a mother take her for granted in much the same way. They accept or criticize her without remarking on the fact that there is a mother there at all—or how it would feel if there were none. I've never had the luxury of being so blasé. Since I lost my mother when I was quite young, I keep pressing my mother-memories into my mind, like the buttons in my cheeks, hoping to deepen an imprint that time has tried to erase.

She was fifty-three when she died; I was fifteen. I had less time with my mother than I've had with my children. Less time than I've known my closest friends, or many colleagues. The truth is, if you subtract the earliest part of my childhood and the darkest months of her illness, my mother and I really knew one another for a scant ten years. I suppose I should be grateful that so little time has left so much to remember. . . .

But her death forced me to live a different life. And since that life has suited me, and I have made gratifying decisions without a mother's advice or counsel, I wonder irreverently, ironically, whether my mother mothered me best by dying. That sentence is bizarre I know, yet it is what I keep thinking. The contra-

dictions are obvious: to mourn this woman so deeply and at the same time feel grateful to her for leaving me alone to grow up by myself; to palpably miss her to this day, and yet simultaneously dread what might have happened between us had she lived. . . .

My father lived for more than twenty-seven years after my mother died, yet he remains a father figure rather than a father. She is the parent I remember and hers is the life I keep mining for gold, running my sieve through the same old streams, searching for precious nuggets that might connect my memories of her to the life I have lived without her. I keep hoping that the missing pieces will turn up in my mother's past.[12]

Unlike Letty, I was a young adult when my mother died, but much of what she writes speaks for me. My father lived on for twenty years after my mother's accidental death at fifty-seven, but I can say with Letty:

She is the parent I remember and hers is the life I keep mining for gold, running my sieve through the same old streams, searching for precious nuggets that might connect my memories of her life to the life I have lived without her.

Like Letty, I secretly envy my friends with mothers, and I also wonder if my choices might have been different if she had lived on and what our relationship would be like if I had been with her to celebrate her eighty-third birthday earlier this week. Sometimes fading memories are more pleasant than the world of reality.

✒ When each of you shall in your nest

Among your young ones take your rest,

In chirping language, oft them tell,

You had a Dam that lov'd you well,

That did what could be done for young,

And nurst you up till you were strong. . . .

Farewel my birds, farewel adieu,

I happy am, if well with you.

ANNE BRADSTREET

10

The Humorous Side of Motherhood

Mother was an enthusiastic horticulturist," recalled Harriet Beecher Stowe, author of *Uncle Tom's Cabin*. But her mother's passion for gardening took a setback one day when little Harriet came upon a package of tulip bulbs sent from her uncle John in New York.

 I remember rummaging these out of an obscure corner of the nursery one day when she was gone out, and being strongly seized with the idea that they were good to eat, and using all the little English I then possessed to persuade my brothers that these were onions such as grown people ate, and would be very nice for us. So we fell to and devoured the whole; and I recollect being somewhat disappointed in the odd, sweetish taste, and thinking that onions were not as nice as I had supposed. Then mother's serene face appeared at the nursery door, and we all ran toward her, and with one voice began to tell our discovery and achievement. We had found this bag of onions, and had eaten them all up.[1]

Like so many recollections of our childhood, this incident was not particularly humorous at the time. There would be no tulips to brighten the springtime garden. But looking back many year later, it was a treasured garden memory that Harriet had of her early years with her mother.

How would any of us ever survive motherhood without fun and a sense of humor? Fortunately our experiences of child-rearing give us plenty of raw material for some good hearty laughs. My own mother survived through her sense of humor, though on many occasions it required time and distance to find a particular incident amusing. I was the center of one such episode. It was a fall day and four of us kids were carrying wood into the house and down to the basement with my mother barking orders. A typical preadolescent, I was lagging behind and complaining and being scolded by my mother, when suddenly, with her back turned, my little brother—the snitch—yelled out, "Mommy, Ruthie stang her tuck out at you!" I think I carried a hundred extra armloads of wood that day, but the incident quickly became a family joke, and Mom laughed the loudest.

My own task of mothering has been made lighter through humor—in part by a son whose high school graduation claim to fame was the "Class Clown Award." He can find humor in almost any situation and plays more than his share of pranks and practical jokes. More than once I've heard his voice on the intercom of our giant Meijer's supermarket, calling me to report to a particular aisle or giving me some message as though I were a clerk in trouble. Embarrassing at the time, but funny as I reflect back on his adolescent antics.

Sometimes the humorous side of mothering comes in reflecting back on experiences of child-rearing. I'll never forget my son's first romance. He was eleven and shy with girls, but tall, blonde, lanky Lisa—also in sixth grade—had captured his heart. They were in Sunday School and youth group together, but nothing more. My mothering mentality does not even include the option for sixth-grade dating—whatever that is. But Carlton was bound and determined to declare his affections, and Valentine's Day offered the perfect opportunity. True to his character, though, he waited until the day after and bought a box of chocolates half price,

knowing that we would be going to the church potluck supper that night where he would see her. Not wanting to give her a red heart-shaped box with a big orange half-price sticker on it, he tore off the cellophane wrapping. As we drove to church I could see he was a bundle of nerves silently contemplating his strategy—until I took a sharp turn and the box of chocolates slid off the dash and spilled all over the floor. I was certain the romantic gesture had been foiled, but I was mistaken. In the darkness and almost in tears he gathered up every last one of the chocolates that had rolled amidst the dog hair and whatever else is on the floor mats from a Michigan winter. "Carlton, you can't give those to her," I gasped. But Carlton is headstrong, and Lisa got her chocolates.

I have a hunch that the humorous side of motherhood goes all the way back to Eve. But the Bible only records one notable occasion of laughter—one indelibly tied to motherhood—an incident so significant that Trevor Dennis pinpointed the incident in the title of his book: *Sarah Laughed.*

Actually Abraham laughed first—apparently dumbfounded that he at one hundred and Sarah at ninety should bear a child. But Sarah's laughter, recounted a chapter later in Genesis 18, was the laughter that gets the most attention from the writer of the Genesis account. She heard what the Lord had said to Abraham, knowing full well she "was past the age of childbearing":

 So Sarah laughed to herself as she thought, "After I am worn out and my master is old, will I now have this pleasure?" (Gen. 18:12, NIV)

The prospect of motherhood caused Sarah to laugh with both skepticism and with pleasure. It is obvious that she was incredulous, but even the possibility of pregnancy must have infected that cynical laughter with joy.

Unlike Sarah, I was only twenty-eight when I learned I was pregnant—and did not consider myself barren—but that was the beginning of the joy and laughter that I have since associated with motherhood.

. . . .

A Guaranteed Grounding

I love history—not facts and figures, but the real life stories of people behind the scenes of great events. In the early centuries of the Christian era, there were terrible times of religious persecution. The names of the emperors responsible and the numbers of the innocent killed are the stuff of history, but behind the scenes are the fascinating details that are often missed in the history books. One of these details has a touch of humor.

How does a mother ground a teenager if he's bound and determined to get out of the house? This was the dilemma Origin's mother confronted in the year 202. She and her husband, Leonides, were devoted Christians—so much so that Leonides was imprisoned during the reign of Septimius Severus for his fearless testimony of faith. Origin, then a teenager, was distraught by the turn of events and he swore he would join his father in prison and die a Christian martyr with him. His mother, with six other children, was horrified by his vow, and was

determined to stop him by whatever means possible. But what could a helpless mother do to stop a headstrong sixteen-year-old boy? Then in a flash the solution came. That night while he slept, she stole his clothes and hid them. He was grounded. His youthful fervor might prompt him to make a rash attempt to die with his father, but surely not to go naked through the streets of Alexandria.

My students find this story amusing—as I do. But for the mother, it was anything but amusing at the time. Leonides did die as a martyr, but Origin was spared—through shame of nakedness—to go on and become one of the early church's great theologians.

. . . .

Eight Birds Hatched in a Nest

The Puritans were not known for their humorous writings. Indeed, their literary style betrayed a very solemn and deeply religious people, not the least of whom was Anne Bradstreet, the most noted female poet in Colonial New England. Vintage Bradstreet are the lines: "And I shall see with these same very eyes, My strong Redeemer coming in the Skies." But Mistress Bradstreet was capable of lightheartedness—Puritan humor in rare guise. Her topic was her brood of eight.

 I had eight birds hatcht in one nest,
Four Cocks there were, and Hens the rest,
I nurst them up with pain and care,
Nor cost, nor labour did I spare,
Till at the last they felt their wing,

Mounted the Trees, and learn'd to sing;
Chief of the Brood then took his flight,
To Regions far, and left me quite:
My mournful chirps I after send,
Till he return, or I do end. . . .
My second bird did take her flight,
And with her mate flew out of sight;
Southward they both their course did bend,
And Seasons twain they there did spend:
Till after blown by Southern *gales,*
They Norward *steer'd with filled sayles. . . .*
I have a third of colour white,
On whom I plac'd no small delight;
Coupled with mate loving and true,
Hath also bid her Dam adieu. . . .
One to the Academy flew
To chat among that learned crew:
Ambition moves still in his breast
That he might chant above the rest,
Striving for more than to do well,
That nightingales he might excell.
My fifth, whose down is yet scarce gone
Is 'mongst the shrubs and Bushes flown,
And as his wings increase in strength,
On higher boughs he'l pearch at length.
My other three, still with me nest,
Untill they'r grown, then as the rest. . . .

When each of you shall in your nest
Among your young ones take your rest,
In chirping language, oft them tell,
You had a Dam that lov'd you well,
That did what could be done for young,
And nurst you up till you were strong. . . .

Farewel my birds, farewel adieu,
I happy am, if well with you.[2]

· · · · · · · · · · · · · · · · · · ·

Baby's in the Slop Jar—

The hectic and harried responsibilities of caring for three lively little ones is sometimes best dealt with through humor. Such was the manner of Harriet Beecher Stowe, who didn't have the advantage of modern conveniences—though she did have the help of Grandmother. In a letter to her good friend Georgiana May, Harriet lightheartedly lays out her daily schedule:

My Dear, Dear Georgiana,

Only think how long it is since I have written to you, and how changed I am since then—the mother of three children! Well, if I have not kept the reckoning of old times, let this last circumstance prove my apology, for I have been hand, heart, and head full since I saw you.

Now, to-day, for example, I'll tell you what I had on my mind from dawn to dewy eve. . . . I apply myself vigorously to sweeping, dusting, and the setting to rights so necessary where there are three little mischiefs always pulling down as fast as one can put up. . . . I start to cut out some little dresses, have just calculated the length and got one breadth torn off when Master Henry makes a doleful lip and falls to crying with might and main. I catch him up and turning round see one of his sisters flourishing the things out of my workbox in fine style. Moving it away and looking the other side I see the second little mischief seated by the hearth chewing coals and scraping up ashes with great apparent relish. Grandmother lays hold upon her and charitably offers to endeavor to quiet baby while I go on with my work. I set at it again, pick up a dozen pieces, measure them once more to see which is the right one, and proceed to cut out some others, when I see the twins on the point of quarreling with each other. Number one pushes number two over. Number two screams: that frightens the baby and he joins in. . . .

. . . Meanwhile number one makes her way to the slop jar and forthwith proceeds to wash her apron in it. Grandmother catches her up by one shoulder, drags her away, and sets the jar up out of her reach. . . .

But let this suffice, for of such details as these are all my days made up. Indeed, my dear, I am but a mere drudge with few ideas beyond babies and housekeeping. . . .

Well, Georgy, this marriage is—yes, I will speak well of it, after all; for when I can stop and think long enough to discriminate my head from my heels, I must say that I think myself a fortunate woman both in husband and children.[3]

. . . .

A Dose of Humor for Mother

Hannah Blackwell, like mothers of every age was worried about her child. Elizabeth was twenty-four, unmarried, unsure of her future, and questioning her childhood faith. Although she would later become famous as the first woman to earn a degree in modern medicine and would serve as a very dis-

tinguished physician, at this point in her life she seemed to be floundering and her mother was concerned about her—and about her own health. Would she even live to see her daughter settled down with a family? Elizabeth responded to her mother the only way she knew how—with humor.

[c. 1845]

 My Dear Mother,

I'm afraid from the sad tone of your letter that you think you're going to die very shortly, but such I assure you is not the case, as I can prove to you if necessary from scripture and common sense; on the contrary I can prophesy many a long and much brighter year in which one of your greatest delights will be to visit me in my beautiful residence near Boston, where I shall present to you my adorable husband, and my three daughters, Faith, Hope and Charity, and four sons, Sounding Brass, Tinkling Cymbal, Gabriel and Beelzebub. (Do not imagine however that I'm going to make myself whole just at present, the fact is I cannot find my other half here, but only about a sixth which would not do.) There are two rather eligible young males here whose mothers have been some time electioneering for wives; one tall the other short, with very pretty names, of good family and with tolerable fortunes, but unfortunately one seems to me a dolt and the other a fool so I keep them at a respectful distance, which you know I'm quite capable of doing. . . . I'm very much obliged to you for your interest in my soul which is quite natural as you had some hand in giving it to me, but you need not be uneasy for I think a great deal on interesting serious subjects,

read the bible and pray in a very good fashion so all will come right presently.

Now my dear mother believe me full of natural affection and with a great desire for your growing fat.

*Your daughter
Elizabeth[4]*

. . . .

A Little Girl's Defiance

Margaret Mead, one of the most widely recognized anthropologists of the twentieth century, spent much of her life studying Samoans and other peoples of the Pacific Islands, with special interest in how their cultures influenced the development of personality and behavior. Her best known work, entitled *Coming of Age in Samoa*, focused on how children develop cultural norms. Her Western readers were fascinated by her studies, but it might have been more interesting if a Samoan had studied Margaret's early development—especially during her "fits" when her security blanket was being washed.

 These "fits" of anger were frequent, but not lasting. Her childhood, Mead recalled, made her think of the story of the little girl who had been shut up in a closet by her mother, and screamed and screamed and screamed. Abruptly the screaming stopped. Alarmed by the sudden silence, the mother went into the closet to see what had happened.

"I spit on your hat and I spit on your shoes

and I spit on your dress," said the child, "and now I'm waiting for more spit." [5]

. . . .

The Woman behind the Magic

The Man behind the Magic is the title of Katherine and Richard Greene's biography of Walt Disney. The title is appropriate, but what few people know is that there was a woman behind the magic and fun of Walt Disney, and she was his mother.

 With rigorously scheduled days, impatient teachers, and a demanding father, Walt might have become rebellious and discouraged. But he never felt sorry for himself.

Flora Disney made sure of that.

A tall woman with high cheekbones, and deep, large, brown eyes, Flora was the heart of the Disney family. If Walt was endowed with a touch of magic, his mother was the person who wielded the magician's wand. Flora encouraged the whole family to have fun and not take themselves too seriously. "She would kid the life out of my dad when he was peevish. . . ."

One day, Walt brought home a mechanical practical joke called a "plate lifter." The little gadget allowed you to push down on a bulb and force air through a tube to make a plate at the other end of the table rise and fall as if by magic. "Let's pull that on your father," she suggested, grinning broadly.

Before they sat down to eat, Walt set the contraption under his father's plate and handed the other end to his mother. *Every time Elias put his spoon anywhere near his soup, the bowl would move around like it was sitting on a toad. Only Elias didn't seem to notice.*

"My mother was just killing herself laughing," recalled Walt. "She kept doing this and finally my dad said, 'Flora, what is wrong with you? Flora, I've never seen you so silly. . . .'"

The more puzzled her husband looked, the harder Flora laughed. Finally, she had to get up and go lie down in the bedroom. Elias never did catch on.

Flora, a former schoolteacher, held the family together. . . .

Walt inherited his perfectionism and willingness to tackle something new from his father. From his mother came an ability to laugh and a down-to-earth delight in the unsophisticated, sometimes slapstick humor of human nature.[6]

· · · · · · · · · · · · · · · · · · · ·

Tom Landry's Bare Bottom

Tom Landry was born and raised in Mission, Texas, a small town in the Rio Grande Valley near the Mexican border. Everyone knew each other, and he learned very early that there was no such thing as privacy or anonymity—especially when Mama was faced with an emergency.

One such occasion occurred when I was five or six and just learning to ride a bike—a true challenge on hard-baked dirt streets full of bumps and ruts like the road that ran along the irrigation canal at the far edge of town. . . . One day I either pedaled

too fast, hit a particularly bad rut, or simply panicked—maybe all three. Whatever the cause, I crashed into the roadbank so hard I flew head over handlebars and landed on my bottom, smack in the middle of a large cluster of cactus.

I jumped up and lit out for home screaming for Mama. But the pain in my posterior was nothing compared to the agony of embarrassment I suffered over her quick-thinking solution to my prickly predicament. Somehow she sent out an alarm, probably by way of my brother and sister, and the next thing I knew I was lying face down and bare-bottom up on a table surrounded by neighbor ladies armed with tweezers.

I have no idea how long it took, but it seemed like hours as my mother and her friends pulled scores of needles from my backside. Looking back I suspect there may have been only two or three women there, but it seemed like a capacity crowd. I felt like a public spectacle and I can still vividly recall horrible embarrassment that lasted far longer than my sore bottom.[7]

· · · · · · · · · · · · · · · · · · · ·

Barbra Streisand's Chicken Soup

Barbra Streisand's biographer depicts Barbra as an abused child—one who was emotionally abandoned as a baby by her traumatized mother, when her father died unexpectedly. Then after her mother remarried, her stepfather ridiculed Barbra and compared her unfavorably with her stepsister. She "was a typical Cinderella story," says one observer. Barbra struggled with her overbearing Jewish mother, Diana, but could not escape her own mother's foibles when she was rearing her son.

 It was a matter of embarrassment to Barbra. In fact, nearly everything Diana Kind did embarrassed her daughter. . . . Diana would leave early from her job in Brooklyn, take the train to Manhattan, trudge up the stage door stairs, and show up unexpectedly in Barbra's dressing room. Invariably, she would be toting, for her daughter's consumption, a carton of chicken soup and some little surprise for dessert. Barbra was enraged by these uninvited visits, which she viewed as an intrusion on her privacy. Eventually, she told her mother to nix the chicken soup act. She was old enough and rich enough to feed herself. Besides, she told her mother, she preferred take-out Chinese.

But what most irritated Barbra about her mother—her unannounced visits and chicken soup— became part of Barbra's own mothering routine.

Surprisingly perhaps, Barbra Streisand is the quintessential "Jewish mother." She is obsessed with the idea of her son's undernourishment and has been known to make a series of unexpected midday appearances at Jason's various homes, wearing no makeup and a babushka wrapped around her head, and clutching a bowl of chicken soup to her bosom as some sort of maternal offering. She would stay for a few minutes and then depart with a single word of instruction: "Eat!"[8]

. . . .

A Revised Version of Cinderella

Barbra Streisand's "Cinderella" story revolves around her mother and a stepfather—not the wicked stepmother typically associated with the fairy tale by that name. But maybe it's time to take a new look at stepmothers and the bad press they've gotten through legends. Is it possible that the fairy tale of Cinderella might be biased and one-sided? Erma Bombeck gives the story an entirely new slant.

 Her name was Buffy Holtzinger.

But to the world of fairy tales, she was identified only as "Cinderella's mean, evil, ugly stepmother." . . .

Buffy was one of the first working mothers in her neighborhood. . . . There was no doubt in her mind that if she continued raising three teenaged girls by herself, she'd end up like Rapunzel sitting in a tower braiding her hair. . . . Her two natural daughters were bad enough. . . . But it was Cinderella's active imagination that drove her up the wall. From the beginning, Cinderella played with the truth like most kids play with their gum—stretching it, rearranging it, hiding it, and disguising it. She told her teacher in third grade that her "stepmother" made her play outside naked in the snow. She told them her stepsisters got silk dresses for Christmas and she got a certificate to be "bled." She told everyone her stepmother hated her because she was pretty and made her wax the driveway. . . .

Cinderella met a shoe salesman that night at the ball and married him several months later. Happiness continued to elude Buffy when Cinderella submitted a manuscript to a publisher called Stepmommie Dearest. *The title was changed to* Cinderella *and the book became an instant best seller.*

It is credited with saving millions of women from a second marriage who are now living happily ever after.[9]

. . . .

Inheriting a Sense of Humor

Joseph M. Stowell, president of Moody Bible Institute, learned from his mother not to take himself too seriously, and she passed on to him her sense of humor—a great asset for the chief executive of a prominent Christian institution. Although she struggled with disabilities all her adult life, she never forgot how to laugh.

Growing up in a minister's home, I became acquainted with some of the unique stresses involved in parsonage life. Of all my mother's strengths, her sense of humor added a positive dimension in our home.

My mother had a great penchant for practical jokes. For one of her favorites, she used the carpeted stairway in the foyer. She glued a nickel to a nail and then nailed the nickel into the carpet. As children, we would hide and snicker as we watched visitors try to pick up that stubborn nickel.

She saved another of her practical jokes for those times when we were entertaining dignified guests such as Vance Havner, or M.R. DeHaan, or J. Sidlow Baxter. She liked to place one of those plastic ice cubes with an insect in it in our guest's crystal water goblet. The highlight of the meal for her children was watching the guest's face as he tried to tactfully explain his dilemma to his hostess.

I remember my mother for her strengths of character as well as for her sense of humor. From the age of eighteen, she had a degenerative nerve condition that totally impaired her nerve control and, to some extent, her speech. I never saw her daunted by those restrictions, however. She accepted them and proceeded with her life. I never heard her complain once about the lot that the Lord had assigned to her. Her perseverance in the midst of that daily trial was a mark of great character.

Today I find that my sense of humor is a strength in the midst of stress. My mother's example in persevering in those things that she could not control has been a great help to me as I face pressures that are sometimes beyond my control.[10]

Joseph Stowell is rich. His mother passed down to him a priceless inheritance—a sense of humor. And how rich we all are if we can look back on a mother's humor and lightheartedness or can enjoy for the present the fun and laughter our children bring.

❧ *Of all the many gifts bestowed on me,*

there is one I treasure above all others—my

dear mother, Lela. My professional life would

have been nothing without her guiding hand.

GINGER ROGERS

11

Stage Mothers

S he had watched the seeds she planted in him burst into an unheard-of-flowering. . . . There seemed to be nothing preventing him going higher and higher.

The one who had planted the seeds was the mother of Albert Schweitzer. She was the one who had "defended him in his dreamy days and encouraged his ambitions." She reveled in the adulation he had won as a young adult from his organ concerts in Paris and his lecturing and preaching.

But now he was throwing it all away. He announced that he would study medicine and then leave all behind to give his life for the underprivileged in equatorial Africa. She was devastated. She did not even bid a warm farewell when he left on Good Friday, 1913. "The train started and they all waved—except for Mrs. Schweitzer. The hard Schillinger spirit would not melt. The will that drove the son to Africa held back the blessing of the mother. He was not to see her again." She died three years later in a tragic accident, but her spirit lived on through him—especially when he returned home and roamed the wooded garden paths he had once wandered with his mother near his home in the German countryside.

 The virtue Mrs. Schweitzer seems to have prized above all was kindness. And she had a deep romantic love of nature, especially of the countryside of her valley; a love bordering on sentimentality. Schweitzer quotes her as saying of a lake where they often walked, "Here, children, I am completely at home. Here among the rocks, among the woods. I came here as a child. Let me breathe the fragrance of the fir trees and enjoy the quiet of this refuge from the world. Do not speak. After I am no longer on earth come here and think of me."

I do think of you, Mother. I love as you did this refuge from the world.[1]

Albert Schweitzer was not an actor, but his mother could certainly be classified as a "stage mother." She wanted to bask in his celebrity as a musician and lecturer. What fame could her son possibly attain by healing people in equatorial Africa? If she had only known. Her son would become one of the most famous medical doctors of the twentieth century, but she missed it all—a "stage mother" buried with her shattered dreams.

The ultimate stage mother story came out of Texas in 1991. According to *Time* Magazine, "Wanda Webb Holloway, organist at the local Baptist church, is an irrepressible stage mother." Indeed, so desperate was she for her daughter to become a cheerleader at the local junior high school, that she plotted to have the mother of her daughter's rival murdered by a hit man. It was not the first time this stage mother became involved in her daughter's competition. Two years earlier she tried to get her daughter's rival disqualified on the basis of a technicality, and the following year, her own daughter was disqualified because Holloway distributed pencils and rulers promoting her daughter.

What a pitiful story of an obviously sick woman. But what was even more troubling were the reflections of the apparently sane principal of the school: "After all, it's the American way. We all want our children to achieve. There is a part of Wanda Holloway in all of us."[2]

I surely hope not. If a part of Wanda Holloway is in all of us, motherhood, I think, is doomed.

The typical stage mother, despite her reputation, is often the most devoted and loving of mothers and truly has her child's well-being at heart. Indeed, almost all mothers are inclined to play the role of stage mother at one time or another. I could hardly describe my own mother as a stage mother, but she was my staunchest supporter and promoter and she was often less than realistic in her estimation of me and my abilities. I'll never forget how she prodded me in my late teens to enter Northern Wisconsin's "Miss Land-O-Lakes" beauty pageant because I was "just as pretty as any of the other girls" in the competition. I have photographs to prove I wasn't, but Mom looked at me—at least in some respects—through the eyes of a stage mother.

There is often a fine line between a stage mother and a mother who transmits to the child a healthy sense of self-esteem, and the difference may lie in the mother's sense of fulfillment in her own aspirations. There is a "Jewish-Mother" joke told in various ways which I have come across as I've been researching motherhood that reflects on the stage-mother mentality. One version puts the mother on the beach, watching in horror as her grown son's sailboat capsizes in the waves. She runs screaming to the life guard: "Help! Help! My son, the doctor, is drowning."

Many of us know a mother like that, who is unable to refer to her son—or daughter—without the added status symbol of a successful career or some other distinction.

Whatever my faults are in the area of motherhood, being a stage mother is not one of them. I'm my son's biggest fan, and no one wants him to succeed more than I do, but I am fulfilled in my own varied activities and I don't need him to boost my ego on the vita of life. But many of our greatest entertainers and sports figures have credited their achievements to the prodding of their mothers—stage mothers whose highest aspiration was to see a child succeed.

· · · · · · · · · · · · · · · · ·

Better an Actor Than a Preacher

"Laurence Olivier," according to his biographer Anthony Holden, "is not merely the greatest actor of this century, perhaps of all time." He is remembered for his critically acclaimed roles in Shakespearean films, *Henry V, Hamlet,* and *Richard III,* as well as in contemporary dramas such as *Wuthering Heights* and *Rebecca.* He was not only an Oscar-winning Hollywood star, but was also knighted at Buckingham Palace in 1947, and was inducted into the House of Lords in 1970—the first actor named a baron in English history. But had it not been for his mother, Olivier might have followed his father into the ministry as an Anglican rector. He was in awe of his father—fascinated by his preaching and desperately wanting his approval, though he later confessed, "everything about me irritated him." Olivier's mother, however, "was determined not to have another clergyman in the family." According to his sister Sybille, "In order to deflect him, Mother encouraged Larry to turn his

mock-sermonizing into recitations of monologues from well-known plays." From his own recollections, Olivier "played shamelessly" to his mother:

 She would mouth the words with me, and whenever I stumbled she would urge me on, applauding deliriously when I got it right and suffocating me with hugs at the end. Soon she started to invite other people in to watch me perform— neighborhood ladies, relatives and the like. And it was always the same at the end—much applause, most of it polite, I'm sure, and a great deal of hugging and "Isn't-he-darling" sort of praise. I suppose you could say that I decided at a very early age that acting was for me.

Olivier's mother died at age forty-eight when he was thirteen. He later described his state of mind as "utter desolation"—so severe that he contemplated suicide. The terrible loss would stay with him the rest of his life, and according to his biographer, would mold his personality and his profession: "The sudden loss of his mother's affection, and his father's failure to replace it, would combine to forge the deep ambivalence in Olivier's character which would prove his making as an actor."[3]

· · · · · · · · · · · · · · · · ·

The Mother of America's Premier Comedian

The mother of four young boys and the wife of Harry who squandered his meager earnings on drink and another woman, Avis Hope might have given up on a happy home. But she was not that kind of woman. She did housework for others to earn money, and she refused to let her circumstances control her outlook on life.

 Avis tried to keep family spirits high. She played her spinet and sang songs and Welsh hymns, teaching her boys to sing along with her. She took them to watch the boardwalk buskers, the puppet shows, magicians, sword-swallowers, and often on picnics.

When her husband decided to emigrate to America in 1906, he left her behind with the boys to follow later. It was not easy traveling with a brood of rowdy boys, but music kept them together—particularly during the last leg of the journey when they were traveling to Cleveland in an immigrant train:

Encouraged and sometimes led by Avis, the Hopes sang, until she nearly choked from embarrassment when the boys passed the hat for coins. The boys were embarrassed when Avis washed their underclothes and held them out the window to dry. And all the while she dreamed about the gold-lined streets of Cleveland.

The streets of Cleveland were not lined with gold, and her Harry was still drinking and underemployed, but again she made the best of life in her new home in America. She held the family together, but most of all: "She saved pennies and finally was able to buy a secondhand upright piano so there would be music in the home."

It was that atmosphere of music in the home that led to Bob Hope's career in Vaudeville and Broadway and finally in Hollywood, and his mother had the thrill of seeing him come home to Cleveland to perform in 1929, before she died.

 From the moment she took her seat, she trembled from head to toe. Tears ran down her cheeks. . . . When she heard the reception by the audience, acknowledging him as a neighborhood boy, she relaxed. She listened to every syllable, nodding her head as though approving every word. . . . Just as he was taking his last bow, he spotted us and proudly he said, "There she is, folks! That's Mahm! The one with the lilies of the valley on her hat. There she is. Way back there. Stand up and let these folks see you, Mahm!"

She didn't really need to. The expression on her face was enough.[4]

· ·

"Ginger Rogers and the Redheads"

My mother told me I was dancing before I was born. She could feel my toes tapping wildly inside her for months.

She was front-page news before she was a year old, but not for her dancing. The headlines of the *Kansas City Star Telegram* read:

 Virginia McMath Kidnapped.

Her father had abandoned her mother before she was born, and her mother assumed he was out of the picture—until a terrifying day in May of 1912, when she suddenly discovered her baby girl was missing. Her husband had come to her place of work in Independence, Missouri, and snatched his daughter and whisked her away to Kansas City. After a harrowing ordeal the mother and baby were reunited, only to face a similar incident two years later. On this occasion the judge imposed a fine and warned the father that "if he tried it again, he'd go to Leavenworth." At age fourteen that same little girl was again making headlines, now as the lead dancer in a three-member troupe, and taking her stepfather's name:

 "Ginger Rogers and the Redheads"

But there was more money to be made in a single act, so Mother and daughter went on the road to stardom together.

 From 1925 to 1928 my mother and I traveled by train in crisscross patterns across the country, from Waco to Chicago, to St. Louis, to Phoenix, to Pittsburgh, and into many cities in California, Oklahoma, Arkansas, Indiana, Wisconsin, Michigan, Massachusetts, and New York. . . . I performed in large theaters and supper clubs, doing my song-and-dance act, sprinkled with vaudevillian humor. . . . Mother's thrifty nature would not allow her to pass up any opportunity to save money. We traveled with a locked suitcase, a portable kitchen in fact, that contained our most important money savers:

a percolator, a hot plate, a toaster, salt, pepper, sugar, and all the necessary implements.

From the road tour to New York to Hollywood to the pinnacle of success, Ginger's mother was with her all the way until she died in 1977. Looking back over her life in May of 1991, seventy-nine years after the kidnapping, Ginger paid tribute to her mother.

 Of all the many gifts bestowed on me, there is one I treasure above all others—my dear mother, Lela. My professional life would have been nothing without her guiding hand.[5]

· · · · · · · · · · · · · · · · · · · ·

"That's All Right Mama"—

"That's All Right Mama" was chosen over "Rock Me Mama" for his first big recording session in 1954, when he was nineteen years old, and that song turned out to be his "breakthrough, his first great moment in the ring." But for Elvis Presley, either song title could be used as a theme of his life. Presley is described as a "mama's boy" by Albert Goldman: "Gladys did not permit Elvis to play out of her sight until he was fifteen. Even then, his whole world outside of school and church was confined to a circle of a few blocks." A few years later when her son was becoming a singing sensation, Gladys was right there to take charge. Those who wanted to cash in on her son had to deal directly with her. Elvis' father, Vernon, wielded far less influence over Elvis.

Vernon Presley, who was both stupid and greedy, was no problem at all. The Colonel made a swift conquest of this spineless creature. The real problem was Gladys. The Colonel, with his shrewd eye for people, knew only too well how vital it was to his success that he get the mother's approval for his takeover.

Later, when they visited their celebrity son in Hollywood, Gladys, the "hillbilly" mama and "simple soul who always wore 'dusters' and spent her life preparing crowder peas and thickenin' gravy," suddenly became the well-groomed mother of a movie star. She retained a "costume coordinator," had her hair styled every day, and bought French poodles, causing a friend to wonder if she had become "screenstruck, just like her son." But the fantasy world that Gladys had created suddenly came crashing down in 1958, when Elvis was drafted into the army.

 The shock of having her baby snatched from her was more than she could bear. Elvis was gone and there was no saying when he would be back. . . . There was no comforting her. All day, she would go about the house wringing her hands and saying, "I feel that something's happened to him."

The distress Gladys felt over the loss of her son contributed to her declining health, and only months after Elvis was inducted into the Army, he was called home from Germany to be at his mother's side. When she died a few days later, Elvis was beside himself. "I heard this horrible wailing," a friend remembers. "It just made my skin crawl. I had never heard anything like that in my life."

 Gladys was as much the source of Elvis' self-confidence as she was the cause of his extreme dependency. She was also his only confidante and his moral governor. Once Gladys died, Elvis found himself desperately alone and naked.[6]

. . . .

Baseball, Mothers, and Apple Pie

When we think of a parent fantasizing about a son's fame in major league baseball, we naturally think of the father living out his own dreams through his boy. But that was not true for Stan Musial, one of the greatest baseball players of all time. For more than twenty years, between 1941 and 1966, he played with the St. Louis Cardinals and "rewrote the record books." One of his longest standing titles was his National League record for most base hits (3,630), which was broken by Pete Rose in 1981. Who was the "cheerleader" behind the amazing athlete known as "Stan the Man"? In his autobiography, Musial tells how the Cardinals were scouting him for their Class D team after he had finished high school, with a contract for $65 a month. His immigrant father strongly objected, insisting that his son should take advantage of an American college education.

I wanted so much to play ball. My mother weakened, but Pop remained firm. French [the Cardinals representative] prepared to leave. This, he said, might be my last chance. I wasn't 17 yet but, for me, the world had come to an end. I cried—tears of disappointment, anger and frustration.

That did it. Mom put an arm around me, dried the tears and told me to blow my nose. Then she stood up. She's a big woman, taller than my father. In typical old-world custom, Pop wore the pants in our family, but now Mom spoke up to him quite sharply.

"Lukasz," she asked, "why did you come to America?"

"Why?" my father said, puzzled, in his broken English. "Because it's a free country, that's why."

My mother nodded triumphantly. "That's right, Lukasz," she said. "And in America a boy is free NOT to go to college too."

Pop grumbled then paused. "All right, Stashu," he said with a sigh, "if you want baseball enough to pass up college, then I'll sign."

Both of my parents and I signed the baseball contract in late summer, 1937. . . . My father wasn't happy that he had relented, and his displeasure increased during the winter. . . .

Stan Musial's father died in 1941, as his professional career was beginning, but his mother lived on to become his biggest fan.[7]

* * * * * * * * * * * * * * *

A Mother and a Child Star

During the 1930s he was the most famous child star in the world, and was no doubt the envy of millions of children of the Depression era who could only dream of his wealth and fame. But behind the innocent pretty face was a little boy bearing the baggage of a thoroughly dysfunctional family and a mother who literally prostituted herself for her son's celebrity. She was a vaudeville entertainer and her husband was a prop man, and their son, who made his first stage appearance before he was two years old, was Mickey Rooney. When he was four years old, Mickey's parents separated, and for a long time he did not even see his father.

 I wasn't sorry we split. I didn't enjoy being "that goddamn kid." I didn't like watching him growl at my mother or hearing her shouting back at him. I didn't want to spend half my life crawling under the bed and behind sofas and cupping my palms over my ears so as not to hear the drunken brawls.

Soon after the separation, Nell headed to California with Mickey, determined to turn him into a child star. To a friend she had said simply, "I have a feeling about Sonny [Mickey] and the movies." But times were hard, and it was then that, in his words, "I lost my innocence." He discovered his mother was making ends meet by bringing men into their tiny apartment for sex. Reflecting back, he writes, "I know, my dear mother, you did it for me."

Mickey Rooney did achieve fame, and Nell's dream had come true, but amidst the fame was pain. Mickey's wife, Barbara, committed suicide with her illicit lover, and ten days later his mother died. He had no tears, only regrets: "I knew her new life, with God, had to be better than it was with me. When I had fallen, she had fallen, too, and she found consolation only in the bottle."[8]

• • • • • • • • • • • • • • • • • •

"Que Sera, Sera"

When Doris Day was thirteen and already an accomplished dancer dreaming of Hollywood, she was involved in a serious car-train crash that left her injured and unable to walk. While she was on the mend, she sustained a second injury that kept her on crutches for more than a year. "My mother was concerned about how I would react to this latest misfortune," she writes, "so to distract me from my idleness my mother decided to give me singing lessons"—which was beyond her means financially.

 My mother helped and encouraged me in every way she could. I've often been asked whether, in light of her involvement with my dancing and singing, she was one of that ogre species of stage mothers. I really can't say. When you're a child you're not aware of your mother in those terms. . . . I don't think my mother was that kind of stage mother. I made up my own mind about everything from the time I was a little girl and my mother respected how I felt. She did exert herself in aiding and abetting me in whatever I decided on, but I don't think she tried to impose her will on mine.

The singing lessons arranged by her mother would eventually pave the way for Doris Day's mul-

tifaceted Hollywood career. Her philosophy of life was inspired by her mother from the time she was little and it would years later become the very message of her most popular hit song.

 It is my nature to accept events as they happen and adjust to them. By sheer coincidence, a song was written for a picture I made twenty years later, "Que Sera, Sera," which precisely stated my philosophy, a philosophy which has not been dented over the years by the arrows of what occasionally has been rather outrageous misfortune. Whatever will be, will be, and I have made the best of it. . . . Our destinies are born with us. They are predestined to happen. . . . This creative planning, that is God.

When I was just a little girl,
I asked my mother, "What will I be?
Will I be pretty?
Will I be rich?"
Here's what she said to me:

"Que sera, sera,
Whatever will be, will be;
The future's not ours to see.
Que sera, sera
What will be will be."[9]

Stage mothers have made their mark on the world, but often only by exacting a heavy price on their own well-being and on the well-being of their children. How fortunate it would be if every mother inclined to be a driving stage mother could sing the words of this song: *"Que sera, sera."*

. . . .

A Stage Mother for God

The stage mother is most often associated with beauty pageants or other "worldly" amusements from New York night clubs to Hollywood. But one of the premier stage mothers of the twentieth century was Minnie Kennedy, the mother of Aimee Semple McPherson, America's most glamorous performer on the revival circuit.

A year after she married, Aimee sailed to China as a missionary with her new husband, only to return months later as a widow with a baby girl in her arms. Less than two years later she remarried and gave birth to a son, but she was unhappy. Unlike her mother, whose family responsibilities had taken precedence over her call to ministry, Aimee believed God's calling was upon her, and with her mother's encouragement, she began preaching. Aimee could vicariously fulfill Minnie's own dreams of ministry.

In the spring of 1919, Aimee wired her mother in New York, asking her to help organize revival meetings in Florida, and that was the beginning of the team enterprise. "She would take charge of booking Aimee's road show, quickly transforming a hobo's odyssey into a continental tour, out of the ragged tent and into the convention hall." With Minnie as her manager, the crowds grew so quickly that the 15,000 seating capacity for the Denver revival in 1922

was insufficient. But Aimee's personal life was as dramatic as was her preaching, and after her alleged kidnapping and rumored extramarital affair in 1926, the bond between mother and daughter began to deteriorate.

In 1927, Minnie moved out of the house they shared together and resigned from the ministry, demanding a fifty-fifty split of all the assets. The feud became bitter and public, culminating in newspaper headlines in 1930 blaring: "MA SAYS AIMEE BROKE HER NOSE!" How could such a rift develop between a mother and daughter so devoted to each other and to God? The issue, more than anything else, revolved around Aimee's lifestyle and those who were influencing her. Minnie's dreams were shattered. Her daughter had not lived up to her expectations. Minnie was a stage mother, bringing in the crowds for her daughter, but first and foremost, she was a stage mother for God.

Aimee continued to speak to large crowds at her own church in Los Angeles and on her revival tours, but the heyday of her ministry was over and her life was filled with turmoil. She died as a result of an overdose of barbiturates—though apparently not taken intentionally to end her life. The funeral and burial took place October 9, 1944. Among the mourners was "a weeping Minnie Kennedy," who had not seen her daughter in seven years.[10]

  Had I been Joseph's mother
    I'd have prayed
  Protection from his brothers:
    "God keep him safe;
  he is so young;
    so different from
  the others."
    Mercifully
  she never knew
    there would be slavery
  and prison, too.

RUTH BELL GRAHAM

12

Reflections on Mothers of the Bible

The Garden of Eden has a terrible litter problem. It is knee deep in our prejudices and pre-
conceptions. No patch of ground is more thoroughly spoiled than that on which Eve walks.
. . . Her story, the little story of a strange
Garden where she is made and a man is formed
also, where she enters into dialogue with a
snake, where God performs marvelous acts of creation and walks in the cool of the day, is one of
the most subtle and compelling in the Bible, indeed
in all literature. . . . The man names his wife,
and calls her Eve. . . . What a name it is!
"Mother of all living!"[1]

The Garden of Eden, with all its flowers and
fruits, was forgotten and forgiven from the
day that heaven came down to earth; from the
day on which Eve got her first-born son from the
Lord God.[2]

From the Garden of Eden to the Garden of
Gethsemane, we find biblical mothers savoring the
joys and enduring the sorrows that have molded
motherhood through the ages. Motherhood begins
with the pain of childbirth and the pleasure of new
life, and that dichotomy of pain and pleasure follows her all her life. So it was with Eve. She experienced overwhelming joy in receiving a baby
boy from the Lord and overwhelming sorrow in
that boy's unspeakable crime, but sandwiched
in between must surely have been the everyday pain
and pleasure of motherhood.

. . . .

Eve, Mother of All Living

Eve, the mother of us all, put motherhood in
proper perspective when she delivered her first-
born son: "I have gotten a man from the Lord."

We like those last words of that quotation from Genesis so much: "I have gotten a man from the Lord." In these words we see Eve's gratitude to God and her acknowledgment of Him as the Giver of this new and wonderful gift, a little baby. That our children come from the hand of our Father is a thought which, when realized, adds much seriousness to our privileges and responsibilities as mothers.

Then, too, she seems to sense not only the little one's babyhood, but his manhood as well—"a man from the Lord"—the time when he shall no longer need his mother's protection and guidance; the time, perhaps, when he shall become a great man and win back the place in Eden that his parents had lost. Who but God can know the hopes of a mother's heart?[3]

. . . .

The Pain of Motherhood

The pain and sorrow and disappointment that mothers experience in child-rearing are powerfully symbolized by the anguish of Eve. She represents the pain of womanhood for all generations.

 There is an unwritten chapter in the life of Eve. She is the mother who sees her favourite first-born branded with shame, while the pitiful Abel becomes a martyr. The idyllic garden vanishes. The streets of London or Paris might surround her, for, in the knowledge of good and evil, she is all the women who have ever lived.[4]

I once heard a minister comment that it was easy to give Mother's Day messages because there were so many model mothers in the Bible: Jochebed (the mother of Moses), Hannah, the Proverbs 31 woman, Elizabeth, and Mary, to name a few. But he went on to say that the same was not true of Father's Day. The Bible, he conceded, simply does not tell the stories of many good fathers. The great men of the Bible like Noah, Abraham, Moses, and David were not particularly outstanding fathers.

One of the best-known mother stories of the Bible comes from the court of King Solomon—a man hardly known as a model father. But he was the King and judge (and womanizer) and the plaintiffs were—amazing as it may seem—both prostitutes and both new mothers of sons and both suffering from the postpartum blues. In this case, their distress came not from hormonal changes and the sudden responsibility of having a new baby but because of the loss of a baby.

 One of them said, "My lord, this woman and I live in the same house. I had a baby while she was there with me. The third day after my child was born, this woman also had a baby. We were alone; there was no one in the house but the two of us.

"During the night this woman's son died because she lay on him. So she got up in the middle of the night and took my son from my side while I your servant was asleep. She put him by her breast and put her dead son by my breast. The next morning, I got up to nurse my son—and he was dead!

But when I looked at him closely in the morning light, I saw that it wasn't the son I had borne."

The other woman said, "No! The living one is my son; the dead one is yours."

But the first one insisted, "No! The dead one is yours; the living one is mine." And so they argued before the king.

1 KINGS 3:17-22

We all know the classic ending of that story. The wise king quickly identifies the mother by her love for her child. Knowing the outcome, he cleverly ordered the child be cut in two in order to satisfy both mothers—as though the disputed possession were a squash or a watermelon. The kidnapper readily agreed. Out of jealousy she had committed the heinous crime, not out of love for the baby. The true mother, of course, cried out in protest. This was her own flesh and blood for whom a deep bond had developed over those three days.

The kings verdict was swift: "Do not kill him; she is his mother."

The biblical story of the two mothers is timeless, as are so many of the stories of motherhood in the Scripture. "Though the ancient world—just as our own—produced bad mothers as well as good ones," writes Virginia Stem Owens, "changing social patterns have probably affected motherhood less than any other human bond, including marriage. The mother-child relationship has endured millennia of pushing and pulling with very little alteration to its essential character."[5]

The pushing and pulling of Sarah is an illustration of this enduring mother-child bond.

· · · · · · · · · · · · · · · · · ·

Sarah's Fear for the Second Son

Sarah is the first great patriarchal wife of the Old Testament, and her story is familiar. She, like so many Old Testament women who will follow her was barren. Infertility in the ancient world was very different than today and more difficult to deal with on a social level. Today a woman who cannot have a child is grieving for herself as much or more than she is grieving for her husband or his family. The loss is hers, and in that sense it is often very understandably self-centered. But in Old Testament times, a wife was expected to bear children—and especially a son—for her husband. It was *his* child she would bear, and if she could not do that, she was inadequate as both wife and mother. So the pain and social ostracism Sarah struggled with was natural—as was her contempt for Hagar who had borne a son by Abraham, her husband. And her joy at conceiving and bearing a son could not be exaggerated. But that joy once again turns into bitter envy during the feast to celebrate Isaac's weaning. Sarah saw Hagar's son Ishmael "mocking" Isaac—or as one commentator suggests, pretending to be Isaac. This enraged Sarah, and it is here where she is most often censured for her behavior. But the same motherly instincts that prompted her desperate desire to bear a child also prompted her jealous protectiveness of that child. A mother's love can be fierce and frightening.

 Now the bitterness which has been simmering for these past fourteen years once more breaks

out. . . . Then Sarah was barren. Now she has a son of her own to defend. She may not know of God's plans for Isaac. God has never communicated them to her, and Abraham . . . has not been especially forthcoming either. For the same reasons, we can presume she does not understand what God has in mind for Ishmael. All she knows is that Isaac has an elder brother, and he is the son of the Egyptian woman who for so long rubbed salt into the wound of her sterility, and that, if things are left to themselves, he will inherit the bulk of Abraham's wealth and power. Already in Genesis we have seen an elder son kill his brother in the story of Cain and Abel. Later in the book we will witness the threat posed to Jacob by his elder brother Esau; and we will hear much about the attempts to get rid of Joseph by his older brothers. One has to be very careful of older brothers in this book. When Sarah has waited so long for Isaac to be born, when his conception and birth have so far exceeded her expectations and given her such surprising joy, can we ourselves be surprised when she is determined at all costs to defend him from the one who represents such a potent threat?[6]

 The single plank that spans the terrible gulf between Isaac's marriage-bed and his death-bed is laid for us in this single sentence. . . . Eloquent with wickedness as the words are—Isaac loved Esau, but Rebekah loved Jacob—yet they make little impression on us till we have read on and on through chapter after chapter, full of the fruit of that wicked little verse. . . .

One of the very first fruits of that devil's garden that Isaac and Rebekah had sowed for themselves was the two heathen marriages that Esau went out and made and brought home, and which were such a grief to Isaac and to Rebekah. That great grief would seem to have been almost the only thing the two old people were at one about by that time. It was a bitter pill to Rebekah, those two marriages of Esau. . . . Esau is greatly blamed by some preachers for his heathen marriages, but surely, quite unfairly. We talk to Esau about the covenant, and what not. . . . And Esau might very well think that he could surely get a mother for his children from nearer home than Padan-aram, who would be as fair, and wise, and kind, and good to them as his covenant mother had been to him.[7]

* * * * * * *

The "Devil's Garden"

Alexander Whyte, known for his studies of Bible characters, is very hard on Isaac and Rebekah as parents—Rebekah especially. They might have had a happy and fruitful family life, but for one problem: "Isaac loved Esau . . . but Rebekah loved Jacob."

* * * * * * *

The Mother of Miriam and Moses

I've listened to many Bible stories and sermons on Moses in the bulrushes, most of them describing the horror of the mother Jochebed when she realized her baby had been found by the Pharaoh's daughter. I didn't buy into that when I was doing a study of Jochebed some years ago, and I've since discovered that other women have viewed this mother as I did—a clever woman determined to beat the system and save her son. Dee Brestin writes with affinity and admiration for Jochebed.

When Moses was born, Jochebed developed an elaborate plan to save him—and her daughter Miriam played a key role. How this drama must have shaped Miriam! If you are an older sister, your mother probably coached you in nurturing your younger siblings, but for Jochebed and Miriam the stakes were life or death. I can picture Miriam hiding with Moses in the closet, honey on her thumb, praying he wouldn't cry when the soldiers prowled past their home. Miriam probably helped Jochebed coat the papyrus basket with tar and pitch, praying with her mother as they worked. And I'm sure Jochebed role played with Miriam how to respond if the princess found Moses. . . .

I have little doubt that one of the reasons that Miriam grew up to be the first woman prophet and a leader of literally millions of women was that she had a mother like Jochebed. Jochebed, because she was determined to choose life for Moses, taught Miriam crucial skills in nurturing, skills that would open up possibilities of love to her for the rest of her life.[8]

Good Mothering without Reward

We all know a woman who is the best mother with the worst kid. This was as true in biblical times as it is today. Sometimes, despite a mother's best efforts, her child went bad or made a series of bad choices. So it was with an unnamed mom and her son Samson.

Samson's mother, known only to us as the wife of Manoah, went to great lengths to raise her boy by all the rules prescribed by the angel who announced her impending pregnancy. Yet all her watchful care did not keep her son from falling into the hands of the designing Delilah.[9]

Ruth's Other Mother-in-Law

The story of Ruth is a compelling biblical narrative that powerfully portrays the bond of love between a young woman and her mother-in-law, Naomi. It is a story of two mothers: Naomi, whose sons die and are lost in history; and Ruth, whose son, Obed, lives on through his grandson David and whose name appears in the genealogy of Joseph, the husband of Mary. There is a missing mother, however, in the Book of Ruth. What about Ruth's other mother-in-law—the mother of Boaz? Did Ruth love her with the same intensity that she loved Naomi? Perhaps she was dead when Ruth and Boaz were married. Tradition tells us that he was an older man. But, living or dead, this woman had already made a name for herself among the Hebrew people, and she is included in Matthew's genealogical line to Joseph.

. . . The compiler of that record tells something new about Boaz— that his mother was Rahab. The only parent of Boaz named in the Hebrew bible is Salmon, the progenitor of the people of Bethlehem. In taking a foreign wife, Salmon follows the examples of Abraham, Jacob, Joseph, and Moses. Ethnic intermarriage thus does not seem to have been a major concern of the Hebrew patriarchs.

If Boaz's mother was a Canaanite prostitute, this could help explain why he is more magnanimous to a poor outsider than others in Bethlehem. Consider the background of the woman who might have become Ruth's second mother-in-law. Rahab collaborates with Israelite spies who are learning about Jericho, which has been targeted for attack by Joshua's army. As a result of her initiative she and her relatives are rescued before the city is destroyed. The story of Rahab concludes with this statement: "Her family has lived in Israel ever since."[10]

. . . .

Jesus and His Mother

Even He that died for us upon the cross, in the last hour was mindful of His mother as if to teach us that this holy love should be our last worldly thought—the last point of earth from which the soul should take its flight for heaven.

HENRY W. LONGFELLOW[11]

Mary has always been a favorite biblical character of mine—not because I see in her the virginal purity of sainthood, but because I find in her a woman whom I can relate to. She was a protective and interfering mother—with a slight tinge of "sow-bear" love that most mothers can identify with. She was very anxious about Jesus' disappearance in Jerusalem when he was twelve; she interrupted Him at the wedding in Cana, expecting Him to handle the wine-shortage problem; and she was so troubled by His ministry at one point that she sought to bring Him home. She was a mother, and we can only imagine the pain she must have endured at her son's death.

Mary stands in my garden—a gray concrete statue barely three feet tall tucked between a blue spruce tree and a shrub. In the winter I often look out the window and see her draped in a cape of fresh white snow. In the spring she is surrounded by lilies and bright purple ajuga, but during the summer and fall, she's partially hidden by foliage. Yet, people notice her, and I've been asked more than once if I'm Catholic. I'm not, but I can understand why I might be asked. But Mary does not belong to any one particular denomination. She's simply a mother for all ages—and a reminder for me of the joy and pain of motherhood.

Memories of a Mother's Reflections on Mary

Dietrich Bonhoeffer, a German pastor and seminary teacher and a leader of the Confessing Church, took a stand against Hitler and the Nazis, and for that he was imprisoned and later hanged. His mother heard the news of her son's death on a radio broadcast—a son in his thirties executed for his faith. For a moment she surely must have known the agony of Mary's seeing her son hanging on the cross. Through his writings, her son's faith has since become an inspiration to Christians around the world—a faith that was nurtured through her family devotions. Married to an "agnostic-humanist," she was the spiritual leader of the family. Her devotional times were memorable, especially her yearly Christmas Eve reflections on the nativity, as Dietrich's sister remembers:

 Christmas Eve began with the Christmas story. We sat in a large family circle . . . all festive and expectant, until our mother began to read. She is unforgettable for me in her black velvet dress with the fine lace collar, her heavy fair plaits bound round her head, and below them her broad serious forehead. She had the pale skin of many blue-eyed people, but now she was flushed with the pleasure of the occasion. She read the Christmas chapter in a firm full voice. . . . I remember that sometimes tears came into her eyes. . . . Also when she read those words in the Christmas story: "but Mary kept all these things and pondered them in her heart."

Dietrich and I talked about this, it affected and oppressed us, and it was a relief when Mother's eyes grew clear again.[12]

Mary, a Surrogate Mother

In Spain and elsewhere in the world, Mary has been elevated far beyond what the Scripture would warrant, but the excesses should not discourage others from seeing Mary as one whose memory lives on to bring comfort and consolation—especially to the motherless.

Teresa of Avila, patron saint of Spain, and a great sixteenth-century Catholic Reformer and mystic, who founded the Reformed Carmelite Order, was deeply indebted to her mother for her spiritual insights.

 Her mother, who had taught her to say her first prayers, died when Teresa was twelve, and Teresa experienced her first real loneliness. She turned from human loss to the infinite resources of God and derived great comfort from thinking of the Mother of Christ, feeling in her the maternal affection she needed.[13]

Childhood Memories of a Godly Mother

In her little volume entitled *Mothers*, published in 1924, Laura Merrihew Adams contends that the lives of the biblical and historical women she features "bear a striking similarity to our own experience today." Now, some two generations later, her words still hold true. One of the women she features is Eunice—a woman who serves as a model for mothers down through the ages.

 Did you ever receive a letter which warmed your heart by the memories it brought to mind, and which dimmed your eyes with tears? Such a letter Timothy received one time from Paul. In the letter Paul said, "I call to remembrance the unfeigned faith that is in thee, which dwelt first in thy grandmother Lois, and thy mother Eunice; and I am persuaded that in thee also."

As Timothy read these words I am quite sure that his heart was warm with tender childhood memories, and his eyes misty. Then he re-read on through the long beautiful letter, which hinged its message upon these words. Because of the faith of his mother before him, because of the faith she had implanted within Timothy, Paul was pleading with him to "stir up the gift of God which is in thee."

A godly heritage: that was Timothy's precious gift from his mother.[14]

. . . .

Prayers from Mothers in the Bible

Had I been Joseph's mother
I'd have prayed
Protection from his brothers:
"God keep him safe;

he is so young;
so different from
the others."
Mercifully
she never knew
there would be slavery
and prison, too.

Had I been Moses' mother
I'd have wept
to keep my little son;
praying she might forget
the babe drawn from the water
of the Nile,
had I not kept
him for her
nursing him the while?
Was he not mine
and she
but Pharaoh's daughter?

Had I been Daniel's mother
I should have pled
"Give victory!
This Babylonian horde—godless and cruel—
don't let them take him captive
—better dead,
Almighty Lord!"

Had I been Mary—
Oh, had I been she,
I would have cried
as never mother cried,
". . . Anything, O God,

anything . . .
but crucified!"

With such prayers
importunate
my finite wisdom
would assail
Infinite Wisdom;

God, how fortunate
Infinite Wisdom
should prevail![15]

· · · · · · · · · · · · · · · · · · · ·

Retelling Old, Old Stories

What message do the stories of biblical mothers have for women today, and how can we keep these stories fresh and relevant for every generation of mothers. In *Daughters of Eve*, Virginia Stem Owens humorously offers some reflections on her own mother's effort to make the Bible relevant to her—using the stories of women to make a statement for today.

 It was my mother who first introduced me to biblical women. For the most part, this was a thinly disguised attempt on her part to socialize my often unsociable nature. She used Hannah, the mother of Samuel, to impress upon me, a child who didn't even like to play dolls, how important children are to women and how important I was to her. Unfortunately, however, the story had the opposite of its intended effect. I was horrified that a mother would abandon her child at the tender age of three to an aging clergyman, a kind of priestly Rumpelstiltskin. Next she tried the story of Miriam, emphasizing her obedience and resourcefulness as a baby-sitter for the infant Moses hidden in the bulrushes. The message was pretty clear. If Miriam could save her little brother from Pharaoh's cruel soldiers, the least I could do was keep mine from running out in the street.[16]

There are many practical lessons and solutions to everyday problems to be learned from biblical mothers, and for this reason alone we should pay more attention to these often obscure and forgotten women. But more than that, we can find memories of motherhood that bind women together in their common cares and commitments from the Garden of Eden to the Garden of Gethsemane—to my backyard garden today, where Mary stands as a reminder of the vitality of motherhood for all generations.

As tender mothers, guiding baby steps,
When places come at which the tiny feet
Would trip, lift up the little one in arms
Of love, and set them down beyond the harm,
So did our Father watch the precious boy
Led o'er the stones by me, who stumbled oft
Myself, but strove to help my darling one;
He saw the sweet limbs faltering, and saw
Rough ways before us where my arms would fail;
So reached from heaven, and lifting the dear child,
Who smiled in leaving me, He put him down
Beyond all hurt, beyond my sight, and bade
Him wait for me. Shall I not then be glad,
And, thanking God, press on to overtake?

HELEN HUNT JACKSON

13

The Motherly Qualities of God

Consider the lilies of the field, how they grow; they
toil not neither do they spin:

And yet I say unto you, That even Solomon
in all his glory was not arrayed like one of these.

Wherefore, if God so clothe the grass of the
field, which to-day is, and to-morrow is cast into
the oven, shall he not much more clothe you, O
ye of little faith.

MATTHEW 6:28-30

In this passage of the Bible, from the *King
James Version* as I memorized it as a child, we see
God as a gardener and God as a mother who cares
for our needs—though God as mother is not
mentioned specifically. Even as a mother cares
for us and clothes us, God does far more—as we
are so powerfully reminded as we enjoy God's
garden in the lilies of the field and nature all
around us.

The lines from a familiar hymn carry the picture of lilies of the field a step further:

 In the beauty of the lilies
Christ was born across the sea,
With a glory in His bosom
That transfigures you and me....

Here Julia Ward Howe exercised a measure of
poetic license as she adorned the birth of Jesus with
flowers, but it reminds us that as God cares for us
even as the lilies of the field, so too Jesus, poetically
speaking, was born among the lilies. And the
lines go on to depict Jesus' care of us, using the motherly term of *bosom*.

Although the Bible speaks of God almost
exclusively in terms of Father, there are passages in both the Old and New Testaments that
refer to the motherliness of God. I relate to these

motherly qualities. It was my mother who comforted me when I was hurting, and it is my mother's comfort that I often long for today, more than twenty-five years after her death. But I know I can find this same kind of motherly comfort in God: "As a mother comforts her child, so I will comfort you" (Isa. 66:13). Indeed, the Lord cares for us and protects us with motherly concern—like a mother hen gathering her brood under her wings for protection (Matt. 23:37). This is a true picture of the God of the Bible—so different than the gods of other religions be they Buddha, Allah, or Krishna. And it is this God of the Bible that down through history has been trusted by Christians around the world as a comforting mother and more.

Motherhood as an ideal and as an institution is almost sacred. It is interesting that fatherhood has had no comparable elevation to religious sanctity, despite the fact that the biblical image of God is primarily that of Father. It is appropriate then, that we look more closely at the motherly qualities of God.

God as a Watchful Mother

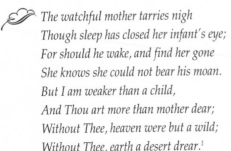

The watchful mother tarries nigh
Though sleep has closed her infant's eye;
For should he wake, and find her gone
She knows she could not bear his moan.
But I am weaker than a child,
And Thou art more than mother dear;
Without Thee, heaven were but a wild;
Without Thee, earth a desert drear.[1]

Jesus as Mother

Some might argue that portraying Jesus as a mother or in feminine imagery is an outgrowth of the modern feminist movement. Not so. Indeed, such portrayals are not as common today as they were in earlier centuries of church history. The Church Fathers—including Clement, Origen, Irenaeus, Chrysostom, Ambrose, and Augustine—all, at one time or another described Jesus as mother. Later, Anselm, an eleventh century theologian and Archbishop of Canterbury, wrote a prayer that spoke of Jesus as mother:

 But you, Jesus, good Lord, are you not also a mother? Are you not the mother who, like a hen, collects her chickens under her wings? Truly, master, you are a mother. . . . It is then you, above all, Lord God, who are mother.

Bernard of Clairvaux, a celebrated twelfth-century monastic reformer and mystic, was even more graphic and personal in his portrayal of Jesus as mother. To a young follower he wrote:

Do not let the roughness of our life frighten your tender years. If you feel the stings of temptation . . . suck not so much the wounds as the breasts of the Crucified. . . . He will be your mother, and you will be his son.

Some critics have argued that celibacy contributed to this need of medieval monks to relate to Jesus as a female, and perhaps there is some truth in that, but women also looked to Jesus as mother. Julian of Norwich, a fourteenth century mystic is an example:

God rejoices that he is our Father; and God rejoices that he is our mother. . . . God almighty is our kindly Father; and God all-wisdom is our kindly mother. . . . The second person of the Trinity is our Mother. . . . Jesus Christ, who does good against evil, is our very Mother.[2]

For Julian and for other medieval mystics, perceiving Jesus as mother was a reflection on motherhood as much as it was a reflection on Jesus. How else could they express the depth of Jesus' love and care for His children than to speak of it in terms of motherliness? Ultimately, they saw God not in terms of gender but in terms of all the attributes that encompass both fatherhood and motherhood.

· · · · · · · · · · · · ·

A Plaque and a Tearful Farewell

God, the Bible tells us, comforts us like a mother comforts her children. What a comfort this truth was to Evelyn Brand two generations ago when was she separated from her children. During the early years of her lengthy missionary career to India, she and her husband returned home on furlough for a year with their children. "The year was blessing," writes her biographer, "and it was tor-

ture." The torture was the constant dread of parting with her young school-age children—leaving them in England to be properly educated. The night before that painful parting, Evelyn gave each child a hand-painted plaque.

For Connie: *As one whom a mother comforteth, so will I comfort you.*

For Paul: *I will be a father unto you.*

The next day the children left for school, and Evelyn knew that she would not see them again for several years.

The pain in that moment and in the days and months and years that followed was soothed by the realization that God could be the mother to her children in a way that she could not be in her absence. The children grew up to be missionaries themselves—Paul, an internationally recognized missionary doctor specializing in leprosy. Evelyn Brand trusted God with her children—God as a mother and God as a father.

· · · · · · · · · · · · ·

God's Motherly Love

The motherly love of God, however, is not just for young children—so writes Herbert Lockyer, who is known for his long association with Moody Bible Institute. He challenges his readers to think in terms of "turning to God as our Mother," and then goes on to refer to Isaiah 66:13:

And mark, the prophet is not thinking of a little child, but of a grown man heartsore and broken, fleeing back for the comfort of his mother's presence. . . .

Many a man weary and broken by a pitiless world,
with things against him, and fortunes ruined, or
with dear ones gone, or faith almost giving way, or
entangled in the net of sin, has retreated in such dark,
lone hours to the mother who gave him being.[3]

Mothers' Hearts Patterned After the Heart of God

The overpowering mother-love for a child is one way to comprehend God's love for us. This is what Harriet Beecher Stowe discovered in 1857 when her son Henry, a student at Dartmouth, drowned in the Connecticut River. In her inconsolable grief, she was consumed by doubts—and fear that God would send an innocent child to hell. To herself she wrote:

 You trusted in God, did you? You believed that
He loved you? You had perfect confidence that He
would never take your child till the work of grace
was mature! Now He has hurried him into eter-
nity without a moment's warning, without prepa-
ration, and where is he now?

She came to terms with her doubts and son's death by reasoning that she could not have a greater capacity to love than God. And if she could love her son so boundlessly, how much more could God love him:

 He invented mothers' hearts, and He certainly has
the pattern in His own.[4]

God Loves as No Mother Could

Sometimes in attempting to describe the motherly love of God, the love of a mother becomes exaggerated and sentimentalized. But in the process we are given a powerful perspective of God's great love for us as wayward children. The words of Herbert Lockyer are an example:

 When in trouble, the mother receives her child with-
out asking many questions. A mother's intu-
ition tells her what is wrong. It is enough for her
to know that her child is in distress. She may guess
much, and fear more, but comfort is her first con-
sideration. Explanations can wait.

How like the motherhood of God! God does not
probe the wound when there is power to heal.
How beautifully tender is the mother comfort of God!
He asks no questions, utters no reproach, demands
no explanation. He has not the scrutiny of a detec-
tive, but the sympathy of a devoted parent. . . .

And God offers us the same motherly tenderness
and sympathy. He heals, gladdens, sympathizes,
loves, cares as no mother could.[5]

A Mother's Prayer

When Elisabeth Howard Elliot was away at boarding school as a teenager, her mother's letters always included expressions of love, and very often a verse from the Bible or a poem or hymn. One of those poems that Elisabeth memorized and copied in her Bible was a mother's prayer for the Lord to be the mother she could no longer be:

As Thou didst walk the lanes of Galilee,
So loving Savior, walk with her for me,
For since the years have passed and she is grown,
I cannot follow; she must walk alone.

Be Thou my feet that I have had to stay
For Thou canst comrade her on every way;
Be Thou my voice when sinful things allure,
Pleading with her to choose those which endure.
Be Thou my hands that would keep hers in mine,
And all things else that mothers must resign.

When she was little, I could walk and guide,
But now I pray Thou be at her side.
And as Thy blessed mother folded Thee,
So, loving Savior, fold my girl for me.[6]

. . . .

From a Mother's Arms to the Arms of God

Helen Hunt Jackson, a nineteenth-century writer known for her impassioned appeal for Native Americans in her books, *A Century of Dishonor* and *Ramona*, suffered her own pain as a wife and mother. Her first son died at eleven months, and then a decade later, as a widow, faced the deepest anguish of her life when Warren, nicknamed "Rennie," died. He was all she had left, and as he lay dying he "must have sensed the look of terrible despair in his mother's face, for he looked

up at her and said, 'Promise me, mamma, that you will not kill yourself,' and the promise was given."

But her reason for living had vanished. She "shut herself up in her room and refused to see anyone. The light in her soul seemed to have gone out, and she walked continuously in the Valley of Despair. She said, 'Anyone who really loves me ought to pray that I may die too, like Rennie.'"

Amidst her grief, however, she found solace in God, who cares for His children even as a mother does. "After three months of struggle, she came up out of the valley with a new light upon her face and a new song in her heart. Her hand was in God's hand, and life was no longer a burden. She had something to give to other mothers." Her gift was a poem that reflected on God who, like a mother, lifts the little one into arms of love—"beyond all hurt."

. . . .

Lifted Over

As tender mothers, guiding baby steps,
When places come at which the tiny feet
Would trip, lift up the little one in arms
Of love, and set them down beyond the harm,
So did our Father watch the precious boy
Led o'er the stones by me, who stumbled oft
Myself, but strove to help my darling one;
He saw the sweet limbs faltering, and saw
Rough ways before us where my arms would fail;
So reached from heaven, and lifting the dear child,
Who smiled in leaving me, He put him down
Beyond all hurt, beyond my sight, and bade

Him wait for me. Shall I not then be glad,
And, thanking God, press on to overtake?[7]

Mother-love and the Love Divine

 Mother-love at its best, and its best is very common, is the nearest thing on earth to the love divine in this respect; it has no reference to the worth of the object. A son may be indifferent, selfish, ungrateful, cruel; his mother loves him just the same. . . . So long as the mother is alive, there is one person in the world to whom he may go with assurance, knowing that nothing he can do can lessen her affection.

WILLIAM LYON PHELPS[8]

Understanding God through Mother-love

Novelist Pearl S. Buck, writing about her mother Carie, who served with her husband for many years as a missionary in China, describes her mother's struggle to find God, and how that discovery came through understanding her own relationship to her children:

All through the years she had looked for a sign from God, a definite sign of approval, and none had come. She could not be sure at any time that the swift emotions of her own heart came from any other source than her own heart and desire. God never came down

to her with visible sound or movement. But it seemed to her after a while that her little children taught her much about the God she hoped in—their dependence on her, their little faces turned to catch her mood, their clinging hands—to the end of her life she would say, "How much more they taught me than I ever could teach them!" She would fall into meditation and say at last, "I suppose we understand God's purposes as little as those babies knew mine, even my purposes for them. They trusted me for all their lives, confident in my love, and because of that, willing to believe that I knew best. I think that must be the way we ought to see God—simply trust that He is there and cares."[9]

Mother is the name for God in the lips and hearts of little children.

THACKERAY, VANITY FAIR[10]

Seeing God through a Mother's—and Father's—Eyes

William F. (Bill) Buckley, Jr., novelist, conservative commentator, and host of "Firing Line," illustrates how significant parental influence can be in one's perception of God. He was brought up in a family where he encountered two very contrasting perspectives of God. His mother, Aloise, according to a friend of his was "one of the sweetest, warmest and gentlest women whom I ever met." In the words of her daughter Jane, "She never said a bad word about anybody." Buckley's father, Will, to the contrary, "was an extremely judgmental person" who was "witheringly sarcastic" in describing political adversaries. Their religious faith was very different as well.

Aloise's religion was more emotional. "She prayed for everything," Priscilla Buckley recalled. "Good weather, bad weather. She had a very personal relationship with God. She said nothing was too unimportant for God." Will's Catholicism was Old Testament, his God stern and unforgiving. Aloise's was the merciful God of the New Testament. Describing the sense of Christ that he had gotten from his mother, Bill once wrote that he found Jesus Christ "endearing" and the God of the Old Testament "a horrible, horrible person, capricious and arbitrary."[11]

William Buckley's perception of God illustrates how easily we can become misled if we rely too much on an earthly mother or father in our understanding of God. No matter how stern and unforgiving and arbitrary Will's Old Testament God may have been, that is not the biblical picture of God. From the Creation story to the cross, the God of the Bible is one God.

From the Old Testament: *As a mother comforts her child, so will I comfort you (Isa. 66:13).*

From the New Testament: *"I will be a Father to you, and you will be My sons and daughters," says the Lord Almighty (2 Cor. 6:18).*

God made mothers before He made

ministers: the progress of Christ's

kingdom depends more upon the influ-

ence of faithful, wise and pious mothers

than upon any other human agency.

THEODORE CUYLER

14

Faith of Our Mothers

One of the most celebrated Christian leaders of the nineteenth century was Frances Willard, a founder and director of the Woman's Christian Temperance Union and an outspoken advocate of women's suffrage. For her, the issues of temperance and suffrage were directly tied to her Christian faith, with a central focus on personal holiness and evangelistic outreach. Her own spiritual pilgrimage began as a child when she "learned the mighty first chapter of St. John's Gospel from her mother's lips." The "school-room" for this instruction in faith was frequently in her mother's garden.

 In the afternoon . . . there were walks with mother, when she clipped a sprig of caraway or fennel for the girls or a bunch of sweet-smelling pinks for Oliver from the pretty little beds in the heart of the orchard, where no one was privileged to go except with mother. "Here she talked to us of God's great beauty in the thoughts He works out for us; she taught us tenderness toward every little sweet-faced flower and piping bird; she showed us the shapes of clouds and what resemblances they bore to things upon the earth; she made us love the Heart that is at Nature's heart. When one of us was afraid of the dark and came to mother with the question "Why," she replied, "Because you do not know and trust God enough yet; just once get it into your heart as well as your head that the world lies in God's arms like a babe on its mother's breast, and you will never be afraid of anything."[1]

 I thank God for my mother as for no other gift of His bestowing.

FRANCES WILLARD[2]

I was recently talking to my son about some issues and problems he's dealing with, and my plea to him was, "What can I do to help you get some of these things straightened out in your life?" His quick response took me by surprise. "Mom, about all you can do is pray. I've gotta handle these things myself." He had caught me up short, and I had no ready response. We are alike in many ways, particularly in being people of action. His answer focused on action. He was giving me permission to passively pray and thus avoid actively interfering in his life, and he would take care of things through his own actions. Prayer, as he seemed to offhandedly imply, probably wouldn't make a whole lot of difference, but it would at least keep me occupied and keep me out of his affairs. Too often I subconsciously act as if that is my own philosophy of life. Prayer is a good thing to do when all else fails, and it may give me some peace of mind, but it's not really going to change things—as the plaque I saw on the wall of a little country church throughout my childhood read:

Prayer Changes Things.

I want to interfere; I want to move full-steam ahead and solve the problem, without pausing and asking, "How does God fit into this?"

I was reminded of how important mothers' prayers have been throughout history when I was paging through a recent issue of *Christian History* and stopped to read an article entitled "Focus on the Frontier Family." It was the frontier mother who was often the spiritual leader of the family. In fact, the article begins with the sentence: "Sallie Norris Hobart was worried." What was she worried about? "There were rough and worldly families among their neighbors, and she feared her children . . . might fall in with their drinking, dancing, gambling, and brawling." Another woman featured in the article was Becky Sullins, who was troubled about raising children on the frontier without family prayers:

 Family prayer yielded a harvest of Christian converts. David Sullins, a Tennessee preacher, recalled that the first convert from his parents' "family altar" was his father. His mother, during one sleepless night, had told her husband, "Nathan, we can never bring up the children right without family prayers."

"Well. . . what are we to do, Becky? I can't pray."

Mother Sullins insisted her reluctant husband could and should pray. She induced him to do his duty by promising to take turns leading. . . . When it came to his turn to pray in his family, it seemed like God had sought him out. "Father dropped on his knees and, stammering and choking, began. Soon under a crushing sense of sin and helplessness, he began to confess and cry for pardoning mercy. Mother prayed and cried, and the Comforter came, and light broke in, and father was converted at family prayers."

Thirteen children were reared around that family altar, and later, all the grandchildren and great-grandchildren "old enough to know and love Jesus" were Christians.[3]

Mothers Before Ministers

God made mothers before He made ministers: the progress of Christ's kingdom depends more upon the influence of faithful, wise and pious mothers than upon any other human agency.

THEODORE CUYLER[4]

John Calvin and a Mother's Influence

John Calvin's mother died when he was three years old—not old enough, some people would argue, for her to have had a lasting influence on his life. But often the hazy memory of a mother long departed has an enduring effect that continues a lifetime—especially if the father is incapable of expressing affection. A biographer of Calvin wrote that his father's style of parenting "consisted in concealing his love from his children, whom he really loved"—"affection which to a young heart is like dew and summer rain." Another biographer of Calvin opens with a story of the boy and his mother coming "out of the dim cathedral into the sunlight." Who was the mother? "She was as pious as she was beautiful, they said, and that meant she was pious indeed."

Years later, though he rarely mentioned his early life, John wrote about a little pilgrimage he had made with his own mother. Together they had walked two hours out into the valley to the shrine of Saint Anne, earthly grandmother of the Lord.

Lifted by his pious mother, young John kissed the precious relic of the skull of Saint Anne as it lay in its golden receptacle, surrounded by candles and flowers and the adoring faces of other pilgrims.

This was John Calvin's visual memory of his mother—the mother who conceived him in her womb, who bore him, who suckled him, and who ever remained his teacher. Such was the embodiment of motherhood for the stern Reformer and theologian from Geneva, who wrote:

Let us learn by the mere name of mother how profitable, indeed how necessary, is the knowledge of her; since there is no other entrance into life, unless she herself conceives us in her womb, unless she bears us, unless she foster us at her breast, unless she guard us under her care and government until we put off this mortal flesh and become like the angels. Our infirmity does not allow us to leave school until we shall have been her lifelong pupils.[5]

The Mother's Hymn

Lord who ordainst for mankind
  Benignant toils and tender cares,
We thank thee for the ties that bind
  The mother to the child she bears. . . .

And grateful for the blessing given
  With that dear infant on her knee,
She trains the eye to look to heaven
  The voice to lisp a prayer to Thee. . . .

All-Gracious! grant to those who bear
A mother's charge, the strength and light
To guide the feet that own their care
In ways of Love and Truth and Right.
                    WILLIAM CULLEN BRYANT[6]

. . . .

A Mother's Prayer
Heard 'Round the World

Hudson Taylor was one of the greatest missionaries of the modern missionary movement. He founded the China Inland Mission—now the Overseas Missionary Fellowship—which has commissioned thousands of missionaries and native Christians to preach the Gospel throughout Asia. Through his own ministry and that of his mission volunteers and Asian evangelists, millions have found new life in Christ. This incredible chain of events began in his youth when he himself found new life in Christ as a result of his mother's prayer. The account is in his own words:

 My mother being absent from home, I had a holiday, and in the afternoon looked through my father's library to find some book with which to while away the unoccupied hours. Nothing attracting me, I turned over a basket of pamphlets and selected from amongst them a Gospel tract that looked interesting, saying to myself, "There will be a story at the commencement and a sermon or moral at the close. I will take the former and leave the latter for those who like it."

I sat down to read the book in an utterly unconcerned state of mind, believing indeed at the time that if there were any salvation it was not for me, and with a distinct intention to put away the tract as soon as it should seem prosy.

Little did I know at the time what was going on in the heart of my mother, seventy or eighty miles away. She rose from the dinner table that afternoon with an intense yearning for the conversion of her boy; and feeling that, absent from home and having more leisure than she could otherwise secure, a special opportunity was afforded her of pleading with God on my behalf. She went to her room and turned the key in the door, resolved not to leave the spot until her prayers were answered. Hour after hour that dear mother pleaded, until at length she could pray no longer, but was constrained to praise God for that which His Spirit taught her had already been accomplished, the conversion of her only son.

I in the meantime had been led in the way I have mentioned to take up this little tract, and while reading it was struck with the phrase: "The finished work of Christ." . . . Then came the further thought, "If the whole work was finished and the whole debt paid, what is there left for me to do?"

And with this dawned the joyful conviction, as light was flashed into my soul by the Holy Spirit, that there was nothing in the world to be done but to fall down on one's knees and, accepting this Saviour and His salvation, praise Him for evermore.

Thus while my mother was praising God on her knees in her chamber, I was praising Him in the old warehouse to which I had gone alone to read at my leisure this little book.[7]

Mother of Missionaries

Mabel Francis was a missionary to Japan for fifty-six years, during which time she conducted evangelism and planted many churches with the help of her brother and sister who joined her in the work. During World War II, she and her sister remained in the country under house arrest, gaining the respect and admiration of the Japanese people. In 1962, the Emperor honored her with Japan's highest civilian award, the Fifth Order of the Sacred Treasure. What was the inspiration behind this missionary trio? A devoted mother.

Mother was a woman of deep faith. She was quiet and gentle, and faithfully taught the family about the things of God. We children were raised with the constant vision of our mother weeping over the lost in all the lands around the world.

Although it has been eighty years and more since that time, I can actually remember being so moved by these times of intercession on the part of my mother that I would say to her, "Don't cry, Mother, and don't worry! When I grow up I will tell the world all about Jesus."

As a teenager, Mabel felt the call of God upon her life.

I then told my mother, "God has called me to Japan."

I can never forget how she wept—and it seemed so unusual that one could weep such tears of joy.

She said, "Mabel, you know how I love Japan, but I could never go myself. I am happy that you can go, and your being in Japan will be a great joy to me."

In October of 1909, Mabel's mother helped load her baggage into a horse-drawn buggy and drove her to the station in Westport, Massachusetts, where she bid a tearful farewell to her daughter—never to see her again. In the years that followed she sent two more children to Japan—children inspired by the prayers of their mother.[8]

Little Cody Learns to Pray

One of the most publicly acclaimed babies of recent times has been Cody, the son of Kathie Lee Gifford, cohost of the popular "Live with Regis and Kathie Lee" TV talk show. Although I don't watch the show, I know about Cody—who has more than once been a topic for lighthearted banter among comedians. As the jokes go, Kathie Lee just can't shut up about her beloved baby. She's the proudest Mom on TV, and people apparently get tired of hearing about him. But some of her Cody stories are worth repeating. One of these comes at the conclusion of her autobiography.

It has been the greatest wonder of my life to know the love of my own child—and to see the way a child develops a loving heart for people. When Cody was about eighteen months old we would pray before bedtime. Every night I'd go down the list—Jesus, bless Daddy, Mommy, Christine, Cousin Shannie, and on and on. I usually include my housekeeper Amanda, who calls Cody "mi nino"—"My little one." So I was about to say Amen when Cody shot me his little frown and said, out of nowhere, "Mi nino." I couldn't believe it. Cody knew the list so well he knew I'd left out Amanda—only he thought her name was Mi Nino. . . .

And as I leave his room I'll look at him and think: The truest pleasures in life don't get any simpler than this.

And I know they don't get any sweeter.

Thank you, Lord. It's so good to be home.[9]

The Key of Our Souls

The real religion of the world comes from women much more than from men—from mothers most of all, who carry the key of our souls in their bosoms.

OLIVER WENDELL HOLMES[10]

"Hymn for the Mother"

My child is lying on my knees;
   The signs of heaven she reads;
My face is all the heaven she sees,
   Is all the heaven she needs.

And she is well, yea, bathed in bliss,
   If heaven is in my face,—
Behind it is all tenderness
   And truthfulness and grace. . . .

Lo! Lord, I sit in thy wide space,
   My child upon my knee;
She looketh up into my face,
   And I look up to thee.

GEORGE MACDONALD[11]

A Mother's Translation of the Bible

There is a story about four clergymen who were discussing the merits of the various translations of the Bible. One liked the King James Version best because of its simple, beautiful English.

Another liked the American Revised Version best because it is more literal and comes nearer the original Hebrew and Greek

Still another liked the Moffatt's translation best because of its up-to-date vocabulary.

The fourth minister was silent. When asked to express his opinion, he replied, "I like my mother's translation best."

The other three expressed surprise. They did not know that his mother had translated the Bible. "Yes, she did," he replied. "She translated it into life, and it was the most convincing translation I ever saw."

THE PIONEER[12]

Learning the Bible from Mother

 Whatever I have done in my life has simply been due to the fact that when I was a child my mother daily read with me a part of the Bible, and made me learn a part of it by heart.

WENDELL PHILLIPS[13]

Charles H. Spurgeon's Mother

 My conversion took place—oh momentous hours— at my mother's knee.

C.H. SPURGEON[14]

"Dedicated to God in Infancy"

 Sir Isaac Newton's mother prayed with and for her son every day of her life. It was the grief of her deathbed that she left a son of seven years at the mercy of a rough world. But Newton said, "I was born in a home of godliness and dedicated to God in my infancy."[15]

A Tribute to Christian Mothers

Only God Himself fully appreciates the influence of a Christian mother in the molding of the character in her children. . . . If we had more Christian mothers we would have less delinquency, less immorality, less ungodliness and fewer broken homes. The influence of a mother in her home upon the lives of her children cannot be measured. They know and absorb her example and attitudes when it comes to questions of honesty, temperance, kindness and industry. . . .

BILLY GRAHAM[16]

Loving Church Like Mama Did

Very often, the responsibility of bringing children up in the church is left to the mother—even when the father professes to be a Christian. This was true of Sarah Ophelia Colley, who was known as Minnie Pearl of The Grand Old Opry and television's "Hee Haw."

Going to church was an event, though it was certainly not out of the ordinary. Mama was there every time the doors opened, and we children had free run of the church as if it was a second home, which in a way it was. As strange as it may sound, the church was another place we played. I don't mean we were ever disrespectful in God's house, but we didn't think a thing about going in anytime we wanted and playing the organ or singing in front of an imaginary congregation. I loved that little Methodist church, and I spent a great deal of time there when I was growing up. We went to prayer meeting on Wednesday night and Sunday School and church on Sunday, and when I was small I also went with Mama to her Women's Missionary Society meetings. There was never a question in our family of not going to church. Church was like school. If you stayed home you got a dose of caster oil on the theory that if you were too sick to go to church or school you were sick enough to need the medicine. . . . Daddy rarely went with us. He said that was the only time he could get the bathroom. . . . His theory about going to church was that he could communicate with God just as well at home. . . . I felt like Mama did about church, even when I was little. I loved going and I still do. One reason might be that it holds such wonderful memories for me of childhood and that long-lost time of innocence. When I go to church, even in a strange city, I have a sensation of going home. I love to sing the Doxology and repeat the Apostles' Creed. I love to hear the hymns and the words of the Bible. I love the stained-glass windows and the pictures of Christ, the quiet, serene atmosphere that gives me time during a busy week to contemplate my life.[17]

. . . .

"Dad Had a Mean Streak. . . . Mom Met the Lord. . ."

A year and a half before he and his twin brother were born, his thirty-eight year-old father killed his "kid brother" (the uncle the boy never knew) with a shotgun blast. The next day this respected businessman was acquitted of the murder charge by a local trial judge on grounds of self-defense. Was it actually self-defense? Under law he was declared innocent on December 29, 1931. But "the sorrow had just begun. Eventually, it would destroy him."

The son of an atheist, this was not the first incident that marred his reputation.

Dad had a mean streak. . . . People didn't mess with my father. Even those who didn't respect him feared him. . . . Dad always carried his gun. . . . The Prohibition era only reinforced Dad's need to carry firepower. He was a "legitimate" bootlegger. He didn't make the stuff. He only bought and sold it. . . . Dad's drinking had increased measurably during those last few years. By the time I entered school, he was drinking a dozen beers a day and downing a fifth or more of whiskey on top of them.

When Jerry was fifteen, his father died—following a deathbed conversion. Even though his father had little time for him when he was growing up, he loved him and missed him, but it was his mother who had held the family together and given him a foundation of faith—faith that has established him as one of America's most noted religious leaders today, Jerry Falwell. The story of his mother was very different than that of his father.

 Mom met the Lord when she was just a child sitting in the family pew. She learned to read her Bible and to pray in those preadolescent years and never stopped reading and praying until the day she died. It was my mother who planted the seeds of faith in me from the moment I was born. . . . My real spiritual development took place at home. Mom led us in a prayer of thanksgiving before our meals. Often she prayed with us a bedtime prayer at night. And she insisted that we accompany her every

Sunday morning to Sunday School and worship whether we wanted to attend or not.[18]

. . . .

"Her God Is My God"

"Her God is my God" sums up Marian Anderson's tribute to her mother who worked as a cleaning lady to support her children after her husband died. As a poor widow, she never could have dreamed that one day her story would be told in the chapter of a book entitled simply "Mother." In *My Lord, What a Morning*, Marian Anderson tells of the struggles she faced as an African-American woman seeking a professional music career. When she was denied the opportunity to sing at Constitution Hall in 1939, because of her race, she was suddenly catapulted into the national spotlight. First Lady Eleanor Roosevelt arranged a concert for her on the steps of the Lincoln Memorial. She went on to become one of the world's leading vocalists, touring America and Europe and featured as a soloist with the New York Metropolitan Opera. Through all her success and acclaim, it was her mother who was her bedrock of support and stability.

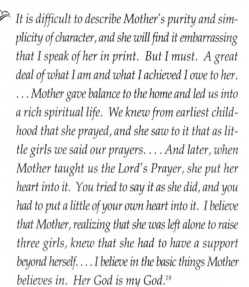

It is difficult to describe Mother's purity and simplicity of character, and she will find it embarrassing that I speak of her in print. But I must. A great deal of what I am and what I achieved I owe to her. . . . Mother gave balance to the home and led us into a rich spiritual life. We knew from earliest childhood that she prayed, and she saw to it that as little girls we said our prayers. . . . And later, when Mother taught us the Lord's Prayer, she put her heart into it. You tried to say it as she did, and you had to put a little of your own heart into it. I believe that Mother, realizing that she was left alone to raise three girls, knew that she had to have a support beyond herself. . . . I believe in the basic things Mother believes in. Her God is my God.[19]

What a legacy a child has who can look to a mother as a role model in prayer and Christian living. As I read these stories of faith from generations gone by and from today, I am challenged to be the kind of mother that my son can one day look back on as a mother who taught him the Scripture, who prayed with him, who took him to Sunday School and church. May he look on me as a mother of faith.

A picture memory brings to me:
I look across the years and see
Myself beside my mother's knee.

I feel her gentle hand restrain
My selfish moods and know again
A child's wrong sense of wrong and pain.

But wiser now, a man gray grown,
My childhood's needs are better known,
My mother's chastening love I own.

JOHN GREENLEAF WHITTIER

15

The Responsibilities of Motherhood

I *found out long ago that those who get the best return from their flower gardens were those who kept no gardeners, and it is the same way with the child garden; those who are too over busy, irresponsible, ignorant, or rich to do without the orthodox nurse, never can know precisely what they lose. To watch a baby untrammelled with clothes, dimple, glow and expand in its bath, is in an intense degree like watching, early of a June morning, the first opening bud of a rose that you have coaxed and raised from a mere cutting. You hoped and believed that it would be fair and beautiful, but ah, what a glorious surprise it is.*[1]

These lines were written by Helen Stough nearly a century ago, in her book, *A Mother's Year.* As a mother and a gardener, she captures the essence of motherhood and the responsibilities it entails—the mother gardener patiently tending her "child garden." In these lines she is making a case for a mother who doesn't hire a nanny. Today the parallel would be a stay-at-home mother. But times have changed. For many women, staying out of the workplace is not a real option. But that doesn't mean that she is not her own gardener, and for women who do forfeit the challenge of a career while little ones are growing up, there truly is a parallel to being one's own gardener and watching the budding rose blossom on that early June morning.

Motherhood carries awesome responsibilities—as, of course, does fatherhood. But as a mother—and as a single mother—I carry the heavy weight of responsibilities of motherhood on my shoulders. I'm continually asking myself what have I done wrong that has caused my son to be less than he ought to be. Or what haven't I done that I should have done to help him sail through adolescence more serenely. But these are questions of the heart more than of the intellect. On a rational level, I refuse to play the blame game. I don't blame my mother for my sins and failures, and by the same token I can't blame myself for my son's. But at the same time I can't try to dodge my responsibility to do the very best that I can as a mother to my son. I spend hours in the backyard nurturing my garden. I take pride in it. The more effort I expend, the better results I get. Can I do less in my garden of memories that I'm nurturing with my son.

The awesome responsibility of motherhood always jars me most when I hear the story of some young man involved in terrible criminal behavior whose mother is blaming herself or wondering what she might have done differently in child-rearing.

Some years ago my son's high school history teacher was charged and later convicted of murdering a prostitute. Her body was found with dozens of stab wounds in a nearby church parking lot, and there was suspicion (though never proof) that he may have killed other local prostitutes, whose murders were unsolved. Because he was Carlton's favorite teacher—"like a father to me"—I too got caught up in the story. It was thrust on me one afternoon, when I learned that Carlton had skipped school to be at the arraignment and was interviewed on the local news that night. So we followed the details of the court case as though we were part of it ourselves.

What haunted me the most during the long weeks of the trial was the pain of the mother.

She and her husband, who made their home in Minnesota, had raised their son in Sunday School and church, and now they were making the agonizing trip every week to stand by him, knowing in their hearts he was guilty. So distressed was I with the pain of this woman whom I knew only through newspaper accounts that I called another teacher at the school to enquire if there was anything I might do for lodging or otherwise while they were in town. I was told that everything was taken care of. But my heart went out to this dear woman—thinking, *But for the grace of God . . . there go I.*

When I think of the ultimate responsibility of motherhood, I can't help but think of the woman who gave birth to Adolf Hitler. But at least I can console myself with the fact that she was spared the pain of living to know her son as an adult. Who was this woman and what was her relationship with her son?

· · · · · · · · · · · · · · · ·

Adolf Hitler was a Muttersöhnchen

 Adolf was a mother's boy, a Muttersöhnchen, one of those who are incurably devoted to their mothers and therefore capable of latent and sometimes open hostility to the father. . . . To the very end of his life, when he was living in a subterranean bunker in the heart of burning Berlin, he kept his mother's photograph with him and found himself continually gazing at it. He did not keep a photograph of his father, and on the rare occasions when

he spoke about his father, it was usually with suppressed fury.

Already the seeds of many future disasters were being sown. By being so devoted to his mother, Adolf was ensuring that he would find no woman equal to her, for she alone represented the ideal. All women would be compared with Klara, and most of them would be found wanting. From his father he inherited the authoritarian temper, the stern dogmatic approach to all problems, and a sense of purpose.

When Hitler was eighteen, his mother fell gravely ill with cancer. He returned home from school to be with her, caring for her every need. "I never witnessed a closer attachment," her doctor wrote. When she died some months later, the same doctor noted: "I have never seen anyone so prostrate with grief as Adolf Hitler."[2]

What might Klara have done differently, I ask myself, to avoid raising a son who would become an Adolf Hitler? Or, do we let his father shoulder the responsibility—or do we put the responsibility squarely on the shoulders of Hitler alone? These are tough questions for a mother contemplating the awesome responsibilities in raising a child.

Sometimes mothers pay dearly for the sins of their children—as was true of Mary Surratt. As an American historian, I have been familiar with her name since graduate school twenty-five years ago, but I never was fully aware of the behind-the-scenes story.

• • • • • • • • • • • • • • • • • •

A Mother Hanged for Her Son's Criminal Involvement

The trial began on May 12, 1865, while the nation was still in mourning. It was less than a month after President Abraham Lincoln had been assassinated, and there would be no mercy for those charged in the conspiracy. Seven men and one woman were on trial. Mary Surratt was the one woman, and most historians have since concluded that she was innocent of any crimes against the President or the country. It was guilt by association—by association with her son John.

The widowed Mrs. Surratt ran a boardinghouse in Washington, and John served as a Confederate courier, "carrying secret papers in and out of Richmond." In this capacity he became acquainted with John Wilkes Booth and joined with him in a plan to take Lincoln hostage in exchange for Confederate prisoners. The conspirators often met at the boardinghouse to plan their strategy, but before the plot could be carried out, the Confederacy fell and an official plan for prisoner exchange was quickly set into motion.

Booth now devised a plot to assassinate the President—a plot which John Surratt and most of the others in the original kidnapping conspiracy renounced or thought too risky. But, as history tells us, Booth went ahead with the dastardly deed. And because of his ties to the boardinghouse, Mrs. Surratt was arrested, while her son fled for his life. The only "evidence" against her was from two men who exchanged their testimony for leniency. They claimed that they had seen Mrs. Surratt talking privately with Booth—though they had never heard any of the words spoken. In addition to that she had traveled back to her hometown before the assassination—allegedly to obtain supplies for Booth—though she testified that she made the trip to collect back rent.

 By the end of the trial, prosecutors had not produced any clear evidence that Surratt was involved with the assassination plot or even that she knew about it. Nevertheless and to the surprise of no one, she and the seven men were found guilty. Surratt and the three most directly involved in the crime were sentenced to hang. . . . Surratt— after two soldiers removed her bonnet—went to the gallows.

Two years later, John Surratt, who had fled the country, was apprehended and brought to trial. At that time "the testimony that had implicated his mother was discredited, and he was not convicted." But few people felt sorry about the wrongful execution of Mrs. Surratt. Many, like President Andrew Johnson, believed she deserved to die. In his words. "She kept the nest where the egg was hatched." She was the mother hen, and for her son's sins she died.[3]

Rousseau's Emile and Motherhood

One of the most influential books ever written on the responsibilities of motherhood was a novel written by a man about a man. Jean-Jacques Rousseau, an eighteenth-century French philosopher wrote *Emile*, a treatise on education in story form about Emile and his wife, Sophie, and their children.

That Rousseau would be perceived qualified to write on family life is astonishing in itself. He himself had a mistress—a servant—who became his common-law wife, and together they had five children, all of whom were given up and raised in an orphanage. Yet, in *Emile*, Rousseau does not hesitate to create a model wife and mother: "Sophie, wife of Emile and the mother of his children, was the ideal woman invented by Rousseau to be the companion of man as Rousseau dreamed she should be." Rousseau speaks through Emile:

 I would prefer a hundred times more a simple and coarsely raised girl than a learned and witty one who might establish in my home a literary tribunal and proceed to appoint herself its head. A female wit is the scourge of her husband, of her children. . . . The true mother, far from being a woman of the world, is as much a recluse in her home as the nun is in her cloister.

Rousseau's ideal of the family and motherhood had wide influence on Western culture—including one of the most powerful figures of the nineteenth century: "The most faithful reader of *Emile* was Napoleon."[4]

Mothers and the Destiny of the Nation

 The future destiny of the child is always the work of mothers. Let France have good mothers and she will have good sons.

NAPOLEON BONAPARTE[5]

A President's Admonition

President Theodore Roosevelt offered timeless advice to mothers. Some might quibble over the fact that fathers carry as much responsibility in properly raising their children as mothers do, but since this volume is about mothers, the advice stands unaltered and unapologetically.

 Into the woman's keeping is committed the destiny of the generations to come after us. In bringing up your children you mothers must remember that while it is essential to be loving and tender it is no less essential to be wise and firm. Foolishness and affection must not be treated as interchangeable terms; and besides training your sons and daughters in the softer and milder virtues, you must seek to give them those stern and hardy qualities which in after

life they will surely need. . . . If you mothers through weakness bring up your sons to be selfish and to think only of themselves, you will be responsible for much sadness among the women who are to be their wives in the future. If you let your daughters grow up idle, perhaps under the mistaken impression that as you yourselves have had to work hard they shall know only enjoyment, you are preparing them to be useless to others and burdens to themselves.[6]

My Trust

A Picture memory brings to me:
I look across the years and see
Myself beside my mother's knee

I feel her gentle hand restrain
My selfish moods, and know again
A child's blind sense of wrong and pain.

But wiser now, a man gray grown,
My childhood's needs are better known,
My mother's chastening love I own.

JOHN GREENLEAF WHITTIER[7]

The Mother as Teacher and Nurturer

The responsibility of the mother as teacher and nurturer of her children has not always been taken for granted. Children have not always been regarded a source of comfort and delight to their mothers.

For mothers of the eighteenth century, such a doctrine was frankly revolutionary. With the high mortality rate suffered by women during childbirth and the fact that about half of all babies born died before reaching adulthood, few women considered motherhood a sacred, tender, and privileged role. Old diaries, letters, and birth records of the seventeenth and eighteenth centuries indicate that the prospect of motherhood was not universally greeted with pleasure.

Mary Wollstonecraft, an outspoken early feminist, was one of the first women leaders of the modern period to strongly argue for the mother's involvement as teacher and nurturer to her young children. The mothers she observed were neglectful of their responsibilities:

 [She] neither suckles nor educates her children, seldom deserves the name of a wife, and has no right to that of a citizen. . . . To be a good mother, a woman must have sense and that independence of mind which few women possess who are taught to depend entirely on their husbands. . . . Unless the understanding of women be enlarged and her character rendered more firm by being allowed to govern her own conduct, she will never have sufficient sense of command of temper to manage her children properly.[8]

Mother Ford and McGuffey's Reader

Henry Ford owed his formative education to McGuffey's Reader and to his mother. Both taught high morals and love of country and love of God. But Mary Ford took her responsibilities as a mother very seriously and was able to enforce and encourage in a way that McGuffey was not.

In addition to McGuffey, Henry's mother provided a similar influence that was just as deep and lasting. Like McGuffey, she was passionate about cleanliness, order, courage, patience, and self-discipline. But where Schoolmaster McGuffey had to operate at long distance, she was as near as the woodshed and the dinner table—and her teachings sank in.

If even a third of the things her son later wrote about her are true, she was a notably clear-headed and straight-thinking woman. Beyond all else she taught him one great lesson about living, about adjusting to people and to life, a lesson that cannot be taught out of books but can only be hammered out in the give-and-take of everyday life:

She taught us what the modern family needs to learn—the art of being happy with each other . . . that if we couldn't be happy here in this house we'd never be happy anywhere else.

But this kind of happiness was never a light-hearted disregard of inappropriate behavior. On one occasion when Henry told a lie, Mary displayed her righteous indignation by refusing to speak to her son for a whole day. It was an experience he never forgot.

> *Shame cuts more deeply than a whip. For a day I was treated with contempt. There was no smiling or glossing over my shortcomings. I learned from her that wrong-doing carries its own punishment. There is no escape.*[9]

. . . .

The Carnegie Family Matriarch

No matter what role they play, mothers are put in a secondary role to fathers by historians. So it is with Andrew Carnegie in my *WorldBook Encyclopedia*. The father is given top billing. But without Margaret Carnegie's responsibilities in leading the family, the millionaire steel manufacturer and philanthropist, Andrew Carnegie, would likely be entirely lost in history.

Will, husband and father, was a social idealist whose interests lay elsewhere than providing for his family. Margaret, a shopkeeper, was the "chief provider" and "the real head of the family," and it was she who made the decision to emigrate from Scotland to America in 1847 to seek a fortune. "Will Carnegie at forty-three was a tired and defeated man . . . but Andrew during these past weeks had shared all of his mother's excitement and none of his father's doubts."

Times were difficult when they first arrived in America, and Margaret needed twelve-year-old Andrew's help, but not at any cost. When she was told by an acquaintance that he could make good money as a peddler, she was adamantly opposed. According to Andrew's later recollections:

> *[She was] an enraged woman. . . . My mother was sewing at the moment, but she sprang to her feet with outstretched hands and shook them in his face.*
>
> *"What! My son a peddler and go among rough men upon the wharves! I would rather throw him into the Allegheny River. Leave me!" she cried, pointing to the door, and Mr. Hogan went.*
>
> *She stood a tragic queen. The next moment she had broken down, but only for a few moments did tears fall and sobs come. Then she took her two boys in her arms and told us not to mind her foolishness. There were many things in the world for us to do and we could be useful men, honored and respected, if we always did what was right. . . . Tom and I could not help growing up respectable characters, having such a mother.*

Three years after they arrived in America, Will Carnegie died, and now Margaret was responsible for her sons only. Andrew's success in the years that followed was directly affected by his relationship with his mother, and she lived to see her son become one of the richest men in the world.[10]

Andrew Carnegie was distraught at his mother's death, but her presence lived on in his garden of memories.

The happiest years of my mother's life were spent here among her flowers. Her love for flowers was a passion. She was scarcely ever to gather a flower. Indeed I remember she once reproached me for pulling a weed, saying "it was something green." I have inherited this peculiarity, and have often walked from the house to the gate intending to pull a flower for my buttonhole, and then left for town unable to find one I could destroy. . . . None could really know her—I alone did that. After my father's early death she was all my own. The dedication of my first book tells the story. It was: "To my favorite Heroine, my Mother."[11]

Scientific Mothering

There are many ways a mother can keep track of her large brood in her efforts to fulfill the responsibilities of child-rearing, but Rose Kennedy the mother of nine children (five girls and four boys, born between 1915 and 1932) developed some clever method all of her own.

 She tried to be "scientific" in her child-rearing techniques. When the family moved to a larger and more elaborate house in Brookline, she designed a series of partitions on the porch so the children could play with no danger of accidentally hurting each other. She kept a card index for each child on which she noted certain data—immunizations, shoe sizes, childhood diseases, growth rates, and so on. . . . She put clocks in every room so that the children would have no excuse to be late for meals; she coded the brood with different-colored bathing caps to keep track of them when they were swimming. She ordered clothes and household items by lots, making space in high walk-in closets for boxes of shoelaces, toothbrushes, combs. She employed an orthodontist who traveled like a circuit rider to their various boarding schools to deal with problems that resulted from having Kennedy teeth in a Fitzgerald jaw.

Sometimes Rose Kennedy's rational scientific mothering got mixed up with pure emotion, as was true in her sense of responsibility for making daughter Rosemary, who was mentally handicapped, feel accepted.

Rose insisted that the two older boys come home from Choate [prep school] to take her to tea dances, explaining their absences by telling school officials that her daughter had an "inferiority complex." She encouraged the boys to get their friends to fill in her dance card, although she danced in an awkward half-trot, and to cut in on each other as they did for the other girls. She tried to create a pattern of normality around her—out of love and pity, but also to protect all the rest.[12]

Golda Meir's Reflections on Working Mothers

Mothers who work outside the home are often racked with guilt, wondering if their children will suffer on account of their absence from home.

Whether she is a minimum-wage, fast-food employee or the leader of a nation, a mother's uneasiness about leaving her child in someone else's care is often expressed through mixed emotions.

Golda Meir's reflections speak for many women. She served as Israel's minister of labor from 1949 to 1956, then as minister of foreign affairs and secretary-general of the Labor Party. From 1969 to 1974, she served as Prime Minister of Israel. But long before she was famous, she was a working mother struggling with her career choices that separated her from her growing children, Menachem and Sarah. She was critical of the stereotypical Jewish mother—"the all-engulfing nurturer who devours the very soul [of her child] with every spoonful of hot chicken soup she gives," and argued that "a working mother could actually bring more to her children than if she were to remain at home." Yet, she herself was never free from guilt.

But one look of reproach from the little one when the mother goes away and leaves it with a stranger is enough to throw down the whole structure of vindication. That look, that plea to the mother to stay, can be withstood only by an almost superhuman effort of will.

At the best of times, in the best circumstances, there is a perpetual consciousness at the back of her mind that her child lacks a mother's tenderness. We believe, above all, in education by example, therefore we must ask ourselves: Whose example molds the child of the working mother? A "borrowed mother" becomes the model. The cute things a child says reach the mother at second hand. Such a child does not know the magic healing power of a mother's kiss, which takes way the pain of a bruise. And there are times, after a wearying, care-filled day, when the mother looks at her child almost as if she did not recognize it; a feeling of alienation from her nearest and dearest steals into her heart.

And having admitted all this, we ask: Can the mother of today remain at home all day with her children? Can she compel herself to be other than she is because she had become a mother? Is there something wrong with me if my children don't fill up my life? . . .

My children have a very close relationship with me, but if I am to be honest with myself there is a little—maybe more than a little—pang of conscience over the injustice I have done to the children, days or evenings I should have remained with them but couldn't. . . . I know that my children, when they were small, suffered a lot on my account.[13]

I resonate with the inner struggles and confessions of Golda Meir. Like her I take the responsibilities of motherhood very seriously, and like her I have a tendency to second-guess some of the decisions I've made. How have these decisions that bear on my motherly responsibilities affected my son, and how will they affect him in years to come? The questions haunt me. The answers elude me.

〜 *Where is the mother who would willingly forget the infant*

that perished like a blossom from her arms, though every

recollection is a pang? . . . No the love which survives the

tomb is one of the noblest attributes of the soul. . . .

WASHINGTON IRVING

16

The Sorrow and Suffering of Motherhood

One blossom of hope, just dawned upon this world, lived but a brief hour, and was transplanted by the all knowing Creator to his gardens of joy.

The sorrow of losing one child is to my mind incomprehensible—and infinitely more painful to lose more than one. How could a mother endure the anguish of losing four little ones? When I read the almost matter-of-fact loss of little ones, I ponder how it could be so. Was the sorrow of mothers in generations past somehow less severe because death was an ever-present reality of life? Was the loss lessened by large size of families? Was faith in God a factor? These questions come to mind as I consider Sarah Everett Hale, a nineteenth-century writer, who reflected on her family on her twenty-fifth wedding anniversary in 1841. Seven children were with her in this world; four were in God's "gardens of joy."

 I have borne eleven children, and have been permitted to keep until this day seven—One blossom of hope, just dawned upon this world, lived but a brief hour, and was transplanted by the all knowing Creator to his gardens of joy.—Another remained with us for seven months, learned to return smile for smile, and was just beginning to show the germs of intelligence when a short space of suffering and anxiety was closed by our laying him away in the dark chamber, which then was but a few paces from the nursery where we had cherished and nourished him.—Then came another bright cherub—our darling "other Susie"—bright and hopeful and promising with her earnest and deep glance, and her thoughtful spirit, and in her seventh year, it pleased God to take her from us. . . . Three weeks had past away after her death, when another little girl was given us—She has been spared to this time—Is like, very like her sister,—God grant

she may be long spared to us, and be so trained here that she may be joined to the "other Susie"—in heaven—Since then another little girl has been given and taken, and now there are seven here, and four awaiting us on the other side of Jordan.[1]

I have never had to endure the sorrow and anguish of losing a child. I simply cannot imagine such searing pain. And I can't imagine how I would react. Would I be so overcome with grief that I could not even make funeral arrangements? Would I be so numbed by the shock that I would function frantically as though on automatic pilot? Would I weep uncontrollably and cry out in piercing agony? Would I stifle my sobs and acknowledge the casseroles and condolences? Would I feel God's comforting presence? Would I mix my tears with laughter and reminisce with Carlton's friends? I desperately hope I never have to experience the answer to those questions.

I'll never forget the day in June twelve years ago while sitting in my car at a red light not far from home at the intersection of Fuller and Fulton. An acquaintance pulled his car up alongside mine and asked, "Did you hear the terrible news?" Before the light had turned green, I had learned that eleven-year old Kimberly VanDyke had been electrocuted near the swimming pool of a Marriott Hotel while away on vacation with her family. Beautiful, bright-eyed, vivacious Kim—it was impossible to believe that her life was snuffed out in an instant.

My heart sank and I felt numb. All I could think of was my dear friend Sharon. Her kids were the light of her life, and Kim was her only daughter.

I ached for Jim too but the mother heart in me went out to Sharon. How can she even keep on going after such a devastating sorrow?

The funeral was memorable. The church was packed. It almost seemed like everyone in Grand Haven, Michigan—school children included—had come to say good-bye. Pictures and memories of Kim filled the easel bulletin board and flower arrangements were everywhere. The service itself was a celebration of God's love and grace. Kim's personality was captured through stories and letters, and there were even points of laughter. It was truly a testimony to the community of the faith of this family. The calm courage of Sharon and Jim and the boys was evident to all. "They're holding up so good," was the universal reflection on this grieving family.

But in the days and weeks and months that followed, Sharon wondered aloud whether she had done her grieving the wrong way. It was at a time when she was hurting so bad she could hardly function and she was asking herself if it might have been better for her emotional well-being if she had flung herself on the floor in anguish and not cared about a "Christian testimony" before others. She had seen a public display of grieving in the Middle East on the television news where the people were physically manifesting their grief—crying out in shrill screams, waving their arms in anguish, and throwing themselves on the ground. *I think they know how to respond to grief better than I did*, she concluded. And maybe they did.

A sorrow that is stifled is often more prolonged and painful than one that erupts in a volcano of emotion. Sharon realized this and sought to come to terms with her grief. Others have been emotionally scarred for life. The sad story of Mary Todd Lincoln is an example.

 Mary Lincoln did not attend Willie's funeral in the White House .... "Tears are not for the gaze," advised one manual, and those who cried in solitude were said to be more sincere in their sorrow for not having "blazoned it upon the housetops." Good Christian women knew better than to mourn excessively; visible emotion only displayed their lack of faith in the doctrine that the dead passed from this world into God's better one. According to one mourning manual, only "jews and heathens howl in impious anguish and they do so because they don't know any better." [2]

The sorrow that Mary Todd Lincoln endured was shared by many other mothers—especially during the bloody battles of the Civil War. More than two years after the death of his own son, Abraham Lincoln, knowing personally the pain of losing a beloved child, wrote a letter to a grieving mother.

· · · · · · · · · · · · · · · · · ·

A Letter of Consolation

Executive Mansion, Washington
November 21, 1864.

 Mrs. Bixby, Boston, Massachusetts.

Dear Madam: I have been shown in the files of the War Department a statement of the Adjutant-
General of Massachusetts that you are the mother of five sons who have died gloriously on the field of battle. I feel how weak and fruitless must be any words of mine which should attempt to beguile you from the grief of a loss so overwhelming. But I cannot refrain from tendering to you the consolation that may be found in the thanks of the Republic they died to save. I pray that our heavenly Father may assuage the anguish of your bereavement, and leave you only the cherished memory of the loved and lost, and the solemn pride that must be yours to have laid so costly a sacrifice upon the altar of Freedom.

Yours very sincerely and respectfully,
Abraham Lincoln. [3]

The price that many mothers paid in the loss of their sons during the Civil War could be viewed indirectly as a debt paid to their black sisters in the South who had lost their children not to the battlefield but to the institution of slavery. I learned in my graduate studies that there were other causes of the Civil War than slavery, but that terrible conflict toppled Southern slavery once and for all. Slaves—and slave mothers particularly—could look to a time when they would no longer anguish over their children snatched from their arms to face a terrifying and uncertain future.

· · · · · · · · · · · · · · · · · ·

An Un-Happy New Year

The most tragic stories of motherhood that I have encountered in my research have been those of slave mothers who have been torn away from their children by heartless masters. Every time I read the accounts I wonder how such pain could have been inflicted upon another human being. And where were the masters' wives, who themselves had experienced the bond of motherhood? Too often they were silent, turning their backs on this most atrocious crime most often associated with slave auctions. But slave mothers had more to fear than the auctions, as Harriet Jacobs described in the narrative of her life as a slave and later as a free woman. The most dreaded day of the year was the New Year when slaves were hired out and separated from their families.

O, you happy free women, contrast your New Year's day with that of the poor bond-woman! With you it is a pleasant season, and the light of the day is blessed. Friendly wishes meet you every where, and gifts are showered upon you. Even hearts that have been estranged from you soften at this season, and lips that have been silent echo back, "I wish you a happy New Year." Children bring their little offerings, and raise their rosy lips for a caress. They are your own, and no hand but that of death can take them from you.

But to the slave mother New Year's day comes laden with peculiar sorrows. She sits on her cold cabin floor, watching the children who may all be torn from her the next morning; and often does she wish that she and they might die before the day dawns. She may be an ignorant creature, degraded by the system that has brutalized her from childhood; but she has a mother's instincts, and is capable of feeling a mother's agonies.[4]

. . . .

"Oh, Lord Jesus, How Long!"

The most unforgettable story that I've ever read of a slave mother's anguish over the loss of children is written by a son, Father Henson, who lived to experience life as a free man, but never without the haunting memories of his last moments of agony with his mother. The setting is a slave auction:

 My brothers and sisters were bid off first, and one by one, while my mother, paralyzed by grief, held me by the hand. Her turn came, and she was bought by Isaac Riley of Montgomery county. Then I was offered to the assembled purchasers. My mother, half distracted with the thought of parting forever from all her children, pushed through the crowd, while the bidding for me was going on, to the spot where Riley was standing. She fell at his feet, and clung to his knees entreating him in tones that a mother only could command, to buy her baby as well as herself, and spare to her one, at least, of her little ones. Will it, can it be believed that this man, thus appealed to, was capable not merely of turning a deaf ear to her supplication, but of disengaging himself from her with such violent blows and kicks, as to reduce her to the necessity of creeping out of his reach, and mingling the groan of bodily suffering with the sob of a breaking heart? As she crawled away from the brutal man I heard her sob out, "Oh, Lord Jesus, how long, how long shall I suffer this way!" I must have been then between five and six years old. I seem to see and hear my poor weeping mother now.[5]

A mother's pain of seeing children sold into slavery can only be matched by a mother's anguish of facing the guillotine—not so much the anguish of dying, but the anguish of leaving little children behind.

. . . .

A Condemned Mother Weeps for Her Children

Marie Antoinette was a controversial queen in her own day and is a much-debated figure in history. Some historians have portrayed her as a selfish and scheming monarch with no sympathy for the suffering peasants. They would argue that the charges of treason were well-founded and that her execution was a natural consequence in the revolutionary atmosphere of France in the early 1790s. Others have viewed Marie Antoinette much more compassionately—that she was a deeply caring queen possessing a personality "that radiated warmth and kindness, that abhorred pretence and found solace in the company of animals and small children." Whoever she was, we know for certain that she suffered unbearable anguish as a mother. In June of 1789, one month before the world would be shaken by the French Revolution, her oldest son died at age ten. Two years earlier, she had lost her darling daughter—only eleven months old. But her greatest anguish of motherhood came when her children were taken from her and she was confined in a prison cell with only memories and some "little packets containing locks of hair from her dead and living children."

After a speedy trial she was condemned to the scaffold, leaving her little ones motherless.

 It was . . . nearly five o'clock on the morning of October 16 [1793], and the death sentence was to be carried out at midday. She wrote a final letter to Elisabeth [her late husband's sister], full of tenderness and feeling, asking her to care for Louis-Charles and Therese as if they were her own children. In her prayer book she wrote, "My God have pity on me! My eyes have no more tears to shed for you, my poor children. Adieu, adieu!"[6]

. . . .

The Love Which Survives the Tomb

 Where is the mother who would willingly forget the infant that perished like a blossom from her arms, though every recollection is a pang? . . . No, the love which survives the tomb is one of the noblest attributes of the soul. If it has its woes, it has likewise its delights; and when the overwhelming burst of grief is calmed into the gentle tear of recollection, when the sudden anguish and the convulsive agony over the present ruins of all that we most loved is softened away into pensive meditation on all that it was in the days of its loveliness,— who would root out such a sorrow from the heart?

WASHINGTON IRVING[7]

The story that will always be symbolic of a mother's pain more than any other made the headlines long before I was born, but it was a story that made a powerful impression on my mother, and I heard it retold as I was growing up.

. . . .

A Diary of Pain and Anguish

The story of the kidnapping and death of baby Charles Lindbergh has brought chills to a generation of a million mothers. The ordeal surrounding the eighteen-month-old son of the celebrated American aviator Charles Lindbergh and his wife Anne captured the world's attention for ten long weeks in the spring of 1932. How could a mother endure such anguish? There's a part of me that doesn't want to know, and yet, when I recently discovered Anne's published diaries and letters that covered this period of time, I rushed out of the library with the book in order to get alone and read those heart-wrenching entries. She introduces the section with some reflections on why she made her private grief public:

> But a deeper reason moving me to publish is that suffering—no matter how multiplied—is always individual. "Pain is the most individualizing thing on earth," Edith Hamilton has written. "It is true that it is the great common bond as well, but that realization comes only when it is over. To suffer is to be alone. To watch another suffer is to know the barrier that shuts each of us away by himself. Only individuals can suffer."
>
> Suffering is certainly individual, but at the same time it is a universal experience. . . . There is no aristocracy of grief. Grief is a great leveler. There is no highroad out.

After the terrifying ten-week ordeal was over and the body of her darling toddler was found, Anne wrote her numbing impressions from her home in Hopewell, New Jersey, on May 12, 1932:

> I feel strangely a sense of peace—not peace, but an end to restlessness, a finality, as though I were sleeping in a grave.
>
> It is a relief to know definitely that he did not live beyond that night. I keep him intact somehow, by that. He was with me the last weekend and left loving me better than anyone, I know that. But all that is merely selfish and small. . . .
>
> May 13, 1932: He has already been dead a hundred years.
>
> A long sleepless night. . . . Then a long day when everything personal flooded back over me, a personal physical loss, my little boy—no control over tears, no control over the hundred little incidents I had jammed out of sight when I was bargaining for my control.[8]

. . . .

Death of a Little One and a Raging River

In her book of family reminiscences, *The Preacher Had 10 Kids*, Frances Bradsher shares the good times and the bad times of a country Methodist preacher. The happy events were often counterbalanced by tragedies, one of which occurred in the spring of 1888. Little Roxy, "the first girl to follow three husky boys, was Papa's special delight, and he was determined to take her along with him on a circuit visit to parishioners even though she had not been feeling well. Her mother reluctantly consented.

Roxy didn't say much on the long trip across the country roads. Most of the time she leaned on Papa's arm and dozed, even when they came to the creek which had to be forded, a venture that had always thrilled her. It had begun to rain by the time they arrived at the Smiths' where they were to stay. . . . Roxy began to choke about midnight. The man of the house came to Papa and said, "The rain is coming down harder, and the creek will rise. I'd better go for a doctor while I can." . . .

"Tell Mrs. Cherry [Roxy's mother] to come with the doctor, too," Papa told the man. . . .

Papa walked the floor, the child in his arms. . . . The rain poured down, and the creek roared with the filling of debris the deluge was dumping into its bands. Would morning never come? Papa thought. Could Mama get there in time?

Daylight, grayed by heavy clouds, began to streak the sky. He could see through the window the buggy with Mama and the doctor standing across the swollen creek. Mama, disregarding the mud, jumped down from the buggy and ran to the bank, separated from her child by surging logs and trash that filled the creek bed. There could be no crossing until the creek went down in its own time.

Papa walked to the window. "See, Roxy, there's

Mama." Maybe the sight of Mama would work a miracle. Roxy made an effort to look, then a fit of choking came and she lay quiet on Papa's shoulder. Her struggle was over.

Papa laid her down and went to the creek bank. No sound could have been heard above the roar of the water, but Mama needed no words to tell her that her first girl child was gone, without the comfort of her mother's arms. A kind of bitterness crept into her heart, she told someone later, bitterness against Papa, who had taken Roxy away when she wasn't feeling well, bitterness against herself for allowing it, and bitterness against God. . . . It was several hours before the creek went down enough to ford, but when Mama stood over her child, wet to the knees, her face streaked with mud and tears, the bitterness vanished. Pity took its place as she looked at Papa, exhausted from his long night's vigil. . . . She could hear the tapping of the hammer as their host made Roxy's small wooden coffin.[9]

* * * * * * * * * * * * *

"Loss"

The name of the young man in the news releases caught my attention because he shared a name with my son: Richard Carlton Meeker, Jr.—the son of a Hollywood celebrity, now dead.

Chapter 10 in Jason Bonderoff's biography of Mary Tyler Moore is titled simply "Loss." Here in less than ten pages, the story of the death of Mary's twenty-four-year-old son in 1980 is recounted. Richie, as he was known, was Mary's only son, and it was not until 1980 that their troubled relationship began to heal. Early that year, Mary admitted to an interviewer what gossip columnists had long been writing, but she added a positive note:

 We went through a fairly long period of not communicating. He had, I think, some resentments of my commitment to my work. He's beginning to understand that I was doing the best that I could at the time. . . . It's nice, I have a new friend.

But that friendship didn't last long. Only months later Richie was killed by a self-inflicted gunshot wound to the head, playing what some reporters called "shotgun roulette." Family and friends insisted the death was accidental, but such an explanation did not ease the pain.

Did Richie purposefully take his own life? No one will ever know for sure. The only certainty is the incredible mixture of sorrow and guilt and shame and anger Mary experienced in coming to terms with the tragedy.

"Pain," Mary had earlier concluded, "nourishes my courage." But any mother would gladly forfeit courage to avoid such unbearable pain.[10]

For another mother—the mother of Hannah Szenes—the cause of the child's death was not suicide, rather idealism and conviction. Nevertheless, it was a death that in the mother's eyes could have been prevented—thus making the pain even more unbearable.

"Mother, Forgive Me"

Today Hannah Szenes is one of Israel's most celebrated heroines—a young woman of remarkable courage and loyalty to her people. "Her poetry and story are taught in Israeli schools, and she has been the subject of a play by one of Israel's major dramatists." She was one of thirty-two Jewish resistance volunteers who parachuted behind the lines of Yugoslavia in March of 1944, when she was in her early twenties, in an effort to stir up opposition to the Nazis among their fellow Jews.

After crossing the border into her homeland of Hungary, she was captured and held in a Nazi prison, and later was executed by firing squad on November 7, 1944.

Hannah had no regrets. She had done what was right for her Jewish people suffering under Nazism. But she was sorry for the pain her widowed mother Catherine was suffering. When her mother first saw her tortured daughter in prison she hardly recognized her. "Her once wavy hair hung in a filthy tangle, her ravaged face reflected untold suffering, her large, expressive eyes were blackened, and there were ugly welts on her cheeks and neck. All Hannah could do was to throw herself into her mothers arms and cry, "Mother, forgive me."

After Hannah's execution, her mother was permitted to retrieve her daughter's belongings. In the pocket of one of her dresses she found a scrap of paper with a note:

Dearest mother: I don't know what to say—a million thanks and forgive me if you can. You know so well why words aren't necessary. With love forever, Your daughter.[11]

Two Generations of Mothers' Pain

When I travel I like to make friends—not necessarily with other tourists, but more often with people I encounter from long ago. One of my newest "friends" is Mary Jemison, "the white woman from Genosee." Her grave marker, statue, and log cabin are located on the Council Grounds at the Letchworth State Park in western New York. Her story fascinates me—especially when I think of the child custody cases that have made headlines in recent years.

In 1758, when she was in her early teens, Mary was taken captive by a band of native Americans. Her family was killed, but she was "adopted" into the tribe. Her mother's last words stayed with her: "Don't forget, my little daughter, the prayers that I have learned you—say them often; be a good child, and God will bless you."

The first months were terrifying, but as the years passed she adjusted to tribal life and married an Indian man. "One thing only marred my happiness," she confessed, "and that was the recollection that I had once had tender parents, and a home that I loved."

It was a hard life—always seeking a place to live that was safe from the encroachment of white settlers—but she refused to return to her heritage. Indeed, when she learned that a Dutchman, in collusion with an Indian chief, was seeking to "redeem" her for a government reward, she hid out and escaped with the help of one of her Indian brothers.

After her first husband died, she married again—a warrior whose "cruelties to his enemies were unparalleled." He was kind to her, but "war was his trade." It was in this atmosphere that her five children were reared, and one day in the midst of bitter sibling rivalry, one of her sons killed his brother. The pain was almost too much to bear.

Mary eventually settled on land granted her by tribal chiefs through the U.S. government. Here her life became more tranquil, and she had opportunity to become reacquainted with the Bible and renew her faith in God, but the pain of one son killing another she carried with her to the grave.[12]

When I think of Mary Jemison, I am reminded of the sorrow associated with motherhood ever since Eve was banished from the Garden.

 Unto the woman he said, I will greatly multiply thy sorrow and thy conception; in sorrow thou shalt bring forth children.

GENESIS 3:16, KJV

I don't think this refers only to the pain of childbirth itself. Eve's sorrows as a mother would be multiplied, and for her the greatest sorrow of all was that of one son killing another. So too for Mary Jemison. We have come full circle. The sorrow and suffering in motherhood continues.

The dream led him first into the garden....

He stretched out his arms, and in the deep peace that

followed mutual recognition and need, the Winged

Presence vanished softly into the darkness, leaving

Mother and Child together in the Garden of Dreams.

KATE DOUGLAS WIGGIN

17

Mothers in Literature and Legend

Kate Wiggin has written a beautiful legend of a motherless boy and his garden of dreams. He "lived very much by himself in a tall building with many windows looking skyward," but then he had a dream:

 The dream led him first into a garden.... The flowers were all dear, familiar, modest ones, such as violets and pansies, clove-pinks and hyacinths; but, loveliest of all, was a clump of Madonna lilies, their tall green stalks crowned with dazzling white blossoms. The Child crept under them and looking up, marveled at the shining purity of the blooms that made a little white heaven over his head.

There were birds in the trees, and the Child sometimes fancied that they tried to speak to him, although he could never puzzle out the meaning of their language. But one night when the birds slept he heard the rustle of great wings, a stirring of the air, a soft flutter, and then, in the darkness, a Voice. There was no Presence, but the Voice was clear, and it said:—

"Do you find the garden beautiful, my child?"

"The most beautiful thing in the world," answered the Child. "Is it you who are making it?" ...

"Yes; for the garden is now finished save for that which you will plant with your own hands.... If you were to plant something precious in the garden, my child, what spot would you choose?"

"I would choose the spot under the Madonna lilies," said the Child....

"Stretch out your hand, my child," said the Voice, "and what you find in the wet grass, that is for you to plant."

And the Child stretched out his hand and touched something soft and warm hidden in a blanket of leaves.

"Is it a bird?" he whispered, for he felt a throb under his hand.

"No, it is not a bird!" said the Voice,—"it is a heart! Make a hollow for it like a nest; do not unwrap it, but lay it gently in the hollow; cover it lightly with soft earth, then step back, for the place on which you stand will be holy ground."

And the Child did as he was bidden. . . . And straightway (for there is not time in dreams) the heart stirred, and trembled, and swelled, and broke through the soft earth, and lifted itself and grew. . . .

And when it came to its moment of full perfection, lo! it was, not a growing and blossoming heart, but—a Mother!

And the Child knew! For knowledge comes swiftly and surely in dreams!

He stretched out his arms, and in the deep peace that followed mutual recognition and need, the Winged Presence vanished softly into the darkness, leaving the Mother and Child together in the Garden of Dreams.

KATE DOUGLAS WIGGIN[1]

The traditional bedtime stories we have learned from our earliest childhood unconsciously penetrate our psyches more than we realize. And our perspective on mothers is no doubt affected by this literature. I am at a loss to recall a story of an evil mother, but the wicked stepmother makes her way into literature all too frequently, and fathers are far less visible than mothers—stepfathers not mentioned at all. When fathers do ap-

pear, they fulfill traditional roles—as does Papa Bear in the story of the three bears. But most often the mother carries on with her children while the father is out of the picture, as is true in many of the Mother Goose rhymes and fairy tales.

· · · · · · · · · · · · · · · · ·

Who Was Mother Goose?

The best-known mother in all of literature and legend is probably Mother Goose. Hardly a child in the Western world has grown up without her, and even as adults we make reference to the nursery rhymes we learned when we were little. But was there really a Mother Goose?

The French tradition behind the Mother Goose nursery rhymes goes back to 1697, when Charles Perrault published a book entitled *Contes de Ma Mere L'Oye,* translated *Tales of My Mother Goose.* It featured many of the traditional stories of the day, including Cinderella, Little Red Riding Hood, and Sleeping Beauty.

The American tradition of Mother Goose dates back to colonial Boston, and in this case there is not only a real mother but a real Mother Goose. She was Elizabeth Foster, who married Isaac Vergoose in 1692.

 He already had ten children and she gave him six more, though the tale about the old woman who lived in a shoe and had so many children she didn't know what to do didn't become a part of the Mother Goose collection until sometime later.

But, if she didn't live in a shoe, she apparently did have so many children that she was constrained to creatively entertain them, and she soon became known for her collection of tales. These stories were later published by her son-in-law in 1719 under the title of *Mother Goose's Melodies*, though no copies are now in existence.

 Whoever Mother Goose might have been, the tales themselves have been passed down by mothers to children for hundreds of years, and fortunately for us we all have that "other mother" in our lives.[2]

Do the stories reflect reality or do they influence reality? Probably both are true, but as we move beyond the fairy tales of children's literature, we encounter a far more diverse reflection on the family—and on mothers' roles. Charles Dickens, for example, deeply scarred by his own mother, sometimes created vicious mothers in his fiction. And other writers of novels and short stories did not hesitate to portray a mother with a dark side who damaged the psyche of her child.

But do mothers fare equally with fathers in literature, and what about the mother-daughter relationship? As in movies today, the best roles are typically reserved for men. The mother-daughter bond, according to Adrienne Rich, is patriarchal society's "great unwritten story." Edith Neisser agrees. In her book, *Mothers and Daughters*, she points out that great literature features few compelling mother-daughter relationships. Such stories, she argues, are comparable to the Dutch "Little Masters" among great artists.

Mothers and Daughters in Literature

...The association of mothers and daughters is rarely material for the heroic stance. That may in itself be sufficient reason why no author has done for this relationship what Shakespeare did for mothers and sons in Hamlet.... During most of the history of the Western world, what two women in the same family felt about each other or how they behaved toward each other simply was not considered important....

The best novels about mothers and daughters might be compared to the paintings of the Dutch "Little Masters." These delicate, detailed portrayals of domestic life illuminate, in all senses of that word, the manner, dress and occupations of the burgher families of the sixteenth and seventeenth centuries in Holland. We do not find fault with Vermeer because he did not choose the subjects which appealed to Michelangelo, nor should we diminish the stature of a Jane Austen or a Rebecca West because they have not dealt with world-shaking themes.

Perhaps one reason why mother and daughter combinations abound in fairy tales and folklore is that the material of these stories is usually not of epic proportions. Girls who are directed by their mothers or stepmothers to sweep the hearth, take the sheep to pasture, or carry baskets of cakes to ailing relatives are such stuff as the interchanges between mothers and young daughters are made of in daily life and may bring out maternal kindness or oppression, daugh-

terly cooperation or resentment. . . .

   Mother and daughter relationships are conspicuous by their absence in Shakespeare, in the Bible and in poetry.[3]

Is it possible, I wonder, that great mother-daughter stories have actually been written, but that the literary critics—primarily men—have not deemed this fiction worthy of high commendation.

A woman who wrote perceptively about the mother-daughter relationship was Edith Wharton. I read her book *The Mother's Recompense* recently for the first time and found the mother-daughter relationship as complicated and unpredictable in that book as it is today in real life and fiction. And I found it ironical that Kate, in a widely read book of the 1920s, ran away from her responsibilities, while Francesca in *The Bridges of Madison County,* one of the 1990s bestselling books, forsook her lover to care for her family.

· · · · · · · · · · · · · · · ·

The Mother's Recompense

The Mother's Recompense was written in 1925, during the "Roaring Twenties," when women were more liberated and daring than they had been in any previous age. Kate Clephane is the main character—the mother—who runs away from a difficult marriage and mother-in-law, and leaves Anne, her little girl, behind to be raised by others. She ends up on the French Riviera, seeking unsuccessfully to regain custody of Anne. The years go by; she has a brief

love affair with Chris, a much younger man, and then one day (her husband now dead) a telegram arrives with the news that her mother-in-law has died, followed by a message from her daughter, asking Kate to come home and live with her.

 It was curious: for the first time she realized that, in thinking back over the years since she had been parted from Anne, she seldom, nowadays, went farther than the episode with Chris. Yet it was long before—it was eighteen years ago—that she had "lost" Anne: "lost" was the euphemism she had invented . . . because a mother couldn't confess, even to her most secret self, that she had willingly deserted her child. Yet that was what she had done; and now her thoughts, shrinking and shivering, were being forced back upon the fact. She had left Anne when Anne was a baby of three; left her with a dreadful pang, a rending of the inmost fibers, and yet a sense of unutterable relief, because to do so was to escape from the oppression of her married life. . . . "I couldn't breathe—" that was all she had to say in her own defence.

Kate responded to her daughter's cable, with two words: "Coming darling," the same words she had used to respond to Anne's cries for "Mummy" when she was alone as a little girl in her nursery at night. But now, anticipating the reunion, Kate's heart was pounding.

She thirsted to have the girl to herself, where she could touch her hair, stroke her face, draw the gloves from her hands, kiss her over and over again. . . .

Kate returned to New York, and she and her daughter had a blissful reunion, epitomized by their night out at the opera. Kate "suddenly exclaimed to herself":

 "I am rewarded." It was a queer, almost blasphemous fancy—but it came to her so. She was rewarded for having given up her daughter; if she had not, could she ever have known such a moment as this? She had been too careless and impetuous in her own youth to be worthy to form and guide this rare creature; and while she seemed to be rushing blindly to her destruction, Providence had saved the best part of her in saving Anne.

But the bliss could not last. During her separation from her mother, Anne had met and fallen in love with Chris, not knowing her mother had also been in love him. When Anne announced her intention to marry him, her mother was horrified and shocked—and wondered to herself if she were jealous of her own daughter. She was determined to prevent the marriage, but in the end, she relented. "I would sell my soul for her—why not my memories?" After the marriage, Anne, who never learned the secret, traveled with her new husband, and Kate returned to the Riviera. This is Kate's reward—this is *The Mother's Recompense.*[4]

Another female literary figure who wrote about motherhood was Jane Austen, whose mother had a major influence on her—in a negative way.

Jane Austen's Malicious Mothers

Jane Austen, the great nineteenth-century English novelist, who wrote *Pride and Prejudice* and many other works of fiction, often portrayed mothers, according to her biographer, very negatively.

 Think, for example, of "Lady Susan," in which there is a mother who hates her daughter and ultimately forgets her existence altogether. In Sense and Sensibility *. . . there is a mother—Mrs. Ferrars—who devotes much of her energy alternately to disinheriting and forgiving her unoffending children. The number of unpleasant mothers in the fiction is striking. . . . Mrs. Hodge reminds us that when Catherine returns home with a broken heart in* Northanger Abbey, *her mother fails to recognize the condition. . . . In* Pride and Prejudice *. . . Mrs. Bennett is a fool.*

Did Jane's relationship with her own mother contribute to the unflattering portrayal of mothers in her writing? Yes, according to her biographer:

 The available evidence suggests that she loved her father, and perhaps felt something less than love for her mother. . . . If parents in her novels are often bad parents, they may stand in for her mother alone, with whom her relations were always less easy. . . . Indeed, the collected edition of Jane Austen's letters does not list a single letter to her mother written during the course of her lifetime, though the two women were

separated often enough and the novelist wrote regularly to other members of the family.

When Jane's sister wrote that their mother was not bearing up well in the unseasonably hot weather, Jane's response betrays her enduring hostility toward her mother, "revelling . . . in the very weather which is making her mother ill."

I am sorry my Mother has been suffering, & am afraid this exquisite weather is too good to agree with her.—I enjoy it all over me, from top to toe, from right to left, Longitudinally, Perpendicularly, Diagonally;—& cannot but selfishly hope we are to have it last till Christmas;—nice, unwholesome, Unseasonable, relaxing, close, muggy weather![5]

Some women writers reflected less on their mothers than on their own perspective on motherhood. To be a great writer was fulfillment in itself. Motherhood could only take away from that ambition. So it was with Margaret Mitchell.

· · · · · · · · · · · · · · · · ·

Motherhood and "Gone With the Wind"

For all his flaws and arrogance, Rhett Butler in *Gone With the Wind*, had parenting skills and inclinations that far exceeded those of Scarlet O'Hara. Her lack of maternal instincts are in many ways a reflection of the author's own feelings toward motherhood. The not-so-subtle inference that "Scarlet dislikes children" could well be a characterization of Mitchell herself, but Mitchell, unlike Scarlet, never had children of her own. This was a conscious decision, as her biographer suggests:

 To have babies or not: this proved a primary dilemma. In 1925, having children hardly seemed an option. Couples wed in order to produce offspring. People did not go childless who had the physical capability of reproducing. The issue was not even "if," but rather "how many." Margaret Mitchell, however, did not want children. . . . Childbirth horrified her; she had no inclination towards biological motherhood and considered her lack of maternal instincts a genetic trait; children made her wince.

Mitchell's correspondence during her early years of marriage contained frequent references to her distaste for childbirth and mothering, and she was eager to share information from "a delightful book" which claimed "that lack of secretion from the posterior pituitary gland causes a total absence of the maternal instinct." So she no longer had to feel any personal guilt for her bias against mothering.

It has sometimes been suggested that writing and publishing a book is like pregnancy and childbirth. For Margaret Mitchell, that is as close as she ever came.[6]

If women writers reflected on mothers and motherhood from all different perspectives, so did men—and they, like their female counterparts, were often influenced by their own mothers.

· ·

The Mother Behind the Little Match Girl

Growing up in a poor family in Odense, Denmark during the early years of the nineteenth century, Hans Christian Andersen often heard stories of his mother's poverty as a little girl. His mother, Ann-Marie, "often told him how much luckier he was than she herself had been, and her account of her parents driving her out into the streets to beg was in her son's mind when he wrote one of the most famous of his tales, that of *The Little Match Girl*, bareheaded and barefoot in the snow on New Year's Eve."

The poverty she endured as a child continued on into her adult years when she worked long days as a washer woman. "All weathers found her scrubbing other people's dirty linen in the river. She was tormented by rheumatism and caught one cold after another, for which she was advised to take juniper drops in brandy, a remedy that was to turn her eventually into a drunkard."

Hans Christian Andersen did not tell of his mother's drinking in his autobiography, but many years after her death, he disclosed that it was his mother who had inspired his story, *She Was Good for Nothing*.

It had its origin in a few words that I heard my mother say when I was a child. One day when I had seen a boy hurrying down to the washing place at the Odense river, where his mother stood in the water and washed her linen, I heard a widow, noted for her frankness, call out from her window and scold the boy: "Are you going down again with liquor to your mother? That's disgraceful! Shame! Never let me see you become like your mother, she's good for nothing!" I came home and told what I had seen. They all said, "Yes, the old washerwoman drinks, she's good for nothing!" Only my mother took her part. "Don't judge her so harshly," she said, "the poor woman works and toils, stands in the cold water, and gets no hot meals for days at a time. She must have something to help her bear up. Of course it's not the best thing for her to take, but she has nothing better. She has gone through a great deal. She is honest, takes good care of her little boy, and keeps him looking neat." My mother's gentle speech made a deep impression on me since I, as well as others, thought ill of the washerwoman. Many years after, another incident led me to think how easily men judge harshly, where it would be just as easy to show kindness. . . . My mother's words were fresh in my mind when I wrote the story She Was Good for Nothing.[7]

· ·

George's Mother

Sometimes it is through literature that we have the clearest windows into our own souls—and too often that view is not flattering. Stephen Crane opens one of those windows in his "masterpiece," *George's Mother*. Crane is better known for *The Red Badge of Courage* and *Maggie: A Girl of the Streets*, but it is *George's Mother* that draws most from his childhood and youth, with the central character patterned after his own mother, a devout Christian who "came from a long line of Methodist preachers." After her Methodist preacher husband died in 1880, she did her best to rear eight-year-old Stephen and his older brothers and sisters in the faith. But with little success—especially with her youngest son, Stephen. *George's Mother* "dramatized the disastrous consequences of a willful young man's alcoholic revolt against his religious mother"—and in many ways it parallels Crane's own story.

 Grim and unsparing, George's Mother *is modern in its story of a destructive relationship. . . . It tells of a possessive, fanatically religious mother's ruination of her son. She believes him to be brilliant, destined for greatness. But the son neither lives up to her expectations nor fulfills his own dreams. Mother and son live in their own worlds with no communication. Alcohol and the flattery of his saloon friends feed the son's growing resentment of his mother's nagging and moralizing. He becomes callous and abusive to her, then loses his job. He tries to borrow money from his friends, but they desert him and he joins a gang of toughs. When George gets word that his mother is dying, he is fighting for a share in a stolen bucket of beer.*[8]

. . . .

The Last "Good Mother" in Literary History

Most fictional mothers in twentieth-century literature are not what could be described as good mothers.

Bad mothers are more interesting than good mothers—except perhaps for Mrs. Ramsey in Virginia Woolf's, *To the Lighthouse.* Here Woolf "laments the loss of a mother-figure whose sole task in life is to comfort, protect, and nurture her children. . . . She gives freely to them without asking anything in return. . . . She is the mother we secretly long for and the mother we would like to be for our own children, but somehow never quite can."

But Mrs. Ramsey, as Woolf creates her, is more than the "Good Mother." She is the *real* mother with eight children "who gives and gives until she is exhausted, yet is still driven to try to fulfill everyone's deepest wishes to be cared for. . . . Through her role as mother and giver, she is defined and thrives, and is ultimately consumed. . . . No one nurtures her," and she is demeaned by her husband who finds her "not clever, not book-learned at all."

When the image or role of the "Good Mother" is inextricably confused with mindlessness and ignorance—even by those who reap the benefits—something in the world has gone terribly wrong. Woolf leaves little doubt as to how humanity has belittled and distorted both the longing for the mother and the object of that longing.

Most readers love Mrs. Ramsey. Indeed, she may be one of the last "Good Mothers" in literary history.[9]

The issue of good and bad mothers is not the focus of a novel that is engulfed in the wickedness of the Nazi political system. Here the mother is forced to participate in that system by making a choice of life and death.

· · · · · · · · · · · · · · · · · · ·

Sophie's Choice

There is probably no greater torture any mother could endure than to be forced to choose which one of her two children should live and which one should die. That the enemy would chose to kill one child and spare the other would be unspeakable anguish for any mother, but that she would be forced to make that choice would be the ultimate torment.

In the novel Sophie's Choice, *William Styron created a scene that epitomizes the limitlessness of human cruelty. Sophie, a Polish mother who has been imprisoned in a concentration camp with her two children, is told that one of her children must die. One will be saved from death, but she must choose which child is to be sacrificed. . . .*

Styron focuses on the SS man responsible for choosing who is to die. He is suffering from depression because of the strain of so much ghastly decision making. To get temporary relief, he makes Sophie suffer the burden of choice instead of himself. On the spur of the moment, when he comes to where Sophie and her children are standing in line, he makes her decide which one of her children must die. Sophie sacrifices her daughter to the SS men.[10]

We learn much about motherhood by looking at literature—literature, an avenue of life that opens so many windows of understanding. I found that to be true in my undergraduate studies. I was a history major, but after taking a riveting course in American literature in my senior year I decided to do a Masters degree at Baylor University in American Studies, where I could combine my love for history and my love for literature. The two disciplines go hand in hand, and they illuminate each other. I utilized these two disciplines recently when I was giving a seminar in Denver for the International Congress on the Family. To show how our views on family life and motherhood have evolved over the generations, I made a brief comparative study of three fictional works and one nonfictional work that show how our perspectives have changed over the years. I jokingly suggested that I should have titled my paper, "From *The Scarlet Letter* to *The Bridges of Madison County*"—a title that reflects my focus on literature. In *The Scarlet Letter*, Hester suffers for her sin, but in the end is redeemed. In *The Mother's Recompense*, the mother puts herself before her child, with little guilt and punishment. In *The Bridges of Madison County*, a book that reflects a turn back toward family values, the mother forfeits an opportunity for romance and an exciting life to fulfill her responsibilities as a wife and mother. Literature reflects and influences patterns of motherhood. Through literature and legend we can better understand where we have been and where we are going.

God made a beauteous garden
With lovely flowers strown,
But one straight, narrow pathway
That was not overgrown.
And to this beauteous garden
He brought mankind to live,
And said: "To you, my children,
These lovely flowers I give.
Prune ye my vines and fig trees,
With care my flowers tend,
But keep the pathway open
Your home is at the end . . ."

And when the sun shines brightly
Tend flowers that God has given
And keep the pathway open
That lead you on to heaven.

ROBERT FROST

18

Mothers and the Fine Arts

Most of the great painters and poets of this world have been men, and when we think of mothers and the fine arts we probably think of mothers who influenced their sons. But Alice Walker reminds us in her book, *In Search of Our Mothers' Gardens*, that mothers have also influenced their daughters—that these very mothers were often artists in their own right. This, she believes, is particularly true of the "creative spirit that the black woman has inherited." Walker discovered this creativity in her mother's garden.

 And so our mothers and grandmothers have, more often than not anonymously, handed on the creative spark, the seed of the flower they themselves never hoped to see: or like a sealed letter they could not plainly read. . . . Only recently did I fully realize this: that through the years of listening to my mother's stories of her life, I have absorbed not only the stories themselves, but something of the manner in which she spoke. . . . The artist that was and is my mother showed itself to me only after many years. . . . My mother adorned with flowers whatever shabby house we were forced to live in. And not just your typical straggly country stand of zinnias, either. She planted ambitious gardens— and still does—with over fifty different varieties of plants that bloom profusely from early March until late November. Before she left home for the fields, she watered her flowers, chopped up the grass, and laid out new beds. . . . Because of her creativity with flowers, even my memories of poverty are seen through a screen of blooms—sunflowers, petunias, roses, dahlias, forsythia, spirea, delphiniums, verbena . . . and on and on. . . . Whatever rocky soil she landed on, she turned into a garden. A garden so brilliant with colors, so original in its design, so magnificent with life and creativity, that

*to this day people drive by our house in Georgia
...and ask to stand or walk among my mother's art.[1]*

Artistic talent is something I neither inherited from my mother nor passed on to my son. (Having written that last sentence before I thought it through, I'm not sure it's true, but rather than delete it from my screen, I'll let it stand—and expose my biases.) Maybe I did inherit creative talent from my mother. She wasn't musical and she didn't paint, but like Alice Walker's mother she had artistic talents that normally don't count. She had an eye for fashion, and my favorite dresses as a little girl were hers, not the "store-bought" dresses.

As for Carlton, he spent hours practicing the violin, the french horn, and the piano, but nothing took. I had thought that my own love for music and the french horn in particular might rub off on him, but it didn't. Neither did my oil painting push him in an artistic direction—though I spent many days at my easel while I was pregnant with him.

No mother can turn a child into an artistic genius, but there's no doubt that a mother can make a profound difference in a child who already has the latent talent and inclinations to excel in the fine arts.

. . . .

An Innocent Son Blamed for His Mother's Death

Of all the classical composers, Mozart is my favorite—perhaps because it was his music that most made my french horn sing. And it was my play-ing a Mozart concerto at the Northern Wisconsin Regional Music Festival that won me a scholarship in my senior year of high school. I was again powerfully reminded of the incredible musical artistry of Mozart more than a decade ago while watching and listening to the Hollywood portrayal of his life, *Amadeus.*

But only recently, with the recent publication of a brand new, six-hundred-page biography of Mozart did I realize the extent of emotional abuse he endured from his authoritarian father as a child and young adult. Leopold Mozart sought to utterly dominate his son and cash in on his talent for personal gain. There was little his mother could do to protect her son, but she tried. "Frau Mozart, with great qualms and mixed feelings, sought to shield her beloved son, and even, on occasion, like an inwardly recalcitrant servant of the state, to undermine her husband's instructions while appearing to carry them out."

It was the occasion of his mother's death in 1778, however, when he was twenty-two, that most vividly displays the cruelty of his father. At the time Mozart was in Paris composing music, being chaperoned by his mother while his father remained home in Austria. Because of bad weather, poor heating systems, and ill health, his mother pleaded in letters to her husband to allow her to come home, but he insisted she stay on in Paris. As her health declined, Mozart did his best to care for her, but she refused to be examined by French doctors—though their "bleeding" of her could hardly have helped her condition. Of his mother's death, he later wrote:

As long as I live I shall never forget it. . . . How cruel that my first experience [of death] should be the death of my mother! I dreaded that moment most of all, and I prayed earnestly to God for strength. . . . Indeed I wished at that moment to depart with her.

To his father in Austria he delayed the announcement of his mother's death, thinking it best to inform him that she was gravely ill. When he divulged his mother's death six days after it occurred, he focused on God's providence:

 Weep, weep your fill, but take comfort at last. Remember that Almighty God willed it thus—and how can we rebel against Him? [I am comforted in] the thought that she is not lost to us for ever—that we shall see her again—that we shall live together far more happily and blissfully than ever in this world. . . . You will easily conceive what I have had to bear—what courage and fortitude I have needed to endure calmly as things grew gradually and steadily worse. . . . I have, indeed, suffered and wept enough—but what did it avail?

Leopold's response to his son was stinging and filled with false accusations. He reminded his son that he had almost caused the death of his mother at his birth, and he scolded him for not having his mother "bled" sooner, and then he put the blame for her death squarely on him.

You had your engagements, you were away all day, and as she didn't make a fuss, you treated her condition lightly. All this time her illness became more

serious, in fact mortal—and only then was a doctor called in, when of course it was too late.

But if that was not enough weight of guilt to lay on his young adult son, the elder Mozart added some more:

 I hope that you, after your mother had to die so inappropriately in Paris, that you will not also have the furtherance of your father's death on your conscience.

How did young Mozart respond? He responded as he always had, according to his biographer:

 For the time being . . . his main task was to carry out his mother's injunction, which had always been the family's central imperative—to provide comfort, solace, and care for a needy and unappeasable father. Thus, Mozart returned to Salzburg, downcast, defeated, having postponed both his need for love and his ambition for greatness, but determined to save his father if he could, as a way of doing what Mama would have wanted.[2]

. . . .

A Mother's Floral Paintings and a Famous Son

Although a pastor's income was modest, Anna had an indoor servant and, despite her growing family and her local duties as the pastor's wife, she was able to pursue her hobby: making pencil drawings of wildflowers for her album or a watercolour of a bouquet she had arranged. . . . We may imagine a winter evening with the family gathered near a wood-fire in their living-room: the chairs of polished wood and leather, patterned tapestry covers on the side tables and large oil lamps of brass and cut-glass by whose light Pastor Theodorus is writing his notes for next Sunday's sermon and Anna is painting a spray of pink hyacinths. The scene embraces the two main strands in Vincent's life, religion and art. They were to tug at him for thirty years until the latter won.

The young boy Vincent was the now famous painter known simply as Van Gogh. His mother Anna was his teacher: "She wanted little Vincent to follow her and his surviving pencil sketches speak well of her encouragement." Like his mother, he painted flowers and gardens, including *Vase with Twelve Sunflowers* and *Daubigny's Garden.*[3]

. . . .

Depictions of Motherhood

Mary Cassatt is one of my newer "friends." Though she herself was not a mother, she painted mothers, and it was through her paintings that I've come to know her. Last fall when I was visiting the National Gallery of Art in Washington, D.C., my good friend Cheryl introduced me to her.

Mary Cassatt, America's most widely recognized woman painter, is known best for her touching depictions of mothers and their children. Perhaps not surprisingly, it was her own mother who was the inspiration behind this focus in her work. According to Mary's biographer, "The extent of Mary's devotion to her mother's memory may be gauged by the course her maternity pictures took, since it was that relationship which had first given them their deep feelings." She goes on to quote Louisine Havemeyer, an art collector and close friend of the family:

 Anyone who had the privilege of knowing Mary Cassatt's mother would know at once that it was from her and from her alone that [Mary] inherited her ability. In my day she was no longer young, [but] she was still powerfully intelligent, executive, and masterful, and yet with that sense of duty and tender sympathy she had transmitted to her daughter.

Mary's paintings are appropriately titled to describe the deep emotion of motherly love: "Mother About to Wash Her Sleepy Child," "The Family," "Emmie and Her Child," "Baby's First Caress," "The Bath," "The Crochet Lesson," and "Mother and Child."[4]

. . . .

Cassatt's Painting Analyzed

I'm not an art critic. When I look at Mary Cassatt's paintings at the National Gallery, I see the emotion and tenderness of motherhood, but I look to others to guide me in how this fits into art history and the Victorian times in which Cassatt lived. In her book, *The Modernist Madonna,* Jane Silverman Van Buren, emphasizes that Cassatt "used new techniques to free the imaginative concepts of women and children from the deadly enclosures of American domestic mythology," while at the same time being very much a part of the Victorian era with her focus on women and the family. "If Cassatt brooded over the oppression of women, or the neglect of children, she overcame her outrage by inventing a new family mythology. Within the body of her mother and child works, women and children exist almost entirely apart from men within an isolated domestic sphere." But her works, influenced by Impressionism and modernism, are clearly differentiated from the classic paintings of mother and child.

Her portrayals of the mother-child relationship as a significant part of here-and-now experience delivered that relationship from its role as a sterile icon of redemption or fertility. . . . In Cassatt's many oils, pastels, and drypoints, mother and baby or mother and her children live through the simple daily life of child rearing. . . . Cassatt's portrayals . . . explore the immediate experience taking place within the family . . . in or to peel away the Christian and Victorian mythologies of madonna and child.[5]

A Mother's Passion for Poetry

She was neither a good housekeeper nor cook, but she was a great storyteller and had a passion for poetry—and wrote stories and poems herself. But her writing would be altogether lost in obscurity were she not the mother of Robert Frost.

William Prescott Frost was an abusive authoritarian alcoholic husband and father, who often seemed distant and uncaring to his son. "Whether it was illness or whiskey that made the man's eyes seem glazed, the boy could not be sure." William Frost died when young Robert was eleven, and from that point onward the boy's behavior deteriorated. During his teenage years while he was living with his widowed mother in Salem, New Hampshire, his mother "admitted that the boy was as stubborn and hot-tempered as his father had been." Sometimes he was so incorrigible that she confessed to her close friend, Mrs. Chase, "I don't know what will ever become of that boy."

Other Baptists in Salem Depot told of a different attitude. More than once, in conversations after a church service, they watched Mrs. Frost put an arm around the boy's shoulders, draw him close, and say with pride, "I have great hopes for Rob." Scornfully and cynically the gossips passed this anecdote around, sometimes with mean comments about silk purses and sow's ears. Most of the townspeople were agreed that the Frost boy was indeed a lazy good-for-nothing and that there was not enough promise in him to justify any hope.

But there was reason for hope—and largely because of the influence of his mother, Isabelle Moodie Frost. From her he developed a love for literature and poetry and nature, and from his pen came the poems America loves—"The Road Not Taken," "Birches," "Mending Wall," "Stopping by the Woods on a Snowy Evening," and many more. Although he later denied writing it, "God's Garden" was one of his earliest poems, probably written with the help of his mother. It draws on his mother's faith and his own—a faith that he later abandoned.

 God made a beauteous garden
        With lovely flowers strown,
    But one straight, narrow pathway
        That was not overgrown.
    And to this beauteous garden
        He brought mankind to live,
    And said: "To you, my children,
        These lovely flowers I give.
    Prune ye my vines and fig trees,
        With care my flowers tend,
    But keep the pathway open
        Your home is at the end. . . ."

    And when the sun shines brightly
        Tend flowers that God has given
    And keep the pathway open
        That lead you on to heaven.[6]

An Arrangement in Gray and Black

James Whistler dismissed those who sought to view with sentimentality the painting of his mother, titled abstractly *Arrangement in Gray and Black*. To him, it was simply another painting that should be appreciated as "art for art's sake"—not as a tribute to his mother. When a friend, however, was admiring the painting as a fine piece of art, Whistler confessed: "Yes, one does like to make one's mummy just as nice as possible."[7]

A Mother's Kiss

 A Kiss from my mother made me a painter.

This famous quote from the celebrated painter, Benjamin West, I have discovered is given time and again without explanation, but there is a story that illuminates the memorable tribute.

We are certain that it was his mother who first discovered and recognized her son's talent. One day a married sister was visiting her parents bringing her baby with her. Having put it to sleep, she left it lying in the cradle. The boy stood watching the sleeping child, and as he gazed, the tender beauty of the little face penetrated to the inner eye which is the special endowment of the born painter. Picking up paper and pencil, he drew a picture of the child. When his mother found him thus busily engaged he tried to conceal the picture. Compelling him to show it, Mrs. West looked in astonishment first at the sketch, then at her grandchild. There could be no mistake about the likeness. Realizing at once that here was considerably more than a mere child's scrawl, she threw her arms about her boy and kissed him. It was at that moment, as the painter himself says, that ambition was born in his soul and his future was decided.

From that day Mrs. West, forgetting her Quaker scruples, encouraged the boy to continue his experiments with pencil and brush.[8]

· · · · · · · · · · · · · · · · · ·

Picasso's Mother

"He was born dead—or so they thought. There was no breathing and no movement from the baby born to Dona Maria Picasso de Ruiz at 11:15 on the night of October 25, 1881." But he was revived and he survived. Today, he is known simply as Picasso. His paintings hang in art museums around the world and are easily recognized as the work of a genius—if not a madman. His creations on canvas are as jarring and discordant as was the mind and personality behind them. Women are a prominent subject of his works, but, according to his most recent biographer, "he was unable to love and was driven to dominate and humiliate the women . . . who fell under his hypnotic spell."

A Freudian analysis of this complex and often cruel man would focus on his mother—and perhaps with good reason. Was he neglected and unloved as a child? Certainly not by his mother. She was the one woman who unconditionally believed in him—and she in turn was idolized by him. Without her overpowering devotion, the name *Picasso* might be just another obscure Spanish name—though it was his father who most wanted him to be a great painter.

[His father] Don Jose was a teacher by profession and a pedagogue by inclination, and Pablo was growing tired of his advice and criticism. Don Jose probably understood his son's strengths and weaknesses all too well, and Pablo soon began to find his mother's adoring incomprehension much less demanding. So even though from the earliest years of his young life it was his father who supported, often at his own expense, his every step as a painter, it was his mother's name that he finally adopted. . . . She believed in him unconditionally. "If you become a soldier," she told him, "you'll be a general. If you become a monk, you'll end up as the Pope!" If her son had not learned anything at school, she felt sure that he knew it all already—or at least, all that was important. As for his egocentricity, it seemed perfectly natural to his doting mother.[9]

Mothers ought to be challenged and inspired by stories that illustrate the formative influence a mother can have in molding a child—especially as it pertains to the fine arts. A word of encouragement or even a fleeting kiss can be the spark that turns latent talent into public genius. And even as we seek to shape our children, we ought to take a backward glance at our mother's formative influence on our own creative talents—our mother's unrecognized artistry be it gardening or quilting or fashioning a little girl's dresses.

❧ *From my mother, I learned the value of prayer, how to*

have dreams and believe I would make them come true. . . .

While my father was filled with dreams of making

something of himself, she had a drive to help

my brother and me make something of ourselves.

RONALD REAGAN

19

Mothers of Presidents and Mothers in the White House

I grew up in the country—rather alone—and one of my favorite pastimes was to walk in the woods, exploring, particularly in the springtime, searching for the first wild violets and starry white blossoms of dogwood, feeling the crush of pine needles underfoot, the wind whispering overhead. In summer barefoot with sand between my toes, I hunted for the Cherokee rose and the black-eyed Susans that grew along the fence rows. . . .

These are the words of the mother in the White House who made the whole country her flower garden. Lady Bird Johnson was a motherless child from age five onward, and part of the result of her loneliness was a love for wildflowers that turned into a gift for a nation. Wildflower preservation was a love that turned into a passion after her husband died. Her own daughters who did not encounter loneliness like she had, had no such passion. She would have been thrilled if this love of hers could have been passed from mother to daughters, but neither joined in her crusade. Their lighthearted excuse was that "It did not come with the genes."[1]

I love reading biographies, and with graduate degrees in American Studies and American History, a particular interest of mine has been behind-the-scenes stories of American Presidents and their wives. One of my favorite "coffee-table" books is *The First Ladies Cook Book: Favorite Recipes of All the Presidents of the United States*. I've never tried one of the recipes, but the book includes far more than recipes. It is filled with kitchen anecdotes and table trivia. The book was published in 1982, and the final chapter is on the Nixons. Here we read that "Mrs. Nixon and her daughters especially enjoy working together to prepare family meals on days when they have the kitchen to themselves."

The final page is devoted to Pat Nixon's favorite recipes: stuffed tomatoes, walnut clusters, vanilla souffle, and vanilla sauce. Nothing that we read is about the secrets of Mom, Dad, and the girls at mealtime in the White House.

What was Mrs. Nixon like as a mother? She was the first "first lady" that I really took notice of. She entered the White House only months after my wedding, and she was setting up housekeeping in the White House at the same time I was making a basement apartment into a home.

It would seem that there would be no better source to learn about a mother than to read a biography written by her daughter, but sometimes memoirs written by close relatives tell much more about the person by what is not said than what is. I found this to be true as I perused *Pat Nixon: The Untold Story* by her daughter Julie Nixon Eisenhower. The subtitle would indicate that here the daughter is introducing to us a woman that the outside world would not have known. But what struck me most about this volume is that the daughter hardly knew her mother better than the rest of us. On page after page we read about public events in "Mother's" life—or just as frequently, events that involved "my parents." Of course, there are behind-the-scenes conversations on politics between "my mother . . . and her husband," but even they sound stilted. When political analysts had become convinced Nixon was a liability on the Eisenhower Presidential ticket, her father asked her mother if he should resign. "Without a moment's notice she answered: 'We both know what you have to do, Dick. You have

to fight it all the way to the end, no matter what happens.'" And so the conversation—at least in the book—ends.

Very little in this book by her daughter tells us what Pat Nixon was like as a mom—but there are some clues that may shed more light on the overall picture than their few sentences in the book would seem to merit:

 Mother's disciplining technique was "the look," as Tricia and I called her freezing, reproachful glance. She did not spank, raise her voice, or whine. If we failed to heed "the look," we had to endure the most dreaded treatment for major offenses: her silence. And because the silence was so impenetrable and such a contrast to the usually loving woman, we avoided provoking it.[2]

The untold story of Mrs. Nixon as a mother remains untold—as is true of many other wives and mothers of Presidents. But we see glimpses of these women in books about their celebrated husbands and sons—and in memoirs of their own lives. They were behind-the-scenes mothers who would be lost in history but for the famous men in their lives. For this reason, if for no other, they offer fascinating reflections on American motherhood.

· · · · · · · · · · · · · · · ·

Presidents and Their Mothers

 There was an enormously strong intellectual-emotional bond between . . . an astonishing number of presidents and their mothers. No less than

twenty-one of the thirty-six American presidents to date [1978] have been their mothers' first boy and almost every one of them were the favorite sons of strong-minded women.[3]

George Washington, as the Father of this country, has been surrounded by myth and legend—even before he died. And what topic is more ripe for exaggeration than the relationship between a great man and his mother? It is difficult to ascertain how Washington felt about his mother, but recent scholarship would tend to dismiss some of the sentimental stories and quotes of bygone years that turn his mother into a saintly mother devoted to her son.

A Tribute to Mrs. Washington

I attribute all my success in life to the moral, intellectual, and physical education which I received from my mother.

GEORGE WASHINGTON[4]

A Sermon Illustration

In a 1926 volume entitled *Sermons on Mothers,* Joseph Baker gives a glowing account of the relationship between George Washington and his mother:

Real men have always been considerate of their parents, especially of widowed mothers. When

Washington was informed of his election as the first President of the United States and that his presence was urgently requested in New York, the first Capital, he hastily set his affairs in order and mounted his swiftest horse, not for New York, but for Fredericksburg, the home of his aged mother.... Though Martha Washington, his wife, was herself a queen among women, and he the cause of the jubilant occasion, the aged mother, beyond a doubt, received the sincerest admiration and the profoundest reverence. Back of the victor they saw the creator.[5]

George Washington and "Mommy Dearest"

It is difficult to imagine a President's mother not bursting with pride over the achievements of her son—especially if he were George Washington, but according to Washington's respected biographer, James T. Flexner, "History does not always draw noble men from noble mothers, preferring sometimes to temper her future heroes in the furnace of domestic infelicity."

 George Washington's mother was an unloving, parsimonious woman who begrudged her son his success, who greatly embarrassed him during the Revolution by complaining publicly that he was permitting her to starve when actually he was providing for her adequately, and who had the reputation for being something of a Tory.... Though she lived into his second term as president, she did

not appear at either inauguration, and there are extant letters showing her "depreciating her son's achievements."[6]

A "Deeply Resented" Mother Jefferson

Sometimes the silence or the very little that a son or daughter says about a mother is more telling than many words. This is the conclusion of Fawn Brodie, the very insightful biographer of Thomas Jefferson.

 If one searches through the scanty documents illuminating the relationship between the great men of American history and their mothers, one finds less about Jefferson and his mother than about any of the others. . . . The astonishing fact is that though he lived with his mother—save for the months he was away at school and studying law— till he was twenty-seven, he did not mention her specifically in the thousands of letters and documents that have come down to us except on two occasions, and these references, one in a letter to his uncle and one in his Autobiography, are laconic and virtually without feeling. . . . Two months after her death Jefferson wrote the news of it to his uncle, William Randolph, one of Jane Jefferson's brothers who had chosen to live in England. The letter begins with some discussion of Randolph's business complaints resulting from hostilities which had broken out between England and her American colonies. Only then comes the brusque announce-

ment: "The death of my mother you have probably not heard of. This happened on the last day of March after an illness of not more than an hour. We supposed it to have been apoplectic."

It is hard to imagine a son being so callous in reporting his mother's death to her own brother. What do the few terse comments and silence tell us about Jefferson and his mother? Merrill Peterson argues that "By his own reckoning she was a zero quantity in his life." Fawn Brodie disagrees:

 No mother is a zero quantity in any son's life, and the fact that Jefferson, whether deliberately or not, managed to erase all traces of his opinion and feeling for her seems evidence rather of a very great influence which he deeply resented, and from which he struggled to escape.[7]

A First Lady's Admonitions to a Future President

Abigail Adams holds the distinction of being the only women to have both a husband and a son serve as President of the United States (though she did not live to see her son attain that office). She was an active citizen, vitally interested in public affairs, but her most consuming passion was her family— particularly their spiritual well-being. She grew up in the home of a New England Puritan preacher, and the faith instilled in her as a child she passed on to her own children. Her deep concern for her children is seen in her letters, including those to John Quincy, who would later become President. To him she wrote:

Adhere to those religious Sentiments and principals which were early instilled into your mind and remember that you are accountable to your Maker for all your words and actions. . . . I had much rather you should have found your Grave in the ocean you have crossed, or any untimely death crop you in your Infant years, rather than see you an immoral profligate or a Graceless child. . . . The only sure and permanent foundation of virtue is Religion. Let this important truth be engraven upon your Heart, and that the foundation of Religion is Belief of the one only God, and a just sense of his attributes as a Being infinitely wise, just, and good, to whom you owe the highest Reverence.[8]

. . . .

Jane Pierce and the Pain of Politics

Jane Pierce prayed for her husband's defeat when he ran for President in 1852, but her prayers were not answered and Franklin Pierce became the fourteenth President of the United States. She did not like the atmosphere in Washington, D.C., fearing it would lead to the ruin of her children—and her husband, with his tendency to drink excessively.

Just weeks before the Pierces moved into the White House their young son, Bennie, was killed in a train accident in front of his parents' eyes. To Jane, who

had doted on Bennie, the tragedy represented retribution for her husband's excessive political ambition—Franklin's capturing the presidency had somehow cost her their son—and the old hatred that she had always felt for Washington and politics revived in her with such force that she could not bring herself to attend the inauguration.[9]

. . . .

"Lemonade Lucy" and the Boys

Rutherford B. Hayes, the nineteenth President of the United States, and his wife Lucy Webb Hayes vowed that they would serve no alcoholic beverages while they were residents of the White House. They were not going to change their temperance commitment just because he had been elected to the highest office of the land. As a result of her position, Mrs. Hayes was dubbed "Lemonade Lucy," and the Hayes' administration was referred to as the "cold water regime."

She later explained to a friend: "I had three sons just coming to manhood and starting out in society, and I did not feel as if I could be the first to put the wine cup to their lips." The oldest son, Webb Cook Hayes, who had just graduated from Cornell University, was serving as his father's secretary. Another son, Birchard, was in Harvard Law School, while a third, Rutherford, was a student at Cornell. The two younger children Fanny and Scott, lived in the White House. Three sons had died in their childhood.

Frances E. Willard, President of the Woman's

Christian Temperance Union, paid this tribute to Mrs. Hayes: "Total abstinence has never had such a standard-bearer as this noble woman, and centuries from now, her steadfast adherence to the truest Christian hospitality will be told as a memorial to her."[10]

Lincoln's Debt to His Mother

President Abraham Lincoln is remembered for an oft-quoted tribute to his mother, later remembered by his biographer and law partner William Herndon. They were riding to court together in the spring of 1851 when Lincoln reflected on his debt of gratitude to his mother, Nancy Hanks Lincoln, who died when he was nine:

 All that I am, or hope to be, I owe to my angel mother.

Some years earlier he confided to a friend "how lonely life was during the months following his mother's death, and how he cherished hearing the Bible stories she had once told him, for they brought her voice back to his mind's ear."[11]

A Mother's Log House Church

 James A. Garfield's mother was an earnest Christian who taught her children that "the fear of the Lord is the beginning of wisdom." A widow with four children, she not only managed her farm, but built with her own hands a log house which was

also used as a church. There she taught her own children as well as others the Scriptures.[12]

Mother McKinley's Aspirations for Her Son

The dream of Nancy Allison McKinley was not that her son would become President of the United States, but that he would become a preacher. She could not prevent him from going into politics, but she was not particularly impressed with his political achievements. "When he was governor of Ohio, she took the train to see him, and when a fellow passenger asked if she had relatives in Columbus, she replied only: 'Yes, I have a son there.'" She served God by helping others, and such were her aspirations for her son.

 Rural isolation and the need for self-help sharpened Mrs. McKinley's sense of responsibility to her family and neighbors. She tended sick friends, helped with welfare cases, bore her share of the community's problems, and acted as peacemaker, for she detested strife. She boarded visiting ministers and teachers. She and her sister had charge of the Methodist church in Niles, and swept, scrubbed, painted, and tended it with the same efficient thoroughness they applied to their own hearths and homes. According to one recollection, they "ran the church, all but the preaching." . . . No amount of world fame could offset in her eyes any man's failure to use all his talents. . . . She longed to give one of her sons to the ministry,

and William's diligence and aptitude for study seemed to mark him for the cloth.

But instead of becoming a minister, Mother McKinley's son became the twenty-fifth President of the United States. "On inauguration eve, the President's brother, Abner, was overheard pleading with her: "But, Mother, this is better than a bishopric." Should she be credited for having produced a President? Not from her perspective: "I don't believe I did raise the boy to be President," she recalled in later years. "I tried to bring up the boy to be a good man, and that is the best that any mother can do. The first thing I knew, my son turned around and began to raise me to be the mother of a President."[13]

- - - - - - - - - - - - - -

A President's Preacher Mother

A good question for a Trivial Pursuit game—if it's not already in the cards—is, "Which President's mother was a preacher—a woman named for a great Old Testament prophetess—Huldah. She was Huldah Hoover, and her son was Herbert, the thirty-first President of the United States—most remembered for the stock market crash of 1929 that occurred during his first year in office. When he accepted his party's nomination in 1928, he described himself as having come from "Quaker stock," reflecting back on his heritage, but his mother wasn't there to hear those words. She had died many years earlier when he was a boy.

 Her shy spirituality made her the butt of her more worldly husband's affectionate chafing. After his death at the age of thirty-four, she became almost wholly the instrument of her spirit and was more in demand than ever in Quaker communities throughout Iowa for the beauty of her preaching. In the two years of her widowhood she took in sewing to support her three children. But her real vocation was preaching. . . . Among the Quakers she had no title or parish or remuneration, except in the love of those whom she instructed. Increasingly she did receive free-will offerings to relieve her of some of the drudgery of the needle so that she might speak the Word of God. Co-religionists even beyond Iowa came to know her soft, unstudied eloquence.[14]

- - - - - - - - - - - - - -

Eleanor Roosevelt's "Withdrawal of Warmth"

Eleanor Roosevelt is remembered as the strongest and most visible First Lady in American history. Her public service is well documented, but what was she like behind the scenes as a mother? An interesting footnote in history comes from her son-in-law, husband of her daughter, the late Anna Roosevelt Halstead.

 Anna always used to tell me that her mother was very unpredictable and inconsistent in bringing up her children. Inconsistent in her feelings—sweet and lovely one hour, and the next hour very critical, very demanding, very difficult to be with. You could never quite tell what she really meant. This

is very troubling to a child, not to be able to rely on the feelings of a parent. Nevertheless, Anna was always very, very admiring of her mother, of course, and also loving of her, so there was great uncertainty, insecurity. I don't think she ever discussed any of that with her mother. She talked to me about it quite a lot.

I think she felt she could count on her father, count on his consistency of affection, in a way she couldn't with her mother. Of course, the most memorable of her mother's withdrawal of warmth—this was when Anna was a mature adult—was when Mrs. Roosevelt returned to the White House right after the President's death, when Mrs. Roosevelt had just found out that Lucy Mercer had been to the White House for dinner, and that Anna had been hostess. Mrs. Roosevelt could show this bitter, cold anger and did, and made Anna feel very badly. Anna tried to explain that her father was lonely and had this great responsibility, and Anna had to make a quick decision as to whether she would give in to the idea of Lucy coming to dinner and spending the evening. And Anna decided in favor of it because it was going to help her father, which was what her job was during that year and a half toward the end of the war.[15]

. . . .

A Mother's Dreams Fulfilled

Lyndon Baines Johnson—"brilliant, formidable, generous, troubled"—was very much a product of his mother's emotional struggles as a young woman, and were it not for her difficulties and the influ-

ence she had on him he might never have become the thirty-sixth President of the United States.

 The image of Rebeckah Baines Johnson that emerges in the stories is that of a drastically unhappy woman, cut off from all the things that had once given her pleasure in life, stranded in a cabin on a muddy stream with a man she considered vulgar and brutish, a frustrated woman with a host of throttled ambitions, trying, through her firstborn son, to find a substitute for a dead father, an unsuccessful marriage, and a failed career. She seemed under a compulsion to renew on her son's behalf all the plans and projects she had given up for herself. The son would fulfill the wishful dreams she had never carried out, he would become the important person she had failed to be. . . .

From his position of primacy in his mother's home, Johnson seemed to develop what Freud has called "the feeling of a conqueror, that confidence of success that often induces real success." The early privilege of his mother's intense love was a source of great energy and power. He learned the alphabet before he was two, learned to read and spell before he was four, and at three could recite long passages of poetry from Longfellow and Tennyson. "I'll never forget how much my mother loved me when I recited those poems. The minute I finished she'd take me in her arms and hug me so hard I sometimes thought I'd be strangled to death."

When Johnson was twenty-nine he was elected to the United States Congress with twice the votes of his opponent—thus fulfilling his mother's dreams as she expressed in a letter to him, beginning "My Dear Lyndon:"

 To me your election not alone gratifies my pride as a mother in a splendid and satisfying son and delights me with the realization of the joy you must feel in your success, but in a measure it compensates for the heartache and disappointment I experienced as a child when my dear father lost the race you have just won. The confidence in the good judgment of the people was sadly shattered then by their choice of another man. Today my faith is restored. How happy it would have made my precious noble father to know that the first-born of his first-born would achieve the position he desired. It makes me happy to have you carry on the ideals and principles so cherished by that great and good man. I gave you his name: I commend you to his example: You have always justified my expectations, my hopes, my dreams: How dear to me you are you cannot know my darling boy, my devoted son, my strength and comfort. . . . Always remember that I love you and am behind you in all that comes to you.[16]

. . . .

Jimmy Carter's "Eccentric" Mother

As Governor of Georgia and as President of the United States, Jimmy Carter was known for his support for integration and his strong stance against racism of any kind. Such an outlook was not one commonly associated with rural Georgia of the 1940s, nor did it reflect the mentality of his father whose racism was not easily disguised. How then did this sensitivity to racial issues develop?

In a New York Times Magazine *article Patrick Anderson observed: "As a boy, Carter saw his parents' differing philosophies on the race issue action out most dramatically.". . . Carter's mother was well known for her intolerance of racial segregation and recalls hearing the epithet "nigger-lover" hurled at her many times although she was never subjected to any significant abuse. Anderson, who later became a Carter speech writer, commented, "Eccentricity is a major art form of the rural South; much is forgiven anyone who breaks the monotony."*

Mrs. Carter's effect upon her son became clear in his mature years when he took courageous stands against racial discrimination in his church, in his community, and in public life.[17]

. . . .

Ronald Reagan's Mother

If I'd gotten the job I wanted at Montgomery Ward, I suppose I would never have left Illinois.

This is the opening sentence of Ronald Reagan's biography, reflecting on his disappointment in not getting a position as the sporting goods manager for the Wards department store chain in his hometown of Dixon, Illinois. He was a college graduate, but jobs were not plentiful in 1932. The nation was in the depths of Depression—and so was he. But his mother came to his rescue.

The influence that Ronald Reagan's mother had on him is best told in his own words as he opens his autobiography in chapter 1:

 I was raised to believe that God has a plan for everyone and that seemingly random twists of fate are all a part of His plan. My mother—a small woman with auburn hair and a sense of optimism that ran as deep as the cosmos—told me that everything in life happened for a purpose. She said all things were part of God's Plan, even the most disheartening setbacks, and in the end, everything worked out for the best. If something went wrong, she said, you didn't let it get you down: You stepped away from it, stepped over it, and moved on. Later on, she added, something good will happen and you'll find yourself thinking—"If I hadn't had that problem back then, then this better thing that did happen wouldn't have happened to me."

After I lost the job at Montgomery Ward, I left home again in search for work. Although I didn't know it then, I was beginning a journey that would take me a long way from Dixon and fulfill all my dreams and then some.

My mother, as usual, was right. . . .

While my father was a cynic and tended to suspect the worst of people, my mother was the opposite. . . . From my mother, I learned the value of prayer, how to have dreams and believe I would make them come true. . . . While my father was filled with dreams of making something of himself, she had a drive to help my brother and me make something of ourselves.[18]

"Mind Your Manners, George"

In his book, *Looking Forward*, George Bush writes of his mother's concern for his manners—not just when he was a boy growing up in Connecticut, but when he was a grown man serving as Vice-President to Ronald Reagan.

 Fifty years later, Mother still stays on the alert for anything that sounds like "braggadocio" coming from one of her children. "You're talking about yourself too much, George," she told me after reading a news report covering one of my campaign speeches. I pointed out that as a candidate, I was expected to tell voters something about my qualifications. She thought about that a moment, then reluctantly conceded. "Well, I understand that," she said, "but try to restrain yourself."

Even after I became Vice President, Mother called to set me straight on my appearance during one of the President's televised State of the Union messages. She said it didn't look right for me to be reading something while President Reagan was speaking. When I explained that House Speaker "Tip" O'Neill and I were given advance copies of the speech in order to follow the President's remarks, she was less than persuaded. "I really can't see why that's necessary," she said. "Just listen and you'll find out what he has to say."

Sometimes Mother is more subtle in her suggestions about my deportment as Vice President. "George, I've noticed how thoughtful President Reagan is to Nancy," she once called to say.

"I've never seen him climb off a plane ahead of her or walk ahead of her. He's so thoughtful!" I got the message.[19]

. . . .

Virginia Kelly and Billy

Virginia Kelly was a very different kind of woman than the prim and proper Mrs. Bush, whose son George, they say, was born with a silver spoon in his mouth. Not so with Bill Clinton. He was born in poverty to a widowed mother, and as a fourteen-year-old stood up to his stepfather and threatened him never to beat his mother again. His mother was proud of her son, not only for standing up for her, but for his accomplishments. Her words in a letter to her mother, reflecting on his high school graduation in 1964, were words that were said again and again in one way or another until she died.

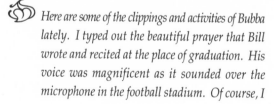 *Here are some of the clippings and activities of Bubba lately. I typed out the beautiful prayer that Bill wrote and recited at the place of graduation. His voice was magnificent as it sounded over the microphone in the football stadium. Of course, I*

was so proud of him I nearly died. He was truly in all his glory that night.

The first lines of the prayer are ones that any mother could say "Amen" to and wish for God's answer in the affirmative:

 Dear Lord, as we leave this place and this era of our lives, we ask your blessing on us. . . . Now we must prepare to live only by the guide of our own faith and character. We pray to keep a high sense of values while wandering through the complex maze which is our society.

Presidents' mothers and mothers in the White House are not much different than ordinary mothers whose lives are largely private. They bask in the glory of high office, but they also endure difficult times of failure and humiliation and public embarrassment. Virginia Kelly was no exception, perhaps often remembering her son's prayer:

We pray to keep a high sense of values while wandering through the complex maze which is our society. . . . Amen.

"I do my best, no more and no less,

and I let them know that I know life

is not easy for them,

but I am realistic enough to know

that I can't be two people."

THE MOTHERHOOD REPORT

20

Single Mothers

One thing in particular that I remember made me feel grateful toward my mother was that one day I went and asked her for my own garden, and she did let me have my own little plot. I loved it and took care of it well. I loved especially to grow peas. I was proud when we had them on our table. I would pull out the grass in my garden by hand when the first little blades came up. I would patrol the rows on my hands and knees for any worms and bugs. . . . And sometimes when I had everything straight and clean for my things to grow, I would gaze up in the blue sky at the clouds moving and think of all kinds of things.

These are the words of Malcolm X, a man we might never imagine took up his mother's fascination and love for gardening. Today he is remembered by many as a hero of black independence and pride, but to others he was a radical and a dangerous man. Whoever he was, Malcolm X was very much a product of his family heritage and environment in Omaha, Nebraska and Lansing, Michigan. His autobiography opens with these words:

 When my mother was pregnant with me, she told me later, a party of hooded Ku Klux Klan riders galloped up to our home in Omaha, Nebraska, one night. Surrounding the house, brandishing their shotguns and rifles, they shouted for my father to come out. My mother went to the front door and opened it. Standing where they could see her pregnant condition, she told them that she was alone with her three small children. . . . Still shouting threats, the Klansmen finally spurred their horses and galloped around the house, shattering every window pane with their gun butts. Then they rode off into the night, their torches flaring, as suddenly as they had come.

When Malcolm X was six, his wife-beating preacher father walked out on his family in a rage. Later that night the child awoke to his mother's screams. She had just learned of her husband's fate—crushed to death on the tracks of a streetcar. In the years that followed, his mother did her best to provide necessities for her eight children, but times were hard during the Depression and the family situation went from bad to worse. As the state welfare agency threatened to take away her children, her mental and emotional health deteriorated, and by 1937, when Malcolm X was twelve and living with another family, she began to lose touch with reality altogether.

Eventually my mother suffered a complete break-down, and the court orders were finally signed. They took her to the State Mental Hospital at Kalamazoo. . . . I can't describe how I felt. The woman who had brought me into the world, and nursed me, and advised me, and chastised me, and loved me, didn't know me. It was as if I was trying to walk up the side of a hill of feathers. I looked at her. I listened to her "talk." But there was nothing I could do.[1]

This is a tragic story of a single mother who didn't make it. Many single mothers have somehow managed to rise up to the challenge and overcome incredible obstacles, but others have fallen under the heavy burden, and some like the mother of Malcolm X, have been so defeated that motherhood itself was stripped away from the cloudy world of reality. Yet as a man, her son could look

back on a mother who reared him to the best of her ability and gave him his own little garden.

The most revered woman of all times, Mary the mother of Jesus, was a single mother. She was single at the conception and single at the cross, and she may have been single when her children were still young and going through adolescence. The last mention of her husband Joseph occurs when Jesus is twelve and left behind at the temple. Mary is a model for all mothers—and particularly for single mothers.

Single motherhood is part of the fabric of our society today—something we all wish was not so prevalent. "Dan Quayle Was Right" summed up the cover-story of a recent issue of *The Atlantic Monthly.* Here was an amazing turn of events—a magazine that appeals to liberal-minded intellectuals suddenly recognizing that the former Vice President's concern about single motherhood was valid. Truly, single motherhood is a massive societal problem, but more than that, it's a painful reality that touches individual mothers and children.

Many women join the ranks of single motherhood when they give birth to their first child. For some of them motherhood comes after a difficult decision to choose life instead of taking the "easy" way out by having an abortion. Others, join the ranks—through the death of a husband or divorce—when their children are growing up.

For me, the single mother status came just at the time Carlton was going through adolescence—at a time when he needed a father the most. It was not easy rearing a strong-willed, thirteen-year-old by myself. Indeed, I've wrung my hands and shed many tears, but through it all our bond of love has grown and a strong and winsome young man has emerged. It's now been more than five years since he's seen, or talked to, or even known the whereabouts of his father, and he commented to me recently, "You've had to be both a mother and father to me." I insisted otherwise. I explained that I've tried to be a good mother, but that's all I can ever be to him. I can never fill the shoes of a father—nor can any single mother.

· ·

Beauty Out of Brokenness

"Broken homes," "broken families," "family breakdown"—these are terms that haunt single mothers who are desperately trying to maintain a semblance of family life despite the dissolution of the marriage. How will this affect the kids? Will they be irrevocably damaged? Can I reverse the trend of wrong choices? These questions flooded my mind as I thought of Carlton struggling through his teenage years in a "broken home." Yet, I know from personal experience and from the stories of others that beauty very often arises out of brokenness.

A story that has always touched my heart is one I write about in *Stories of Faith*:

When she entered the world on October 31, 1896, she had more than two strikes against her. Her twelve-year-old mother was alone in a run-down Philadelphia slum dwelling when she went into labor, and would have delivered the baby by her-

self, had not her cries been heard by a neighbor. She did not want the baby, who had been conceived when she was brutally raped at knife point. Her pregnancy had been a disgrace, and she was rejected by her church.

In spite of these terribly unfortunate circumstances, the baby grew up to become one of the most beloved soloist of the Billy Graham Crusades—Ethel Waters. Hers was not an easy childhood, and while still a teenager, she was married and divorced. But God brought beauty out of brokenness, and she could sing with gusto the words to her trademark Gospel song:

I sing because I'm happy;
 I sing because I'm free.
His eye is on the sparrow,
 and I know he watches me.

God truly does watch over us, as Ethel knew so well from her own experiences, and as single mothers we can trust God with our children, knowing He will watch over them through the storms of life.[2]

· ·

Struggles of Single Mothers

One of the struggles single mothers face is trying to fill the role of both mother and father—an impossibility that creates tension for both the parent and child, as testimonies of single mothers from *The Motherhood Report* illustrate:

I do my best, no more and no less, and I let them know that I know life is not easy for them, but I am realistic enough to know that I can't be two people.

 I tried so hard to be everything to my son, but after squeezing myself dry I realized that I could not be a stand-in for his father. Now I try to make him understand that I am only one person and he has to be patient and wait until I have time to help him.[3]

. . . .

Jesus and the Little Children of Unwed Mothers

Nan Britton was an unwed mother—a circumstance that created a scandal in the 1920s, but more than that the father of her little girl was the President of the United States.

 As a fourteen-year-old schoolgirl in Marion, Ohio, she decorated her bedroom with photographs of Warren Gamaliel Harding, the dapper, married editor of her home-town newspaper. Later, when Harding moved to Washington as a U.S. Senator, the schoolgirl crush incandesced into a full, flaming passion, and in 1919, on a couch in his Senate office, a child was conceived. Nan Britton bore Harding's baby in the same summer he was summoned into the historic smoke-filled room in Chicago and made the compromise Republican candidate for President. The illicit relationship continued on through most of the affable Ohioan's presidency, remaining a secret even in the glare of publicity brought about by the Administration's involvement in the famous "Teapot Dome" oil-lands scandal. Only after the scandal-scarred Chief Executive's death in 1923 was the nation informed that he had been unfaithful to his marital vows as well as to his presidential oath of office.*

When Nan's efforts to obtain child support from the Harding family failed, she wrote a tell-all book, *The President's Daughter*. She dedicated the book to "all unwed mothers, and to their innocent children," and went on to remind her readers that the "illegitimate" children are not to be blamed for their circumstances:

 It is to be remembered that . . . Jesus of Nazareth did not say, "Suffer little children born in wedlock to come unto me for of such is the kingdom of heaven." Jesus loved and honored all little children and didn't bother at all about who their parents were or about the manner of their birth. He himself was born in a manger which was most unconventional.[4]

. . . .

A Legacy of Divorce and Single Mothering

One of the most painful struggles a single mother can endure is a divorce that involves a custody battle over a child—an ordeal far more prevalent today than a generation ago. But the anguish then was no less than now, and then as now a mother often blames herself, as was true of Lena Horne, one of the most popular and celebrated African-American performers of the twentieth century. When she divorced her husband and the father of her two young children, the arrangement was that she would "share custody" of Teddy, but it meant that she could see him "only during school holidays and vacations." She caved into the agreement, but she later lamented that decision.

I regret most bitterly that I did not press my fight for him harder, yet at the time I could see the point my lawyers and agents raised. There would have been a great deal of unpleasant newspaper coverage, with all the sympathy going to Louis as the husband seemingly dropped by the ambitious wife with no concern but her own career. More important to me, however, was that I had myself been the child of divorce. When I remembered the bitterness I had been exposed to by my mother after her divorce, and thought how much worse it would be for our children if Louis and I began slinging mud in a courtroom and the papers, it sickened me.

And so my son grew up as a partial stranger to me. I only saw him a few months out of the year.

Even as Lena struggled with her on-again, off-again relationship with her own mother, so did she struggle with that relationship with her children. As children and as young adults, their bond of love with their mother was less than secure—the legacy of single mothering and of children being torn between two parents.

 My mother and I will probably be working at understanding one another until we die. And then there's my son, Teddy, proud, sensitive, tremendously brilliant, mystic, poet, writer, loyal to two parents under difficult situations—I know I love him for himself, not because he is mine. He and I are still not as close as I wish we could be. I hope these things will change. But if they do not, I hope I will have the grace not to torture them about it. Or myself. I hope I will at least be able to set them free of the pose we share and in the process, allow myself to be completely free, too.

In 1963, my daughter married. . . .

"You're a good friend, Mother, but I don't think you really love me," she said to me one time. Now she was leaving. How could I prove to her that she was wrong—that I did love her, even if I had not let her see it. I was afraid she would never know. And so, secretly, I resented her marriage.[5]

. . . .

Single Mothering on the Screen and in Real Life

Sally Field, the Emmy Award winning star of *Norma Rae* and *Places in the Heart*, and of the three-part television drama, "A Woman of Independent Means," has lived a life that is not so different off the screen than it has been in the movies as she freely admits: "I'm a mother before anything else . . . I'm committed to my children. I cook, I make jam, I make quilts. I'm really very much a homebody. . . . Without my kids, I'm not worth a damn."

Faith of our Mothers from Generation to Generation

Naomi Judd and her daughter Wynonna (Chris) teamed up for many years as country music's favorite female duet until poor health forced Naomi to step aside. Wynonna continued as a top country singer in her own right. The story of Naomi's struggles as a child with her father's drinking and her parents' estrangement, and her own failed marriage and relationships as a young adult followed a pattern that had come down through the generations. Indeed, she had come from a long line of "dysfunctional" families. But along with the terrible problems came a strand of faith that was passed down from one generation to the next.

 Grandmommy Judd was the voice of the Judds, the matriarch who ran the family, similar in that way to my Great-Grandmother Cora Lee. . . . Mother believed in the rewards of Proverbs 22:6: "Train up a child in the way he should go: and when he is old, he will not depart from it." She'd experienced its truth already in her own life. The greatest thing Miss Cora Lee ever did for Mom was take her to church. Her grandmother's own kids wouldn't go, and Mom had seen them wind up with crippled lives, but it taught my mother the deepest source of her identity was God. She developed a personal accountability to Him.

Naomi dedicated her biography, *Love Can Build a Bridge*, "to my future grandchildren and their descendants. This is who we are and how we lived." In that book she tells how she passed the faith on to her daughters:

 I told Chris and Ashley, "The truth is the truth! It's God's domain and it will stand up to your questions. But never presume there's only one way to find the truth!" We read stories about Buddha and Confucius and other important teachers and discussed their contributions. When Chris and Ashley wanted to know the difference between them and Jesus I replied, "These good men wanted to show the world the way, the truth, and the light. Jesus, however, was the way, truth, and light."[6]

Sacrificing a Scholarship for a Son

Today if a fifteen- or sixteen-year-old girl gets pregnant by a much older married man living next door, the man might likely serve time in prison and the girl might get an abortion. But there was no such justice in Greenville, South Carolina in the early 1940s—especially among black folks; and abortions, fortunately, were very difficult to get. So baby Jesse was born without a last name—later given the surname Burns by his grandmother, and adding the name Jackson when he was adopted by his stepfather. That underprivileged young boy went on to college and seminary to became a minister and later a Presidential candidate—all of which he owed to the sacrifice of his mother.

In 1941, Helen Burns, Jackson's mother, was a pretty high school student, living at home with her mother, Matilda Burns. Helen had grown up, like many blacks, as an "outside child," never knowing a father. His grandmother was illiterate and worked as a maid for a white family and spent the little money she earned on her daughter, who had a beautiful singing voice. Then, as Jackson would say, "the cycle of pain" was repeated, and his sixteen-year-old mother got pregnant by a married man, their next-door neighbor, Noah Robinson, a relatively wealthy black man.

Jesse's mother had to give up her singing ambitions and the scholarships to music colleges she'd just won. She first went to work as a maid, like her mother, and later went to beauty school and became a hairdresser. . . . Years later the preacher-politician would cite his illegitimacy in his inspirational speeches to young blacks and then to America in general: "You are God's child. When I was in my mother's belly, I had no father to give me a name. . . . They called me a bastard and rejected me. You are somebody! You are God's child!"[7]

Several years ago, I wrote a cover story for *Christianity Today* entitled "Working Mothers." In it, I included a sidebar on why women work. There I wrote the following:

Perhaps the most compelling reason that mothers have entered the work force in recent years is the rise of single-parent households. By 1986, 10 million families in America—one in every six—were financially supported by a woman. This situation has been caused largely by the increased divorce rate and the escalation of teenage pregnancies, which have forced women into full-time work to provide the bare necessities for themselves and their children.[8]

When I wrote the article, I thought that paragraph and the rest of what I had to say was fairly straightforward and matter-of-fact, and thus I was surprised when a following issue contained a barrage of criticism from women condemning working mothers—and, I suppose, though not outwardly stated, condemning single mothers at the same time.

No mother chooses as an ideal to be a single mother. Bad choices and unfortunate circumstances are typically the culprit. But for single mothers who are struggling to be homemakers and financial providers at the same time, it is encouraging to learn about single mothers of yesterday and today—ones like the mother of Ethel Waters—whose children go on to be caring and loving people and productive members of society. And it is sometimes helpful to be reminded that Mary was a single mother, and that "Jesus loved and honored all little children and didn't bother at all about who their parents were or about the manner of their birth."

For the mother is and must be, whether she knows it or not, the greatest, strongest and most lasting teacher her children have. Other influences come and go, but hers is continual; and by the opinion men have of women we can generally judge of the sort of mother they had.

HANNAH WHITALL SMITH

21

Motherly Influence and Advice

In the garden of the Somersby Rectory where he spent his childhood days, "hollyhocks, sunflowers, lilies, and roses grew in charming disorder to match the life of the family." Alfred Lord Tennyson was the second oldest of eleven children in a household where there was a stark contrast between the blooming flowers of the gardens and his father's "black depression," epilepsy, alcoholism, and abusiveness. His mother, on the other hand was a dreamer, "who was said to forget to order food for her family until they were nearly ready to sit down at a meal, then to send hurriedly to the neighbouring farm for two or three ducks."

 Mrs. Tennyson was probably more genuinely religious than her melancholy clergyman husband, and she passed on to Alfred her spirit of reverence, although he early deserted her strict Evangelical beliefs. For her he reserved the love he was half afraid to show to his father. He liked to read poetry aloud, and she listened sympathetically to her children's poems, so that they grew up scribbling verse nearly as easily a prose. . . .

The informality and warmth of her affection were necessary to offset her husband's nervous sternness to the children, and without it they might have grown up far more crippled emotionally than they did.[1]

From all accounts, Mrs. Tennyson had a positive influence on her children as they were growing up. But I know all too well from personal experience that motherly influence is not always a positive one. More than once when my son has said or done something that has distressed me, I have suddenly realized that I'm looking in the mirror at myself. Why, I ask myself, did he have to inherit all my negative traits—but those are the bad days, and fortunately most days are not.

But negative motherly influence did not begin with me, and I recently discovered an interesting confirmation of this from my studies in American History. Foreign travelers to America in the nineteenth century often had mixed reviews of Yankee motherhood. "Virtually every visitor praised her conscientiousness and devotion," writes Page Smith, "although there was less agreement as to whether her influence was wholly desirable." Overindulgence was the most obvious parental shortcoming of the day—as it has been in more recent generations as well (and one of my own shortcomings). Captain Marryat reconstructed a typical conversation between a mother and son:

"Johnny, my dear, come here," says his mamma.
"I won't," cries Johnny.
"You must, my love, you are all wet, and
*   you'll catch cold."*
"I won't," replies Johnny.
"Come, my sweet, and I've something for you."

Does that conversation sound familiar? The reason for such lax discipline, in the opinion of Marryat, was due to "the total neglect of the children by the father, and his absence in his professional pursuits." Maybe so.[2]

For better or for worse, mothers continue to be primarily responsible for the care of our children. We are the ones who have the greatest influence over the character development of these little ones, and for that reason I accept my task of mothering with great humility and seriousness.

"Other Influences Come and Go"

For the mother is and must be, whether she knows it or not, the greatest, strongest and most lasting teacher her children have. Other influences come and go, but hers is continual; and by the opinion men have of women we can generally judge of the sort of mother they had.

HANNAH WHITALL SMITH[3]

How to Reform the World

If you would reform the world from its errors and vices, begin by enlisting the mothers.

C. SIMMONS[4]

Advice for Sleepyhead Sons

What mother at one time or another is not distressed over her children's sleeping habits—"long lying in bed"? I sometimes think I have a lot in common with Lady Bacon in Elizabethan England—though surely not in my economic status. She was the wealthy and well-married wife of Sir Nicholas Bacon—a woman who would be lost in history were she not the mother of the celebrated philosopher and statesman Francis Bacon.

She "was a woman of almost terrifying energy and strength of moral purpose, a Puritan before the word was current, and all her life a hot gospeller." Though she ruled with authority over the servants in her lavish household, keeping her sons in line was another matter. But she never stopped trying. Even when they were in their thirties, living together away from home, she sent messengers after them "bearing admonitory letters, anxious, shrewd, most of them addressed to Anthony." She was a nagging mother, but she cared desperately about her sons' well-being—both physically and spiritually. To Anthony she admonished:

 Procure rest in convenient time. It helpeth much to digestion. I verily think your brother's [Francis's] weak stomach to digest hath been much caused and confirmed by untimely going to bed and then musing nescio quid [I know not what] when he should sleep, and then in consequence by late rising and long lying in bed, whereby his men [servants] are slothful and himself continueth sickly. The Lord our heavenly father heal and bless you both as his sons in Christ Jesu.[5]

. . . .

Words of Advice to a Depressed Daughter

Catherine Booth, cofounder of the Salvation Army, counseled many women in distress, including her depressed daughter Evangeline. To her she sent a monthly letter of encouragement and love:

I can better counsel you—not to give way to lowness while you are young.... Rise up on the strength of God and resolve to conquer. My love for you

makes me desire your highest good. How can love desire less? Anything that desires less is selfishness, not love. You may have others who will be more demonstrative but never who will love you more unselfishly than your mother or who will be willing to do or bear more for your good.[6]

. . . .

A Mother as Role Model for Son

How can a mother best help her son to mature into a loving and responsible adult? Sonya Friedman, a nationally known clinical psychologist, offers some suggestions that could be adapted to daughters as well:

 Such a woman tells her son that women are to be loved, considered, and respected.... A mother's demonstration of affection will show her son that, in fact, affection is natural, important, and not necessarily a prelude to sex. A good mother prepares her son to take care of someone else. She gives him a sense of worth, a clear idea of his place in the world—neither exalted nor debased. She will be instrumental, as well, in determining the nature and level of his ambitions. Finally his understanding of a woman's desires and needs will come from her.[7]

What if Mary Morrison had heard and heeded the words of Sonya Friedman. How different the relationships and family life for one very prominent American might have been.

Mary Morrison and Her Son Marian

Marian Morrison, known around the world as the actor John Wayne, was haunted throughout his life by negative influences—at least as he perceived them—from his mother. He was married and divorced three times—with cultural differences complicating his second and third marriages. (His second wife was Mexican and his third wife was Peruvian.) There is no evidence that Mary Morrison was a mean-spirited "Mommie Dearest," but she may have unwittingly damaged her son whose insecurities were evident in his marriages and passed on to the next generation. In *John Wayne: My Father*, Aissa Wayne writes:

 His mother chose her youngest boy to shower with love, saving only what trickly drops remained for my father. My dad resented his mom, even while aching for her love. Perhaps the rejection he felt as a child later influenced the unsettling way my father behaved toward me—lavishing me with affection, demanding my constant reassurance that I loved him back. Perhaps, after all those years, he was still trying to fill a void that cast such painful shadows over his childhood.

As she was growing up in the early 1960s, Aissa's relationship with her father became more and more strained.

It was also the time that I began fearing him. More and more in our home, my father insisted I demonstrate my affection. It might have related to the mortality he must have been feeling. Or perhaps it went all the way back to his relationship with his mother, his sense that she never loved him as much as his younger brother.... Whatever the cause, he now required ongoing proof of my love. For nearly the next ten years, if he was in a room and I entered it, I could not pass by without kissing him and telling him I loved him. ... Now, in supposedly the sanctuary of home life, I felt scrutinized and pressured by my own father. My affection for him, expressed so spontaneously when I was a little girl, sprung from fear and obligation as much as free will. ... Since his rage was always delayed and indirect, it all became so unfathomable, so disquieting, trying to decipher what might set him off. So I learned to be cautious of my actions and words. I learned to walk small around my father.[8]

There truly is a negative side to motherly influence and advice, but I'm convinced through my studies on motherhood that the positive side outweighs the negative. From great inventors and statesmen to writers and physicians, mothers have had a profound behind-the-scenes influence on their children.

Thomas Edison's Mother

Thomas Edison is remembered as one of America's greatest inventors, and he symbolizes American individualism and ingenuity. He grew up in America's heartland, Milan, Ohio, "with its old tree-shaded central square and its quiet lanes of white wooden frame houses." His story is part legend and part reality, and like so many American legends and true stories, the mother has a profound impact on her son. She was a stern disciplinarian, and according to Edison's own testimony she used a birch switch on him so regularly that it had "the bark worn off." But more importantly, she took an interest in her son's interests.

Nancy Edison . . . sensed, or discovered by chance, the real direction of her son's interests; for one day she brought forth an elementary book of physical science, R.G. Parker's School of Natural Philosophy, *which described and illustrated various scientific experiments that could be performed at home. Now his mother found that the boy had truly caught fire. This was "the first book in science I read when a boy, nine years old, the first I could understand," he later said. Here, learning became a "game" that he loved. He read and tested out every experiment in Parker; then his mother obtained for him an old Dictionary of Science, and he went to work on that. He was now ten and formed a boyish passion for chemistry, gathering together whole collections of chemicals in bottles or jars, which he ranged on shelves in his room. All his pocket money went for chemicals purchased at the pharmacist's and for scraps of metal and wire.*

Thus his mother had accomplished that which all truly great teachers do for their pupils: She brought him to the stage of learning things for him-self, learning that which most amused and interested him, and she encouraged him to go on in a path. It was the very best thing she could have done for the boy.

Unfortunately, Nancy Edison did not live to see her son become a famous scientist. She died when he was in his early twenties, after a period of physical and mental illness. Edison's father outlived his mother by a quarter century and died at the age of ninety-two, but the father and son did not have a close relationship, and "there is no record of his having ever said anything complimentary on the subject of his father." A later reference to his father indicates resentment on the part of the son: "My father thought I was stupid, and I almost decided I must be a dunce." His reflection on his mother stands in stark contrast:

 My mother was the making of me. She was so true and so sure of me. I felt that I had someone to live for—someone I must not disappoint. The memory of my mother will always be a blessing to me.[9]

• • • • • • • • • • • • • • • • • •

"The Determination of an American Mother"

Harold Macmillan, the son of a devout Methodist mother from Spencer, Indiana, is remembered as one of Britain's greatest Prime Ministers in modern times. His term of office from 1957 to 1963 were years of "unparalleled prosperity for postwar Britain" but, according to his biographer, they were "only the culmination of a lifetime of extraordinary service and astonishing accomplishment." Were it not for his mother, Macmillan might have lived and died in obscurity. She was the one who "pointed his footsteps towards a political career; and indeed fanned his ambition all through his life." How did the son regard his mother?

No-one who has not experienced it can realize the determination of an American mother. . . . She had high standards and demanded equally high performances from all about her. She had great ambitions, not only for herself but for her children. This was sometimes embarrassing both to my father and us. But I can truthfully say that I owe everything all through my life to my mother's devotion and support. . . .[10]

The Hand that Rocks the Cradle

They say man rules the universe,
That subject shore and main
Kneel down and bless the empery
Of his majestic reign
But a sovereign, gentler, mightier
Man from his throne has hurled,
For the hand that rocks the cradle
Is the hand that rules the world.

WILLIAM STEWART ROSS[11]

When Carlton was little—and on through elementary school—I told more stories to him than I read to him. My made-up stories were his favorites, and I was sometimes as interested in where they would go the following night as he was. It was thus with some pleasure that I read the story of Goethe's mother.

A Mother's Gift of Story-Telling

From little mother my happy nature,
And joy of story-weaving.

These are the lines of Johann Wolfgang Goethe who inherited the gift of story-telling from his mother. She was a woman with a vivid imagination who might have become a great fiction writer in her own right—if she had been relieved of some of her domestic duties and if women of her day had been encouraged to pursue literary endeavors. But instead she passed her gift on to her son whose works became classics. As an avid story-teller, Frau Aja, as she was known, found as much delight in creating imaginary tales as her children found in listening to them.

 As we thought of paths that led from star to star, and that we should one day inhabit the stars, and thought of the great spirits we should meet there, I was as eager for the hours of story-telling as the children themselves; I was quite curious about the future course of my own improvisations, and any invitation which interrupted these evenings was unwelcome. There I sat, and there Wolfgang held

me with his black eyes; and when the fate of one of his favorites was not according to his fancy, I saw the angry veins swell on his temples, I saw him repress his tears. He often broke in with, "But, mother, the princess won't marry the nasty sailor, even if he does kill the giant." And when I stopped for the night, promising to continue on the morrow, I was certain that he would in the meantime think it out for himself, and he often stimulated my imagination.[12]

. . . .

The "Grandmother" of Little Women

It was her mother, more than anyone else who influenced Louisa May Alcott in her writing. When she wrote a poem, "To a Robin," as a little girl, her mother enthusiastically predicted, "You will grow up a Shakespeare." According to her biographer, "Louisa remembered the words as if they had been laid on her as a mission and accolade." On her tenth birthday, Louisa opened her present from her mother and found a note enclosed: "I give you the pencil case I promised, for I have observed that you are fond of writing and wish to encourage the habit." Another gift from her mother was a print of a mother and daughter, and a note attached: "I enclose a picture for you which I always liked very much, for I imagined that you might be just such an industrious daughter and I such a feeble but loving mother, looking to your labor for my daily bread." In the words of her biographer, "Louisa pasted the picture and the note in her journal and kept them there always as a steady reminder to herself of her high destiny."[13]

When her first book, *Flower Fables*, was published, Louisa sent a copy to her mother with this note attached:

20 Pickney Street, Boston, Dec. 25, 1854.

 Dear Mother,—Into your Christmas stocking I have put my "first-born," knowing that you will accept it with all its faults (for grandmothers are always kind), and look upon it merely as an earnest of what I may yet do, for with so much to cheer me on, I hope to pass in time from fairies and fables to men and realities.

Whatever beauty or poetry is to be found in my little book is owing to your interest in and encouragement of all my efforts from the first to the last, and if ever I do anything to be proud of, my greatest happiness will be that I can thank you for that, as I may do for all the good there is in me, and I shall be content to write if it gives you pleasure.

Jo is fussing about;
My lamp is going out.

To dear mother, with many kind wishes for a happy New Year and merry Christmas.

I am your ever loving daughter,

Louy.[14]

The Mother of America's Baby Doctor

Dr. Benjamin Spock's *Baby and Child Care* is the book I turned to many times during my early years of child-rearing. As a wholly inexperienced child-care-giver, I needed ready advice about such things as diaper rash and dependence on a pacifier. On issues of behavior and discipline, I usually set Dr. Spock aside. He was too permissive for my tastes— and no doubt for his own mother's. Yet, it was Dr. Spock's mother who had the greatest influence on his life and profession. He begins his autobiography with her story:

My mother had all of her babies at home in New Haven, Connecticut. She wouldn't think of going to a hospital. She made the obstetrician set up a delivery room in a bedroom of our house. For a while she had a baby every two years (the sign was always the same: her craving for guava jelly). It was very exciting for us children, and the whole house was turned upside down. . . .

By the time Bob came along, I had changed a lot of diapers and given a lot of bottles. Since I was nine years older than Bob, I related to him more as a parent than as a brother. I was really Bob's regular sitter. I'd change his diapers, give him bottles, and rock him to sleep in the baby carriage on the long porch of the summer cottage in Vinalhaven, Maine. That summer's experience identifying with Mother in her love of babies was no doubt the main influence in my decision, a dozen years

later, to go into pediatrics. . . . My mother was certainly the person who most influenced my life and my attitudes. Some writers of profiles about me have implied that I got into pediatrics and wrote a book to rebel against her. To be sure, it was easy for me to conclude that there must be easier, pleasanter ways to bring up children than my mother's. But what is more fundamental and positive, I identified with her in her love of children. And her influence clearly lingered. Though I became somewhat skeptical, for instance, about her emphasis on early bedtime and on fresh air, I found them difficult to shake entirely, and they turn up in Baby and Child Care.[15]

A Mother's Strong Spirit Passed On to Her Daughter

For more than a half century she has been known as one of Hollywood's strongest and most spirited actors, and she has continued acting on into her eighties. As a woman who is not easily pushed around or manipulated, Katharine Hepburn inherited her strong will from her mother for whom she was named. Although she does not subscribe to all the tenets of modern feminism, her stand on women's rights developed early—through the influence of her mother.

 Time passed and mother was walking through the park one day. Tom, her first son, was walking along by her side, with me, Kathy, being wheeled. Well, thought Mother, here I am, these two adorable *children, a handsome, brilliant husband looking forward to his brilliant career. But me, what of me, what of me? Is this all that I'm here for? There must be something. I have a Bachelor's degree, I have a Master's degree.*

She went home sort of Puzzled, and Daddy came rushing in and said, "Look here in the paper. A woman named Emmeline Pankhurst is speaking about women and the vote tonight, let's. . . . " They went. Dad obviously had begun to realize that Mother was getting restless about her spot in the world. He found the solution. Mother became the head of the Connecticut Women's Suffrage Association. . . .

Mother had a booth at the Connecticut Fairgrounds, and we had a gas cylinder in the booth so that we could fill balloons. VOTES FOR WOMEN balloons, purple, white and green. I was about eight. I used to fill the balloons, tie a six-foot string onto them, go out into the street, pursue visitors to the Fair, follow them till they were willing to accept one of our balloons, whether they wanted one or not. In what was a rather insistent voice I'd say, "Votes for Women—here, take it— Votes for Women," and they took it.

When the men were voting about something, the Suffragettes always had their own voting booth right next door. There was a large sign on it saying (one of Dad's gems): WOMEN, IDIOTS AND CRIMINALS VOTE HERE. Mother was one of their favorite debaters. She was quick-witted, lots of fun and proof for your eyes and ears that women were not fools, they deserved the vote.[16]

· · · · · · · · · · · ·

A Surgeon General's Mother and Home Surgery

C. Everett Koop, "America's top doctor" of the 1980s, has warm memories of his mother as having a very strong influence in his early character development and his interest in medicine.

My mother, Helen Apel, grew up in a large Brooklyn family. . . . Well read and intelligent, she entered the work force in a secretarial/managerial capacity when many women were excluded. She was a wonderfully kind and generous woman who adored me, doted on me, and felt I could do little wrong. She possessed an extremely strong personality. When my mother was in good spirits, the group around her became lively; when she was glum, conversation went flat and the party proved dull. We were very close during my growing-up years, and her high expectations of me are in part responsible for much of my striving for achievement.

My mother should have been a nurse or a doctor. She had all the compassion needed, and a good deal of know-how as well. In her earlier years— before I came along—she administered anesthesia for surgeons who did certain operative procedures in the patient's home. . . . Many times I heard Mother's story about trying to give anesthesia to a neighbor's child while the doctor chiseled away his mastoid bone. She once held the head of her own maternal grandmother between two bed pillows while the famous ophthalmologic surgeon Dr. Willie Meyer removed a cataract from the old woman's eye. And, of course, my mother stood anesthetic watch over many a tonsillectomy. Indeed, I had my tonsils out at home.[17]

. . . .

A Mother and a Son's Military Career

Douglas MacArthur, who commanded the troops in the South Pacific during World War II and later served as the United Nations commander in Korea, is remembered as one of the great Army generals of the twentieth century. His father, Arthur MacArthur, and grandfather had also served with distinction in the military, but it was his mother, Mary Pinkney MacArthur, who had the greatest influence on his own military career—through her behind-the-scenes connections. After he graduated top in his class from West Point, he served at various Army bases until the outbreak of World War I.

 Pinky was her son's most ardent supporter. She had begun her campaign for his further promotion on October 6, 1917, two weeks before he had even left the United States. Writing Secretary of War Baker from the Garden City Hotel on Long Island, where she had been supervising MacArthur's supervision of the Rainbow [the "famous 42nd Division"], she went straight to the point: "I am taking the liberty of addressing you on a matter very close to my heart, and in behalf of my son— Douglas. . . . I am deeply anxious to have Colonel

MacArthur considered for the rank of Brigadier General, and it is only through you that he can ever hope to get advancement of any kind. All men— even the most able—must first get the opportunity in order to achieve success, and it is this opportunity I am seeking from you—for him." After summarizing his career in five paragraphs ("He is today the soul and body of the 42nd Division") she concluded. . ."He is a loyal and devoted officer and I present his name for your consideration, as I believe his advancement will serve—not only to benefit his own interest, but on a much broader scale, the interest of our beloved country in this great hour of her trial. With great esteem, Very cordially yours, Mrs. Arthur MacArthur."

In 1918, her son was promoted to rank of Brigadier General, but that was not the end of her efforts on his behalf. Some years later she contacted an influential attorney, once under her son's charge, again lobbying for his cause: "I wish you would get busy and get his promotion. He's been a Brigadier General for five years now. . . . I don't care what it costs. Just go ahead and send the bill to me personally. Don't tell Douglas." She then wrote to General John J. Pershing:

 . . . . I am presuming on long and loyal friendship for you—to open my heart in this appeal for my Boy—and ask if you can't find it convenient to give him his promotion during your regime as Chief of Staff? . . . You are so powerful in all Army matters that you could give him his promotion by a stroke of your pen! You have never failed me yet—and

somehow I feel you will not in this request. . . . Won't you be real sweet—The 'Dear Old Jack' of long ago—and give me some assurance that you will give my Boy his well earned promotion before you leave the Army? . . . God bless you—and crown your valuable life—by taking you to the White House. Faithfully your friend—Mary P. MacArthur.[18]

Douglas MacArthur, through his mother's influence—and interference—became one of the great military leaders of modern times. He was arrogant and controversial, especially in his defiance of President Truman, but he remains a hero to many. He's a hero to me too, not just because of his leadership during and after World War II, but because of his flair for writing and his ability to articulate my own thoughts. He wrote a personal prayer for his son that I have copied and framed and hung in the hallway just outside Carlton's door.

Build me a son, O God, who will be strong enough to know when he is weak and brave enough to face himself when he is afraid; one who will be proud and unbending in honest defeat, but humble and gentle in victory. Build me a son whose wishes will not replace his actions—a son who will know Thee and that to know himself is the foundation stone of knowledge. Send him, I pray, not in the path of ease and comfort but the stress and spur of difficulties and challenge; here let him learn to stand up in the storm, here let him learn compassion for those who fail.

Build me a son whose heart will be clear, whose goal will be high; a son who will master himself before he seeks to master others; one who will learn to laugh, yet never forget how to weep; one who will reach into the future, yet never forget the past, and after all these things are his, this I pray, enough sense of humor that he may always be serious yet never take himself too seriously. Give him humility so that he may always remember the simplicity of true greatness, the open mind of true wisdom, the meekness of true strength; then I, his father, will dare to whisper, "I have not lived in vain."

GENERAL DOUGLAS MACARTHUR[19]

Then, I, his mother, will dare to whisper, "I have not lived in vain."

He who takes the

child by the hand

takes the mother

by the heart.

DANISH

22

Mothers from All Nations

A *Walled Garden* is the title of a book describing traditional Jewish family life—a family guided by the injunction to be fruitful and multiply, a family insulated from blight from the outside, and a family in which "the young flourished and the old declined." The mother's role was crucial. It was she in this garden "who created the environment for earthly bliss." And the girls who would one day become mothers were "the brightest flowers in the garden."

> *The powerful, enveloping and sometimes suffocating love of the Jewish mother for her children is a theme reiterated in modern novels [but there is also a] Jewish ideal of motherhood. . . . The traditional Jewish family has been called "a walled garden."*[1]

Motherhood forms a universal bond that knits women together across language and cultural and geographical barriers. I recognized that in a very profound sense a few years ago when I was visiting a remote area of northern Kenya. The people in that region live on the land as their ancestors have for generations without any of the amenities of the modern world. They are impoverished by Western standards, but for them wealth means something entirely different than it means to the typical Western mother.

Mothers are the backbone of Kenya. They spend many hours a day working in their *shamba*—the garden plot that is part of their very identity, even as their children are. Indeed, motherhood and gardening are entwined into one "vocation" for many African women.

I found that to be true while visiting Molly, a missionary acquaintance in Allele, in the northern part of Kenya. There I had an unforgettable encounter with African motherhood that has left an indelible visual imprint on my heart. As we walked through the countryside, my missionary friend led us along the edge of a corn field to an isolated *shamba* and beyond that to a thatched hut to meet one of the tribal women. She lived alone away from the rest of her family tending the crops, planting and hoeing and making preparations for harvest—never missing a day's work until two days earlier. She had taken a break in order to give birth to a baby boy right there in the tiny thatched hut next to her garden. We were her first visitors, and she was a proud African *Mamma*. I introduced her to Carlton—my tall, lanky teenage son who towered over her—and she introduced me to her son and put him in my arms. As I held that little bundle in my arms she peered at his face inside the blanket and we shared the moment together as mothers.

Spending time in Kenya has expanded my perspective on motherhood. In many ways, mothers are the same from one culture to another—and yet we are so different. Motherhood is as natural as the maternal instincts that drive us, but motherhood is also embedded deep in tradition. As an American I have much to learn from mothers of other cultures. In America, motherhood has become tied to materialism. Not so in Kenya. A mother's worth is not related to how many video games her children have or whether their bikes are shiny and new. Rather, her worth arises out of a cultural heritage that recognizes the mother's indispensable role in the family as caregiver and provider.

On the negative side, however, sometimes her worth, unfortunately, is related too much to how many children she is able to bear and how much work she is able to accomplish, and her place in the family is not always secure. When her husband is polygamous—as is still true for many African women—she may feel pushed aside and be jealous of a favored wife. I've always been taken aback by my African students who speak of their "mothers." To Gabriel, his birth mother was not his beloved mother. The one he truly loved was another one of his father's wives.

I know better than to romanticize motherhood in other cultures, and if I'm tempted to I am quickly reminded of how arduous and difficult rearing a family can be in societies where resources and education and medicine are severely limited. Nor is the mother immune from long separations from her children—not because she drops them off at a day-care center, but separated just the same. I have a photo of three African women walking up a steep path with huge bundles of firewood on their backs—a common scene in Kenya. They are mothers who have been at work all day away from home. Who is taking care of the little ones? Other siblings? An aunt? A grandmother? Will all be well when they arrive home? I can close my eyes and see them still—walking up that steep hill. And I say to myself again and again, "But for the grace of God . . . there go I."

. . . .

India's Hannah and Samuel

Hannah has been an inspiration for mothers around the world wherever the Christian Gospel has penetrated, and every culture has its own "Samuels" reaching out with the Gospel as a result of their mother's prayers. K.P. Yohannan, an Indian evangelist and the president of Gospel for Asia, is one of those "Samuels."

His Christian mother, Achiamma Yohannan, prayed that God would call at least one of her six sons into the ministry. She set aside every Friday for fasting and prayer, but one by one her boys were drawn in other directions. Only one son remained without a chosen vocation—the "scrawny and little baby of the family" who was "so shy and timid" that he "trembled when asked to recite in class." But Achiamma refused to abandon her conviction that God would answer her prayer. K.P. was sixteen when he heard God's call:

 Alone that night in my bed, I argued with both God and my own conscience. By two o'clock in the morning, my pillow was wet with sweat and tears. I shook with fear. What if God would ask me to preach in the streets? How would I ever be able to stand up in public and speak? What if I were stoned and beaten?

By himself he knew he could never fulfill the call to ministry, but he gradually sensed he was not alone. The very presence of God filled the little room and he fell on his knees and responded to God's call in answer to his mother's prayers.[2]

Today as he travels the world and speaks before audiences of thousands, he is never far away from the memory of his mother's prayers.

The Mother

 From out the South the genial breezes sigh,
They shake the bramble branches to and fro
Whose lovely green delights the gazer's eye:
A mother's thoughts are troubled even so.
From out the South the genial breezes move,
They shake the branches of the bramble tree:
Unless the sons fair men and honest prove
The virtuous mother will dishonored be.

The frigid fount with violence the spray
By Shiyoun's town upcasts its watery store:
Though full seven sons she gave to life and day,
The mother's heart is but disturbed the more.

When sings the redbreast, it is bliss to hear,
The dulcet notes the little songster breeds;
But ah! more blissful to a mother's ear,
The fair report of seven good children's deeds.

TRANSLATED FROM THE CHINESE
BY GEORGE BARROW[3]

Housekeeping Tips

How does a mother of ten children manage to keep her primitive dwelling in the Kalahari desert clean? This was the dilemma confronting the early nineteenth-century Scottish missionary Mary Moffat who ministered alongside her husband, Robert Moffat, for most of a half century in the Kuruman Valley of Southern Africa. "You will perhaps think it curious," she wrote, "that we smear all our room floors with cow dung." She had resisted implementing "that dirty trick," but was finally convinced by African homemakers who knew how to keep house far better than she in that inhospitable climate.

 I had not been here long but I was glad to have it done and I had hardly patience to wait till Saturday. It lays the dust better than anything, kills the fleas which would otherwise breed abundantly, and is a fine, clear green. . . . It is mixed with water and laid on as thinly as possible. I now look on my floor smeared with cow dung with as much complacency as I used to do upon our best rooms when well scoured.[4]

. . . .

Proverbs about Mothers

 Whom will he help that does not help his mother.

TURKISH

A mother's love will draw up from the depths of the sea.

RUSSIAN

No mother is so wicked but she desires to have good children.

ITALIAN

 He who takes the child by the hand takes the mother by the heart.

DANISH

Heaven is at the feet of mothers.

PERSIAN

Buy land that slopes toward the center and marry a girl whose mother is good.

JAPANESE

 An ounce of Mother is equal to a pound of clergy.

SPANISH

An elephant does not carry heavy on its tusks. Interpreted means: It is no burden for a mother to take care of her child.

WEST AFRICAN

God could not be everywhere, and so He made mothers.

JEWISH

A mother understands what a child does not say.

JEWISH

Half an orphan is the fatherless child; whole orphan, the motherless.

FINNISH

A Mother's love, the best love; God's love, the highest love.

GERMAN

Happiness on the Inside

A traditional Chinese term for a pregnant mother: "The woman with happiness inside her."[5]

A Russian Babushka and a Great Statesman

During the many decades that communism ruled the Soviet Union, the Christian faith was shunned. The old women—grandmothers or Babushkas, as they were called—clung to their beliefs, but atheism was the religion of the State. But when the reign of communism came to an end, Christianity had not disappeared, as had been predicted. The faith of the mothers lives on. Among those mothers and grandmothers were those who had an influence on one of "the great visionary statesmen of our century Mikhail S. Gorbachev," a man who "has transformed the world, while hesitating at the brink of his own radical psychological transformation." Who were these remarkable women in his life?

 Misha [Mikhail] was also very close to his Grandmother Gopkalo, a tall woman with a spotless white babushka tied down over her forehead as tightly as a nun's wimple. A devout Russian Orthodox Christian, she took the boy to church and made certain he was immersed in a tub of holy water and properly baptized. In open violation of the state-decreed atheism she kept icons, those shimmering images of saints rendered on wood with a veil of gold. When Stalin's Terror reached its peak, she, like other peasants of the older generation, hid their wooden saints behind ordinary pictures.

Gorbachev's mother is also a believer to this day, according to Archbishop Antony of Stavropol. Russian mothers have breathed basic Christian values into their sons for a millennium, and the Archbishop has no doubt that Mikhail would have "absorbed the idea that connects all Christians—that God is the one who created the world and in every human we must see the image of God and treat him with love."[6]

An Eastern Legend for a Grieving Mother

Anne Morrow Lindbergh who knew from experience the grief of a mother whose child had died, tells a thought-provoking Eastern legend on how to find a cure for such sorrow:

 It is . . . the story of Buddha's answer to a mother who had lost her child. According to the legend, he said that to be healed she needed only a mustard seed from a household that had never known sorrow. The woman journeyed from home to home over the world but never found a family ignorant of grief. Instead, in the paradoxical manner of myths and oracles, she found truth, understanding, compassion, and eventually, one feels sure, rebirth.[7]

Nelson Mandela's Mothers

Today South African black children are likely to grow up in massive "shanty-towns" teeming with millions of people and blighted by poverty and a high crime rate. Not so sixty years ago when A-a-a Dalibhunga was growing up in Qunu. After spending more than a quarter century in prison, Nelson Mandela emerged as Africa's foremost leader, to serve as South Africa's first democratically elected President. What are his roots, and what role did his mothers play in his early years of development? His great-great grandfather was King Ngubengcuka, who ruled over all the Thembus before he died more than a century ago. His father had four wives, his mother being the third, and Nelson, as is true of many African children, grew up knowing the love of more than one mother. The details of his early years are told in the words of his sister Leabie:

> We lived with our mother in her three rondavels. That was myself, my two older sisters and Buti, as we called Nelson. Our mother had built them herself, with the help of the men in our family who put on the thatch. We used the one hut for cooking, one for sleeping and one for storing our grains and other food.
>
> There was no furniture in our "house," that is no European furniture: We slept on mats, without pillows, resting our heads on our elbows. Our mother's "stove" was a hole in the ground over which she put a grate. When the food was cooking, there was usually a lot of smoke for there was no chimney in our "kitchen." The smoke escaped through the window. . . .
>
> Our father was not a Christian. Our mother Nosekeni (known as Fanny in our church), was a devout Christian. She was most worried about Buti's future. . . .

When the boy was ten his father died, and after that he went to live with a cousin who was the regional chief and could afford to give the boy an education. The chief's wife Jongintaba, according to her daughter, "took him under her protective wing. I think she loved him as much as she did her own boy. . . and Nelson returned that love and came to see her as if she was his own mother."[8]

The African Mother and Child

In the West, the primary love relationship is assumed to be between the husband and wife—or, perhaps to an even greater extent between courting couples. This is not true in many cultures throughout the world—certainly not in Africa. I'll never forget asking Teddy, one of my African students, about the woman I had seen him holding hands with over the lunch-hour break.

It was my first term of teaching at Moffat College of Bible, and I was new to African culture. I assumed he must be courting her—though she did appear somewhat older then he. I wondered if he was "dating" her. He broke into gales of laughter, and finally when he got control of himself, explained that she was a family friend—another mother to him. Never, he insisted, would he publicly hold hands with the young woman who might one day become his wife.

In her book, *Surviving without Romance,* Mary Lou Cummings tells the stories of African women, and almost without exception the women speak of their relationship with their children as their strongest love bond. For them there is no real expectation or desire for romance with a lover or husband.

 African women make no apologies for their sense that the prime love relationship in life is that between mother and child. A husband is certainly an emotional support system. But he is rarely the soul's twin, the cherisher of my deepest self, that Americans idealistically describe him to be. He is an authority figure, a provider, and gives the family identity in his clan. African women respect their husbands, but they love their children.[9]

* * * * * * * * * * * * * * *

The Mother of Mao Zedong

When I was in graduate school, the Maoist revolution in China was seen in a positive light by many of my professors and fellow students. I was never carried away with this sort of idealism of the early 1970s, but I did have my own little red bound copy of *The Sayings of Chairman Mao.* Today there are few Western scholars who would idealize Mao. His ruthless regime is too well documented. Yet, he had millions of loyal followers who truly believed that he could bring prosperity to the impoverished masses of China. Much of Mao's ideology was developed as a young adult, but his early family relationships set the stage for his later political career. As a child he resented the fact that his comparatively prosperous father took advantage of their impoverished neighbors, and that he himself was sent out to collect money they owed. He became increasingly bitter toward his father and his "tight-fisted" usury, while joining with his mother to help those in need.

 Mrs. Mao indulged her eldest son, and he never lost his deep affection for her. Zedong was the only child in the house during the crucial early years and he did not have to share with others the attentions of his mother. . . . She could not read or write. And like most others she was a Buddhist. Before and during his school days, Zedong used to go with her to sing hymns and appease the gods at the Buddhist temple on Phoenix Hill high above the valley.

Mr. Mao did not believe in Buddhism and this bothered Zedong. At the age of nine, he discussed with his mother the problem of his father's impiety and how the two of them might deal with it. "We made many attempts then and later to convert him," Zedong recalled years afterward, "but without success. He only cursed us." . . . Zedong's own struggle with his father went on unabated and the household was painfully polarized.

Zedong joined forces with his mother in efforts to curb Mr. Mao. They furtively gave away rice to a villager in dire need. They allied with the hired laborer to defeat Mr. Mao's stingy ways. . . .

As Zedong grew older, however, the spirit of generosity turned into an angry ideology. He turned away from his Buddhist upbringing and from the influence of his mother. His deep affection for her would continue, but revolutionary Marxist writings would guide his conscience.[10]

. . . .

Indira Gandhi and Motherhood

Indira Gandhi grew up in a culture where womanhood is not highly valued, even by other women. Her own mother, Kamala, was treated with contempt by her husband and his family, and Indira, through her mother's influence, vowed it would be different with her family.

Kamala, lonely and miserable, retreated into religion. Indira was taught to appreciate Hinduism by her mother. She heard endless tales from the Hindu classics, stories of wars, loves, adventures, which made an undoubted impact on her and left a permanent mark on her consciousness. Kamala, who had only received lessons in English after her engagement to Jawaharlal, ensured that her daughter was not simply interested in religion, but was also fluent in Hindi and felt at home in India, unlike her aunts who had been brought up in a completely English style. Perhaps Kamala felt that this was the best way of showing her resentment of Jawaharlal. In any event, the experience was important and, in later life, very useful to Indira. At the same time Kamala talked to her daughter about men and how they ran women's lives and

had caused so much unhappiness. The only way women could challenge this was by being independent. Kamala was certainly bitter about her own experience, but she did not attempt to generalize it and her daughter always valued the advice. She proudly confessed many years later that having seen her mother's unhappiness had made her determined never to be dependent on any man in the same fashion.

Indira Gandhi's commitment to be an independent woman did not mean that she was less involved in her own family life. In fact, the opposite was true. While many affluent Indian women left their children in the care of servants, she vowed that she would be different. In an article entitled, "On Being a Mother," she wrote:

When Rajiv and Sanjay were babies I did not like the idea of anyone else attending to their needs and tried to do as much for them as I could. Later when they began school, I took care to have my engagements during school hours so as to be free when the boys returned home. Once when Sanjay was quite small, a nursery-school friend of his came to our house with his mother. The mother, a society lady of means, commenting on my public work remarked that I could not be spending much time with my sons. This hurt Sanjay and before I could think of a reply he rushed to my rescue with the words—"My mother does lots of important work yet she plays with me more than you do with your little boy." It seemed his little friend had complained about his mother's bridge-playing![11]

This past summer I was able to expand my cross-cultural horizons when I was invited to conduct seminars and lectures in Singapore. There, once again I was reminded in so many ways that motherhood is essentially the same the world over. Here in this tiny country, education is prized, and mothers are deeply involved from the preschool to university and beyond. Eating is the favorite pastime in Singapore, and around those delicious "10-course" meals, the conversation with career-driven "working" mothers often focused on our children. Their concerns were my concerns. We had a bond in our motherhood. Carlton accompanied me on the trip, and that gave me a little extra "status"—as if I really needed it—as a mother.

After a very pleasurable and fast-paced working vacation, with eighteen speaking engagements, I said good-bye to my old and new friends in Singapore, knowing that one day I would return. One of those to whom I said farewell was a very special *Mamma*—the mother of my good friend Suraja. After I returned home I wrote to Suraja, and I added a line for her mother:

Please . . . give your Mom a great big hug and "I love you" from both of us. I lost my mother more than 25 years ago, and when I find a Mom like yours, it almost makes me a little envious. She is truly special.

Mothers from many nations—drawing from so many different traditions and cultural norms. Yet, in many ways we are so much alike.

What a wonderful thing
is a mother!
Other folks can love you,
But only your mother understands;
She works for you—
looks after you—
Loves you, forgives you—
anything you may do;
And then the only thing
bad she ever does do—
Is to die and leave you.

BARONESS VON HUTTON

Walking through the Valley
of the Shadow of Death

So sorrowful was the poet Robert Browning when he received word of his mother's death that "he swore it was impossible to visit England again and it would break his heart to see his mother's garden once more."

It should have been a happy time for Browning. It was the spring of 1849, when he and his wife Elizabeth Barrett Browning, were living in Florence. The news that has mother had died suddenly from a heart attack came only days after the announcement they sent back to England of the birth of their baby. Elizabeth was deeply concerned about his well–being, knowing that he had "loved his mother as such passionate natures only can love."

It was a time when his emotions were chaotically pulled in opposite directions. "The coincidence of birth and death afflicted Browning with terrible force, 'and just because he was too happy when the child was born, the pain was overwhelming afterwards.'" When baby Robert was baptized he took his grandmother's maiden name "Wiedemann," at which time Robert lamented:

 "I have been thinking over nothing else, these last three months, than Mama and all about her."

The grief continued, as he wept over the letters from his sister telling of his mother's final days. How could he ever again walk through her garden that had such sentimental emotion to him?

Some years earlier, Robert had written a poem reflecting on his mother and that garden:

 Here's the garden she walked across,
   Arm in my arm, such a short while since:
Hark, now I push its wicket, the moss
   Hinders the hinges and makes them wince!...

Down this side of the gravel-walk
    She went while her robe's edge brushed the box:
And here she paused in her gracious talk
    To point me a moth on the milk-white flox.
Roses, ranged in a valiant row,
    I will never think that she passed you by!
She loves you noble roses, I know;
    But yonder, see, where the rock-plants lie!

This flower she stopped at, finger on lip,
    Stooped over, in doubt, as settling its claim;
Till she gave me, with pride to make no slip,
    Its soft meandering Spanish name....

Where I find her not, beauties vanish;
    Whither I follow her, beauties flee;
Is there no method to tell her in Spanish
    June's twice June since she breathed it with me?[1]

For Robert Browning it was his mother's garden that flooded his emotions when he learned of his mother's death. For me it was my mother's voice—the realization that I would never talk to her again.

It was 6:30 on the evening of September 23, 1969, just as I had turned on the NBC evening news—a moment that will be forever etched in my memory as one of shock and horror and indescribable grief. The phone rang in our tiny New Jersey apartment, and the message from my brother Jonnie conveyed the terrible news that my mother had been killed in a car accident late that afternoon. As I hung up the phone, my words of anguish summed up the finality of that broken bond:

"I can never talk to her again—never again."

As I've reflected back on that first expression of despair, I now understand why talking to Mom was so terribly important to me then and why I continue to miss that talk so much even today. A teacher turned farmer's wife, my mother, for good or ill, lived for us five kids. It was her dream to see us all graduate from college. We all did, but unfortunately she did not live to see it. She was proud of our accomplishments, and it was impossible to "brag" too much to her. Indeed, she would literally interrogate us about our achievements and success. She adored her two grandchildren, and Carlton would have been the apple of her eye if she had lived to know him.

My mother would have been eighty-three this summer and I continue to miss her and all the mother-daughter talks we might have had through the years. But I sometimes wonder what it would be like if she were still alive. Would she comprehend the world around her and be able to converse with me about my activities and aspirations or would she be in her own world of the past. If she were living in a bygone era of raising little children and canning bushels of peaches and pears, would I be frustrated or would I be able to join in and travel with Mother back in time?

• • • • • • • • • • • • • • • •

Traveling with Mother Back in Time

In his best-selling book, *Growing Up,* Pulitzer Prize winning author Russell Baker tells how he came to terms with his mother's mental condition before she died. She was out of touch with his reality but strangely, very much in touch with her own. Hers was a bygone era when life was fulfilling and more meaningful, and it was only in this world that Russell came to truly appreciate his own heritage.

At the age of eighty my mother had her last bad fall, and after that her mind wandered free through time. Some days she went to weddings and funerals that had taken place half a century earlier. On others she presided over the family dinners cooked on Sunday afternoons for children who were now gray with age. Through all this she lay in bed but moved across time, traveling among the dead decades with a speed and ease beyond the gift of physical science. . . . For ten years or more the ferocity with which she had once attacked life had been turning to a rage against the weakness, the boredom, and the absence of love that too much of age had brought her. Now, after the last bad fall, she seemed to have broken chains that imprisoned her in a life she had come to hate and to return to a time inhabited by people who loved her, a time in which she was needed. Gradually I understood. It was the first time in years I had seen her happy. . . . I soon stopped trying to wrest her back to what I considered the real world and tried to travel along with her on those fantastic swoops into the past. . . .

These hopeless end-of-the-line visits with my mother made me wish I had not thrown off my own past so carelessly. We all come from the past, *and children ought to know what it was that went into their making, to know that life is a braided cord of humanity stretching up from time long gone, and that it cannot be defined by the span of a single journey from diaper to shroud.*[2]

The Shadow of Death

In his book *Facing Death and the Life After*, Billy Graham tells a story of the death of a young mother that may appear to offer an easy answer in the face of grief, but it brings out the truth of Psalm 23 in a way that few accounts of death do.

 Dr. Donald Grey Barnhouse was one of America's great preachers. His first wife died from cancer when she was in her thirties, leaving three children under the age of twelve. Barnhouse chose to preach the funeral sermon himself. What does a father tell his motherless children at a time like that?

On the way to the service, he was driving with his little family when a large truck passed them on the highway, casting a shadow over their car. Barnhouse turned to his oldest daughter who was staring disconsolately out the window, and asked, "Tell me, sweetheart, would you rather be run over by that truck or its shadow?"

The little girl looked curiously at her father and said, "By the shadow, I guess. It can't hurt you."

Dr. Barnhouse said quietly to the three children, "Your mother has not been overrun by death, but by the shadow of death. That is nothing to fear."[3]

"It's All Right, Mother"

During the summer after her mother's ninetieth birthday, Madeleine L'Engle took her dying mother into her home at Crosswicks, and became a mother to her, caring for her as she had once been cared for by her mother when she was a little girl. Their roles were now reversed, and Madeleine felt frightened and vulnerable. Her story has a different twist than that of Russell Baker's.

 I put my arms around her and hold her. I hold her as I held my children when they were small and afraid in the night; as, this summer, I hold my grandchildren. I hold her as she, once upon a time and long ago, held me. And I say the same words, the classic, maternal, instinctive words of reassurance. "Don't be afraid. I'm here. It's all right."

> *"Something's wrong. I'm scared. I'm scared."*
> *I cradle her and repeat, "It's all right."*
> *What's all right? What am I promising her? I'm scared too.... What's all right? How can I say it?*
> *But I do. I hold her close, and kiss her, and murmer, "It's all right, Mother. It's all right."*

When is a mother no longer a mother? Is it possible to lose one's mother before she dies? These questions haunted Madeleine as she cared for the woman who was once her mother.

 Who is this cross old woman for whom I can do nothing right? I don't know her. She is not my mother. I am not her daughter....

I know that it is a classic symptom of arteriosclerosis, this turning against the person you love the most, and this knowledge is secure above my eyebrows, but very shaky below. There is something atavistic in us which resents, rejects, this reversal of roles. I want my mother to be my mother.

And she is not. Not any more. Not ever again....

One morning I dress Mother in a fresh nightgown while Vicki and Janet finish with the bed. Most mornings, Mother hardly seems to notice what has happened, or to care. She will murmur, "I'm cold. I want to go back to bed"—she who used to be so fastidious, so sweet-smelling. But this morning as I sit with my arms around her while the girls ready the bed, she leans against me and, suddenly herself, she says, "Oh, darling, I'm so ashamed about everything."

My heart weeps.[4]

Mothers

 What a wonderful thing
> *is a mother!*
Other folks can love you,
> *But only your mother*
> *understands;*
She works for you—
> *looks after you—*

Loves you, forgives you—
anything you may do;
And then the only thing
bad she ever does do—
Is to die and leave you.

BARONESS VON HUTTON[5]

· · · · · · · · · · · · · · · · ·

A West Point Graduate Returns

His father was "Light-Horse Harry" Lee, "gallant" officer in the Southern campaigns of the American Revolution, and later the Governor of Virginia, but it was his mother, Ann Carter Lee, who made her son, General Robert E. Lee, the man he would become as the Confederacy's greatest general.

The traits that characterized Robert . . . were instilled by his mother. . . . In Robert she possessed that rarity of a son who lived completely in his mother's ideal for him.

The debt he owed her could never be repaid, but his deep gratitude was evident when he returned from West Point Military Academy to be at her side.

When all the counts were in for the four years' work—including tactics and artillery, which were given no yearly grades—Lee graduated as second in his class, as the top cadet, and as the first to complete the course without receiving a single demerit. However, there was no proud home-coming. His mother was in the last stages of her terminal illness. . . .

The newly graduated honor student became her full-time nurse. . . . He was beside her when her eyes closed in death. The vision remained vividly with him the rest of his life. When he was himself an old man, at Ravensworth for another funeral, he lingered at the doorway of the room where she had died and said, "Forty years ago I stood in this room by my mother's deathbed. It seems now but yesterday."[6]

· · · · · · · · · · · · · · · · ·

The Best Friend You'll Ever Have

Dora Sloan was a Jewish mother who never came to terms with her son Bernie's marriage to a Protestant woman. It is her story—and a family story—that Bernard Sloan tells in his book *The Best Friend You'll Ever Have*. After his widowed mother was diagnosed with multiple myeloma (cancer of the bone marrow), Bernie flew to Arizona, where she lived, helped her sell her apartment furnishings, and moved her back to Larchmont, New York to live with him in his modest home with his wife Ethel and two sons. The months that followed proved to be a demanding trial and test of family harmony. Ethel's selfless efforts to care for her mother-in-law were often met with silent glares. Nothing she did pleased her, and Bernie feared that his mother could bring down their marriage.

As her condition temporarily improved, Bernard was able to set his mother up in an apartment of her own close by, but the strain of living and dying continued. Later when she knew her time was short and was confined to a hospital, she made clear how her possessions should be dispersed—insisting that nothing go to Ethel, still harboring grudges against her. This should have been the time "she would release her prejudices, clear her soul, regret her treatment of Ethel," but that was not to happen. She lapsed into a coma.

 I felt I should talk to her. It would be my last chance. But I had nothing to say. What could I tell her? That I was angry? Was I supposed to agree with her that Ethel was foxy? Was I supposed to love her for leaving this world without a kind word for the only person who had really sacrificed for her?

Bernard was angry when he left his mother's side, and surprised later that night at the explosion of his emotions when he got the news his mother was gone.

 I wanted no one to step through the door and stand over me and touch my shoulder. I wanted no one to talk about grief and how they understood. No one could understand. I did not want anyone to know that I cared for her. I was astonished at the depth and intensity of my feelings that I thought had long atrophied; they were like the roots of a tree that appears dead—buried but very much alive. Nothing she did could destroy them.

I was bawling at her death, and there was nothing I could do to stop.[7]

Words Left Unspoken

Faye Moskowitz, a woman of words who makes her living as a commentator and journalist, regrets that she left too many words unspoken when her mother was dying of cancer many years ago. The words unspoken between mother and daughter became a deafening silence as a motherless Faye looked back to what might have been.

 I suppose I realized from the beginning that my mother's illness was a serious one: I had seen the fearful loss of symmetry where the breast had been, the clumsy stitching around it, like that of a child sewing a doll's dress. I had caught her one morning weeping in front of the mirror as she poked at the rubber pad that kept working its way up the open collar of her blouse. But I was sixteen years old and worried enough about keeping my own physical balance. One false step and I might fall off the edge of the world. I was afraid to walk the outer limits of her sickness; I dealt with death the way the rest of my family did . . . by denying it. . . .

Alone for a moment, she called to me one day as I tiptoed past her bedroom. . . . I stood next to her, watched her pluck at a fold in the bedclothes, smooth them, try to make the question casual by the homely gestures. "Faygele," she said, finally, "do you think I will ever get better?"

How could I answer her truthfully, being bound as inextricably as she was by the rules of the complicated deception we were playing out? Perhaps I understood in my heart's core that she was doomed, but I hadn't the permission of knowledge; I could only answer, "Of course, of course," and help to wrap her more tightly alone inside her fear. She never asked me that question again. . . .

I still grieve for the words unsaid. Something terrible happens when we stop the mouths of the dying before they are dead. A silence grows up between us then, profounder than the grave. If we force the dying to go speechless, the stone dropped into the well will fall forever before the answering splash is heard.[8]

Unlike Faye's mother, my mother died very suddenly of accidental injuries, and I did not have the opportunity to have that one last talk with her before she passed through the valley of the shadow of death. But since then I have had the privilege as a "surrogate" daughter to say good-bye to two mothers on two different occasions, and I will always cherish those memories.

The most recent occasion was in 1987, after my friends Joan and Bud Berends took early retirement and departed for Kenya for a two-year mission assignment. At the airport, Joan gave me a letter asking if I would stand in as a daughter to her mother while they were gone. I agreed without hesitation, never imagining that the next day her mother would be hospitalized and would be on and off the road to recovery until she died some seven weeks later. My daily visits to the hospital provided a much-needed escape for me during a time when I was going through turmoil in my own life. I felt needed and wanted. The night before she died was a sweet time of talking and kissing her good-bye before she entered into the presence of God.

Ten years earlier, I had said good-bye to Gertrude in a somewhat similar manner. In this case, however, the daughter, Mary, refused to see her mother in the weeks before she died and I was a self-appointed "surrogate." I'll never forget entering their tiny apartment one evening—not knowing this would be her last night. She was lying on the sofa, her sister nearby, and her husband in the kitchen. Nobody was talking. Everyone was in denial—convinced she was on the mend. She obviously wasn't.

I was a young pastor's wife at the time, and I'd never had any training or experience in dealing with death. I didn't know what to say. What can one say at a time like this? So I simply greeted her and knelt beside her and held her hand. I could sense she wanted to talk, so I quoted some Scriptures and said nice things and spoonfed her some soft ice cream. But what she really wanted was me. So I put my arms around her and kissed her head, now bald from chemotherapy, and told her I loved her. After a few minutes I pulled back, but she was tenacious in her weakness, and she didn't want me to go. So I stayed and held her and kissed her and told her I loved her—for what seemed to be most of an hour—until she had fallen asleep. The next morning when the phone rang early, I knew what the message would be. She had passed through the valley of the shadow of death.

How tragic, I sometimes think, that her daughter Mary, wasn't the one to have that tender embrace and sweet, sweet communion. But, oh how privileged I am to have been a daughter saying good-bye to a mother on these two occasions.

She always leaned to watch for us,
Anxious if we were late,
In winter by the window,
In summer by the gate;

And though we mocked her tenderly,
Who had such foolish care,
The long way home would seem more safe
Because she waited there.

Her thoughts were all so full of us—
She never could forget!
And so I think that where she is
She must be watching yet,

Waiting till we come home to her,
Anxious if we are late—
Watching from heaven's window,
Leaning from heaven's gate.

MARGARET WIDDEMER

Beyond the Grave to Glory

I come to the garden alone,
 While the dew is still on the roses;
And the voice I hear, falling on my ear,
 The Son of God discloses.

And He walks with me, and He talks with me,
 And He tells me I am His own,
And the joy we share as we tarry there,
 None other has ever known.

C. AUSTIN MILES

"In the Garden" was my mother's favorite hymn—the hymn we sang at her funeral. I often reflect on that hymn as I'm sitting under the awning on my back deck looking out into the garden. I'm often most alone in my garden and its a good place to reflect—on God and on memories gone by.

It's more than a quarter century since my mother died, and most of the time my life goes on as if that terrible day in 1969 had never happened. I think of her on special occasions, and wish she could have known Carlton through his growing up years. I no longer cry—except when caught by a moment that I'm not prepared for.

I thought of her tonight as I was watching Sally Field starring in *A Woman of Independent Means.* Sally was playing a woman who had lost her husband some years earlier, and her oldest son had died during the previous year. But here she was at the cemetery all day in deep grief over her mother who had died long ago. "Its strange," she lamented, "how grief doubles back on you, ambushes you."

Yes, it is strange after all these years. The wound has still not completely healed, and the grief does double back on me and ambushes me when I'm least expecting it. But I will always have a garden of memories with all its color and fragrances, and when I think of heaven, I think not so much of streets of gold, but of beautiful gardens—gardens far more glorious than my mother's ever were or mine will ever be.

· · · · · · · · · · · · ·

"Where Is My Mother?"

She knew her faithful Christian mother had gone to be with the Lord, but the physical loss of this one she loved so profoundly brought such a sense of separation that she often wondered aloud where she was. The grieving daughter was Frances Willard, founder and director of the Woman's Christian Temperance Union—one of the most celebrated women of her time. Her deep love for her mother—greater than that of her siblings, she was convinced—may have been intensified because she herself never married or had children of her own. She often spoke of motherhood in idealized sentiments—a perspective that emerged out of her own relationship with her mother.

 I thank God for my mother as for no other gift of His bestowing. My nature is so woven into hers that I almost think it would be death for me to have that bond severed and one so much myself gone over the river. She does not know, they do not any of them, the "Four," how much my mother is to me, for, as I verily believe, I cling to her more than ever did any other of her children. Perhaps because I am to need her more.

Her mother's death was not death for Frances. She lived on for six more years, dying in 1898, at the age of fifty-nine. But, again and again, penned in her journal was the question, "Where is my mother?" It was "a question that was to persistently reiterate itself until, like a tired child, she had been restored to her mother's arms."[1]

· · · · · · · · · · · · ·

Come Back to Your "Mother's Religion"

 "Come down to the mission tonight . . . if you've wandered far away from God and your mother's religion."

These words caught the attention of a professional baseball player who was sitting on a Chicago curb with some of his buddies on a Sunday afternoon in 1886. The words "your mother's religion" pierced his heart, and he was determined to heed the appeal. That night he went to the meeting at the Pacific Garden Mission and his life was forever changed. There he heard the songs his mother and grandmother used to sing—and there he found his "mother's religion"—and his grandmother's. The young man was Billy Sunday, the best known American evangelist of the early twentieth century.

Both his mother and his grandmother had died long before the time of his own conversion—and not all of his childhood memories with them were good ones. But their faith in God had its grip beyond the grave, and son Billy could not resist. He came back to his "mother's religion."[2]

"Tell Mother, I'll Be There"

A hymn that captures the story of Billy Sunday often rang through the auditorium of the Pacific Garden Mission. Its message brought back memories, and grown men wept and prayed for God's forgiveness.

 When I was but a little child how well I recollect
How I would grieve my mother with my folly
 and neglect;
And now that she has gone to heav'n I miss her
 tender care:
O Saviour, tell my mother I'll be there!

One day a message came to me, it bade me quick-
 ly come
If I would see my mother ere the Saviour took her
 home;
I promised her, before she died, for heaven to
 prepare:
O Saviour, tell my mother I'll be there!

Chorus *Tell mother I'll be there in answer to her pray'r;*
 This message, blessed Saviour, to her bear!
 Tell mother I'll be there, heav'n's joys with
  her to share:
 Yes, tell my darling mother I'll be there!

C.M. FILMORE

The Watcher—Mother

She always leaned to watch for us,
 Anxious if we were late,
In winter by the window,
 In summer by the gate;

And though we mocked her tenderly,
 Who had such foolish care,
The long way home would seem more safe
 Because she waited there.

Her thoughts were all so full of us—
 She never could forget!
And so I think that where she is
 She must be watching yet,

Waiting till we come home to her,
 Anxious if we are late—
Watching from heaven's window,
 Leaning from heaven's gate.

MARGARET WIDDEMER[3]

A Mother Remembered

If my son were to memorialize me in some way, how would I want that to be inscribed in history? If he were to name something for me, maybe it would be a park and botanical garden—or maybe just his backyard garden, even as I have named mine, *Carlton Gardens*, for my grandmother, my mother, and for him. He talks about one day having his own boat. Maybe he'll name it for me. No. I don't expect to be memorialized by my son—on a boat or anything else.

But neither did the mother of Paul Tibbets. Her name will forever be remembered for a B-29 bomber—a weapon that would create some mixed emotions if my son had named it for me.

Colonel Paul Tibbets was the pilot who dropped the atomic bomb on Hiroshima, on August 6, 1945. His bomber he named *Enola Gay* for his mother, and the bomb that would be the death warrant for more than 100,000 people, he named "little boy." He tells about the naming in his autobiography:

 As the time approached for the Hiroshima mission, I gave serious thought to a name for my plane. Considering the historical importance of the event, it seemed hardly fitting to announce that the world's first atomic bomb had been dropped from an unnamed B-29 bearing the number 82. . . .

My thoughts turned at this moment to my courageous red-haired mother, whose quiet confidence had been a source of strength to me since boyhood, and particularly during the soul-searching period when I decided to give up a medical career to become a military pilot. At a time when dad thought I had lost my marbles, she had taken my side and said, "I know you will be all right, son." . . .

Her name, Enola Gay, was pleasing to the ear. It was also unique, for I had never heard of anyone else named Enola. It would be a fine name for my plane: Enola Gay.[4]

 · · · · · · · · · · · · · · ·

"Fold Her, O Father"

 Fold her, O Father! In Thine arms,
     And let her henceforth be
A messenger of love between
     Our human hearts and Thee.

Still let her mild rebuking stand
     Between us and the wrong,
And her dear memory serve to make
     Our faith in goodness strong.

And grant that she, who, trembling here,
     Distrusted all her powers,
May welcome to her holier home
     The well-beloved of ours.

JOHN GREENLEAF WHITTIER[5]

· · · · · · · · · · · · · · ·

A Mother Watching from Above

Arthur Ashe is remembered as one of the world champion tennis players in the 1960s and 1970s, and the first black man to win the men's single's title at Wimbledon. The opening lines of his memoirs, *Days of Grace*, pay tribute to his mother, Mattie Cordell Cunningham Ashe, a faithful member of the Westwood Baptist Church in Richmond, Virginia.

 If one's reputation is a possession, then of all my possessions, my reputation means most to me. Nothing comes even close to it in importance. . . . I know that I haven't always lived without error

or sin, but I also know that I have tried hard to be honest and good at all times. When I fail, my conscience comes alive. I have never sinned or erred without knowing I was being watched.

Who is watching me? The living and the dead. My mother, Mattie Cordell Cunningham Ashe, watches me. She died when I was not quite seven. I remember little about her, except for two images. My last sight of her alive: I was finishing breakfast and she was standing in the side doorway looking lovingly at me. She was dressed in her blue corduroy dressing gown. The day was cool and cloudy, and when I went outside I heard birds singing in the small oak tree outside our house. And then I remember the last time I saw her, in a coffin at home. She was wearing her best dress, made of pink satin. In her right hand was a single red rose. . . . Every day since then I have thought about her. I would give anything to stand once again before her, to feel her arms about me, to touch and taste her skin. She is with me every day, watching me in everything I do. Whenever I speak to young persons about the morality of the decisions they make in life, I usually tell them, "Don't do anything you couldn't tell your mother about."[6]

. . . .

A Futile Search for a Mother Through Seances

Harry Houdini is remembered as America's greatest magician and escape artist of the early twentieth century. He was born Ehrich Weiss in Budapest, Hungary, in 1874. Soon after his birth, his father killed a man in a duel and fled with his wife and four children to America. Ehrich found odd jobs to help support the family, but as a teenager his interests turned to magic and performing, and he convinced his brother to join him, encouraged by his mother.

 She made satin stage costumes—jackets and short pants—and was a tolerant audience of one whenever they wished to try out a new trick.

In 1913, when Houdini received word of his mother's death during a news conference, he sobbed "Mother—my dear little mother—poor little mamma."

 The death of his beloved mother had almost shattered his life. He had gone to seances hoping to hear her soft voice and encouraging words again. The shabby deceptions he encountered in seance rooms sickened him. He was willing to believe; he wanted to believe.

Houdini's futile search for his mother through mediums convinced him that spiritualism was a fraud, and in that way he left a legacy to his mother who had been his strongest supporter and biggest fan.

From coast to coast, on stages and lecture platforms, Houdini demonstrated how messages were written on slates, not by spirit hands but by the substitution of a message-bearing surface for a blank one.

So it was that the great master of illusion became known for exposing spiritual deception—

the deception that so callously pretended to bring back the mother of a grieving son.[7]

* * * * * * * * * * * * * * * *

Sensing a Mother's Presence After Her Death

Norman Vincent Peale, the well-known minister of the Marble Collegiate Church in New York City, and the author of *The Power of Positive Thinking* was very close to his mother, and she had a profound influence on him in life and in death. Reflecting on his mother he wrote:

 It would be quite difficult, even impossible, for me to describe the influence my mother had on my life. . . . Everything for her had charm, romance, color, beauty, and I marvelled at this, and believe that among the many gifts which she gave to me is this insatiable and never-ending interest in life.

But it was also in death that she gave her son an interest in death. When she died in 1939, he was forced to come to terms with a personal loss that might have pushed him into utter despair. Instead, he was comforted by his mother's presence that followed him the rest of his life.

 Going instinctively to the church on hearing that she had died, he went to his office and placed his hand on a Bible she had given him. At that moment, he said he felt two hands resting on his head, and "knew" it was his mother's presence.

Several years later, after buying at auction a pair of expensive hurricane lamps for Ruth, he heard his mother's voice, reassuring him about the gift and her affection for Ruth. He reported to a friend that the bond with his mother was so strong that for him she had "never really died."[8]

* * * * * * * * * * * * * * * *

Mother Most Beloved

 The years roll on, Mother dearest, that bring me nearer to you, but you have never seemed far away.

The wheels of time have left their tracks on all about us, but your dear face has remained just the same.

What you said to us and the memories of what you did for us come back and back to your children in the silent seasons of the night and the busy hours of the day, and never is there a sickness or trial nor a joy that you are not present in some form.

More than a thousand times since you journeyed on we have said, if only mother were here as of old that we might say the word and do the thing we postponed or forgot.

JOHN WANAMAKER[9]

* * * * * * * * * * * * * * * *

"My Mother's Message to Me"

Helen Steiner Rice is known by all of us as the woman behind so many of the sentimental messages on greeting cards. She had a way of putting into words what we so often felt. But behind those words and behind that woman, was Anna

Steiner, a strong, independent woman who had a powerful influence in her daughter's life.

She taught her daughters important lessons about womanhood. . . . She instilled in them the belief that women could love and respect men but need not be totally dependent on them. It was a lesson neither girl forgot. Anna also paid special attention to the spiritual development of her children. A deeply religious person, she did her best to ground them in the fundamentals of Christian living.

Helen was a poet for all occasions, especially for celebrations of joy and family togetherness, and her biography is appropriately subtitled "Ambassador of Sunshine." But it was on the occasion of her mother's death in 1945, that she wrote one of her most memorable poems. She had endured other tragedies, yet this was "the darkest hour" of her life. Her only comfort was in her mother's words some years earlier on her anticipated "journey into eternity." From her recollection of that sweet time of intimate sharing, Helen wrote a poem to help heal her broken heart, not realizing that it would speak to countless grieving hearts, as the message in a best-selling sympathy card. It was titled, "My Mother's Message to Me."

When I must leave you for a little while
Please do not grieve and shed wild tears
And hug your sorrow to you through the years,

But start out bravely with a gallant smile;
And for my sake and in my name
Live on and do all things the same,
Feed not your loneliness on empty days
But fill each waking hour in useful ways,
Reach out your hand in comfort and in cheer
And I in turn will comfort you and hold you near,
And never, never be afraid to die
For I am waiting for you in the sky![10]

The words of Helen's mother, are words that I would leave behind to Carlton—though expressed somewhat differently. It's only natural for me to assume that he will survive me and be left behind without my watchful concern and unconditional motherly love. To him I write:

When I am gone and you are left alone, I know your heart will ache and the tears will fall. The pain will sometimes be almost unbearable. But when you weep, just remember you are weeping for yourself. That's all right. Don't stifle your sorrow. Let the tears fall. But when you smile and laugh and sing and dance, you smile for me; you laugh for me; you sing and dance for me. When you celebrate the joy of life, think of me. And don't ever forget the happy times and the good times we have had together. Plant a flower for me, my beloved son, not on my grave— oh, sure, that's okay, too—but in your garden and let it bloom as a reminder of my love for you and the joy we've shared during the fleeting span we call life—our very own garden of memories.

NOTES

INTRODUCTION

1. Eleanor Doan, *Speakers Sourcebook* (Grand Rapids: Zondervan, 1988), 169.

2. Cited in Rebecca Merrill Groothuis, *Women Caught in the Conflict* (Grand Rapids: Baker, 1994), 165, 210.

3. Nancy Gibbs, "Power Gardening," *Time* (June 19, 1995), 54.

4. Gail MacDonald, *High Call; High Privilege* (Wheaton, Ill.: Tyndale, 1986), 58–59.

5. Anne Morrow Lindbergh, *Hour of Gold, Hour of Lead: Diaries and Letters*, 1929–1932 (New York: Harcourt, Brace, Jovanovich, 1973), 215.

6. Mabel Barbee Lee, *The Gardens in My Life* (Garden City, N.Y.: Doubleday, 1970), xiv.

CHAPTER 1

1. Tim Hilton, John Ruskin: *The Early Years*, 1819–1859 (New Haven: Yale University, 1985), 10, 12, 170–71.

2. Louis M. Notkin, ed., *Mother: Tributes from the World's Great Literature* (New York: Samuel Curl, 1943), 141.

3. Elisabeth Badinter, *Mother Love, Myth and Reality: Motherhood in Modern History* (New York: Macmillan, 1980), 234–35.

4. Sue Hubbell, *A Country Year: Living the Questions* (New York: Random House, 1983), 89–91.

5. Anne Fremantle, ed., *Mothers: A Catholic Treasury of Great Stories* (New York: Stephen Daye, 1951), 7.

6. Thomas Curtis Clark and Esther A. Gillespie, compilers, *1000 Quotable Poems* (Chicago: Willett, Clark & Company, n.d.), 253.

7. William Lyon Phelps, compiler, *The Mothers' Anthology* (New York: Doubleday, Doran & Co., 1940), xvii.

8. Louis M. Notkin, 101.

9. Johanna Johnston, *The Heart That Would Not Hold: A Biography of Washington Irving* (New York: J.B. Lippincott, 1971), 35–39; Washington Irving, *The Sketch Book* (New York: Literary Classics, 1848), 108–9.

10. Hugh T. Kerr and John M. Mulder, eds., *Conversions: The Christian Experience* (Grand Rapids: Eerdmans, 1983), 212–13.

11. Nancy Friday, *My Mother, My Self* (New York: Dell, 1977), 28.

12. Faye Moskowitz, *A Leak in the Heart: Tales From a Woman's Life* (Boston: David R. Godine, 1985), 54–55.

13. Louis Genevie and Eva Margolies, *The Motherhood Report: How Women Feel About Being Mothers* (New York: Macmillan, 1987), 84–85.

14. Betty Mahmoody with William Hoffer, *Not Without My Daughter* (New York: St. Martin's, 1987), 221, 354, 367, 369, 404, 417, 418.

CHAPTER 2

1. Katie May Gill, *Mother: Poems for Mother* (Richmond, V.A.: Cavalier Press, 1957), 43.

2. Page Smith, *Daughters of the Promised Land: Women in American History* (Boston: Little, Brown and Company, 1970), 212.

3. Mabel Bartlett Peyton and Lucia Kinley, *Mothers: Makers of Men* (New York: Robert M. McBride, 1927), i.

4. Ibid., 17.

5. Eleanor Doan, *A Mother's Sourcebook of Inspiration* (Grand Rapids: Zondervan, 1969), 29; Lyle W. Dorsett, *Billy Sunday and the Redemption of Urban America* (Grand Rapids: Eerdmans, 1991), 9.

6. James G. Watson, ed, *Thinking of Home: William Faulkner's Letters to His Mother and Father, 1918–1925* (New York: W.W. Norton, 1992), 32, 47, 185, 201, 208.

7. Bernard Ruffin, *Fanny Crosby* (New York: United Church Press, 1976), 56; Louis M. Notkin, ed., *Mother: Tributes from the World's Great Literature* (New York: Samuel Curl, 1943), 195.

8. Liz Smith, *The Mother Book* (Garden City, N.Y.: Doubleday, 1978), 109.

9. Quoted in *The Mothers' Anthology*, compiled by William Lyon Phelps (New York: Doubleday, 1940), 162.

10. Susan Tracy Rice, compiler, *Mothers' Day: Its History and Origin* (New York: Dodd, Mead and Company, 1927), 76.

11. Thomas Curtis Clark and Esther A. Gillespie, compilers, *1000 Quotable Poems* (Chicago: Willett, Clark & Company, n.d.), 255.

12. Helen Keller, *The Story of My Life* (New York: Bantam Books, 1990), 10, 153–54.

13. William Lyon Phelps, 213.

14. Karen Payne, ed, *Between Ourselves: Letters between Mothers and Daughters, 1750–1982* (Boston: Houghton Mifflin, 1983), 336–39.

15. Barbara and Kathy Miller, *We're Gonna Win* (Old Tappan, N.J.: Fleming H. Revell, 1983), 52–55.

CHAPTER 3

1. Liz Smith, *The Mother Book* (Garden City, N.Y.: Doubleday, 1978), 104–5.

2. Nancy Friday, *My Mother, My Self* (New York: Dell, 1977), 26.

3. Liz Smith, 442.

4. Christina Crawford, *Mommie Dearest* (New York: William Morrow, 1978), 34–35.

5. Patti Davis, *The Way I See It: An Autobiography* (New York: G.P. Putnam's Sons, 1992), 33–34, 330.

6. Otto H. Frank and Mirjam Pressler, eds., *Anne Frank: The Diary of a Young Girl*, translated by Susan Massotty (New York: Doubleday, 1995), 61–64, 99.

7. Anthony Summers, *Goddess: The Secret Lives of Marilyn Monroe* (New York: Macmillan, 1985), 6–7.

8. Malcolm Forbes with Jeff Bloch, *Women Who Made a Difference* (New York: Simon and Schuster, 1990), 111–13.

9. General H. Norman Schwarzkopf with Peter Petre, *The Autobiography: It Doesn't Take a Hero* (New York: Bantam, 1992), 19, 21.

10. Judy Sullivan, *Mama Doesn't Live Here Anymore* (New York: Arthur Fields, 1974), 222, 236–39, 243.

CHAPTER 4

1. Gigi Graham Tchividjian, *Sincerely . . . Gigi* (Grand Rapids: Zondervan, 1984), 47–48.

2. Stephanie Coontz, *The Way We Never Were: American Families and the Nostalgia Trap* (New York: HarperCollins, 1992), 151–54.

3. Liz Smith, *The Mother Book* (Garden City, New York: Doubleday, 1978), 32.

4. Mabel Bartlett Peyton and Lucia Kinley, *Mothers: Makers of Men* (New York: Robert M. McBride, 1927), 4–5.

5. Malcolm Forbes, with Jeff Bloch, *Women Who Made a Difference* (New York: Simon and Schuster, 1990), 134–37.

6. Kaye Halverson and K.M. Hess, *The Wedded Unmother* (Minneapolis: Augsburg, 1980), 60–61, 74.

7. Octavus Roy Cohen, "Mothers' Day," in *The Mothers' Anthology* compiled by William Lyon Phelps (New York: Doubleday, Doran & Co., 1940), 100–10.

CHAPTER 5

1. Mabel Barbee Lee, *The Gardens in My Life* (Garden City, N.Y.: Doubleday, 1970), 113–14, 143.

2. Annie Dillard, *An American Childhood* (New York: Harper & Row, 1987), 233–36.

3. Dale Hanson Bourke, "Ruth Bell Graham: Tough and Tender Moments," *Today's Christian Woman* (September/October 1991),

53, 129.

4. Domini Taylor, *Mother Love* (New York: G.P. Putnam's Sons, 1983), 7.

5. William Lyon Phelps, *The Mothers' Anthology* (New York: Doubleday, 1940), 156–57.

6. Ibid., 19–21.

7. Judith Walzer Leavitt, *Brought to Bed: Childbearing in America, 1750–1950* (New York: Oxford University Press, 1986), 34.

8. Nathaniel Hawthorne, *The Scarlet Letter* (New York: Dodd, Mead & Company, 1948), 46–51, 113, 165, 178, 207.

9. Catherine Bramwell-Booth, *Catherine Booth* (London: Hodder and Stoughton, 1970), 341.

10. Jeb Stuart Magruder, *An American Life: One Man's Road to Watergate* (New York: Atheneum, 1974), 16, 304.

11. Barbara Johnson, *Beyond Heartache: Comfort and Hope for Hurting People* (Grand Rapids: Zondervan, 1978), 73–76.

12. Jane Swigart, *The Myth of the Bad Mother: The Emotional Realities of Mothering* (New York: Doubleday, 1991), 144.

13. Louis Genevie and Eva Margolies, *The Motherhood Report: How Women Feel About Being Mothers* (New York: Macmillan, 1987), 408.

CHAPTER 6

1. Wyn Wachhorst, *Thomas Alva Edison: An American Myth* (Cambridge, Mass.: MIT Press, 1981), 70–74.

2. Liz Smith, *The Mother Book* (Garden City, N.Y.: Doubleday, 1978), 40–43.

3. Ann Jones, *Women Who Kill* (New York: Holt, Rinehart and Winston, 1980), 249.

4. Paula Caplan, *Don't Blame Mother!* (New York: Harper & Row, 1989), 52.

5. Adrienne Rich, *Of Woman Born: Motherhood as Experience and Institution* (New York: W.W. Norton, 1986), 196–98.

6. Bruce Mazlish, *James and John Stuart Mill: Father and Son in the Nineteenth Century* (New York: Basic Books, 1975), 15–16.

7. *A Mother's Journal: A Book of Days* (Boston: Museum of Fine Arts, 1991), 14.

8. Ernest Jones, *The Life and Work of Sigmund Freud: The Formative Years and the Great Discoveries, 1856–1900*, Vol. 1 (New York: Basic Books, 1953), 3, 5, 16–17.

9. Bruce Mazlish, 17.

10. Ibid., 3, 152–54, 314.

11. Richard W. Wertz and Dorothy C. Wertz, *Lying-In: A History of Childbirth in America* (New Haven: Yale University, 1989), 188–89.

12. Ibid.

13. Jane Swigart, *The Myth of the Bad Mother: The Emotional Realities of Mothering* (New York: Doubleday, 1991), 33–37.

14. Elisabeth Badinter, *Mother Love, Myth and Reality: Motherhood in Modern History* (New York: Macmillan, 1980), ix, 215.

CHAPTER 7

1. Elizabeth Cady Stanton, *Eighty Years and More: Reminiscences, 1815–1897* (Boston: Northeastern University Press, 1993), 112.

2. Richard W. Wertz and Dorothy C. Wertz, *Lying-In: A History of Childbirth in America* (New Haven: Yale University, 1989), 115.

3. Liz Smith, *The Mother Book* (Garden City, N.Y.: Doubleday, 1978), 15–16.

4. Antonia Fraser, *The Weaker Vessel* (New York: Random House, 1984), 448–50.

5. Cited in Naomi Ruth Lowinsky, *Stories from the Motherline: Reclaiming the Mother-Daughter Bond, Finding Our Feminine Souls* (Los Angeles: Jeremy P. Tarcher, 1992), 37.

6. Richard W. Wertz and Dorothy C. Wertz, 22–23.

7. Selma R. Williams, *Divine Rebel: The Life of Anne Marbury Hutchinson* (New York: Holt, Rinehart and Winston, 1981), 188, 194.

8. Louis M. Notkin, ed., *Mother: Tributes from the World's Great Literature* (New York: Samuel Curl, 1943), 13.

9. G.H. Napheys, *The Physical Life of Women: Advice to the Maiden, Wife, and Mother* (Walthamstrow, Miss.: Mayhew, 1879), 141–93.

10. Madeleine L'Engle, *The Summer of the Great-Grandmother* (San Francisco: Harper & Row, 1974), 77–78.

11. Laurel Thatcher Ulrich, *A Midwife's Tale: The Life of Martha Ballard, Based on Her Diary, 1785–1812* (New York: Alfred A. Knopf, 1991), 203.

12. Malcolm Forbes with Jeff Bloch, *Women Who Made a Difference* (New York: Simon and Schuster, 1990), 143–46.

13. Suzanne Arms, *The Immaculate Deception: A New Look at Women and Childbirth in America* (New York: Houghton Mifflin, 1975).

CHAPTER 8

1. Katie May Gill, *Mother: Poems for Mother* (Richmond, Va.: Cavalier Press, 1957), 229.

2. Ruth A. Tucker, *From Jerusalem to Irian Jaya: A Biographical History of Christian Missions* (Grand Rapids: Zondervan, 1983), 101.

3. Kaye Halverson and K.M. Hess, *The Wedded Unmother* (Minneapolis: Augsburg, 1980), 77–78, 105, 121.

4. Cited in John Van Regemorter, Sylvia Van Regemorter, and Joe S. McIlhaney, Jr., *Dear God, Why Can't We Have a Baby?* (Grand Rapids: Baker, 1986), 59.

5. Anne Taylor Fleming, *Motherhood Deferred: A Woman's Journey* (New York: G.P. Putnam's Sons, 1994), 15–17, 134.

6. Ann Kiemel Anderson, *And with the Gift Came Laughter* (Wheaton: Tyndale, 1987), 18–20.

7. Elizabeth Wade White, *Anne Bradstreet: "The Tenth Muse"* (New York: Oxford University, 1971), 127–28.

8. Anna A. Gordon, *The Beautiful Life of Frances E. Willard* (Chicago: Woman's Temperance Publishing Association, 1898), 222.

9. Linda Atkinson, *Mother Jones: The Most Dangerous Woman in America* (New York: Crown, 1978), 32–36, passim.

10. Susan Tracy Rice, compiler, *Mothers' Day* (New York: Dodd, Mead and Company, 1941), 199–200.

11. Rita Kramer, *Maria Montessori: A Biography* (New York: G.P. Putnam's Sons, 1976), 94.

12. Louis M. Notkin, ed., *Mother: Tributes from the World's Great Literature* (New York: Samuel Curl, 1943), 77.

13. C. David Heymann, *A Woman Named Jackie* (New York: Carol Communications, 1989), 191–92, 200.

CHAPTER 9

1. Frances Hodgson Burnett, *The Secret Garden* (New York: J.B. Lippincott, 1949), 124–25, 127, 267, 276, 280, 282.

2. Cynthia Pearl Maus, *Christ and the Fine Arts* (New York: Harper & Brothers, 1959), 576.

3. Katharine Holland Brown, "The Mother," in *The Mothers' Anthology* compiled by William Lyon Phelps (New York: Doubleday, Doran & Co., 1940), 77–86.

4. Liz Smith, *The Mother Book* (Garden City, N.Y.: Doubleday, 1978), 1–2.

5. Louis M. Notkin, ed., *Mother: Tributes from the World's Great Literature* (New York: Samuel Curl, 1943), 64.

6. Eileen Simpson, *Orphans: Real and Imaginary* (New York: Weidenfeld & Nicolson, 1987), 164–65.

7. Susan Tracy Rice, compiler, *Mothers' Day* (New York: Dodd, Mead and Company, 1941), 296.

8. William Raeper, *George MacDonald* (Batavia, Ill.: Lion, 1987), 364, 383.

9. Anne Arnott, *The Secret Country of C.S. Lewis* (Grand Rapids: Eerdmans, 1975), 85–95.

10. Art Buchwald, *Leaving Home: A Memoir* (New York: G.P. Putnam's Sons, 1993), 11–12.

11. Christopher Andersen, *Madonna* (New York: Simon and Schuster, 1991), 23–26.

12. Letty Cottin Pogrebin, *Deborah, Golda, and Me: Being Female and Jewish in America* (New York: Crown, 1991), 15–16, 19–21.

CHAPTER 10

1. Susan Tracy Rice, compiler, *Mothers' Day* (New York: Dodd, Mead and Company, 1941), 256–58.

2. Elizabeth Wade White, *Anne Bradstreet: "The Tenth Muse"* (New York: Oxford University, 1971), 310–14.

3. Joan D. Hedrick, *Harriet Beecher Stowe: A Life* (New York: Oxford University Press, 1994), 128–29.

4. Karen Payne, ed, *Between Ourselves: Letters Between Mothers and Daughters, 1750–1982* (Boston: Houghton Mifflin, 1983), 91–94.

5. Jane Howard, *Margaret Mead: A Life* (New York: Simon and Schuster, 1984), 26–27.

6. Katherine and Richard Greene, *The Man Behind the Magic: The Story of Walt Disney* (New York: Penguin, 1991), 14–15.

7. Tom Landry with Gregg Lewis, *Tom Landry: An Autobiography* (Grand Rapids: Zondervan, 1990), 41.

8. Randall Riese, *Her Name Is Barbra: An Intimate Portrait of the Real Barbra Streisand* (New York: Carol Publishing, 1993), 22, 30, 206, 451.

9. Erma Bombeck, *Motherhood: The Second Oldest Profession* (New York: McGraw-Hill, 1983), 99–101.

10. Jeanne Hendricks, *A Mother's Legacy* (Colorado Springs: NavPress, 1988), 30.

CHAPTER 11

1. James Brabazon, *Albert Schweitzer: A Biography* (New York: G.P. Putnam's Sons, 1975), 27, 173–74, 266, 445.

2. Nancy Gibbs, "Murders They Wrote," *Time*, April 1, 1991, 29.

3. Anthony Holden, *Laurence Olivier* (New York: Atheneum, 1988), 15–22.

4. William Robert Faith, *Bob Hope: A Life in Comedy* (New York: G.P. Putnam's Sons, 1982), 32–33, 37, 71.

5. Ginger Rogers, *Ginger: My Story* (New York: HarperCollins, 1991), xii, 1, 3–12, 49, 399.

6. Albert Goldman, *Elvis* (New York: McGraw–Hill, 1981), 77, 115, 229–30, 283, 330, 345.

7. Stan Musial as told to Bob Broeg, *Stan Musial: "The Man's" Own Story* (Garden City, N.Y.: Doubleday, 1964), 19–20.

8. Mickey Rooney, *Life Is Too Short* (New York: Villard, 1991) 14–16, 23, 278.

9. A.E. Hotchner, *Doris Day: Her Own Story* (New York: William Morrow, 1976), 24–30, 147.

10. Daniel Mark Epstein, *Sister Aimee: The Life of Aimee Semple McPherson* (New York: Harcourt Brace Javanovich, 1993), 5–7, 131, 323, 339–41, 439.

CHAPTER 12

1. Trevor Dennis, *Sarah Laughed* (Nashville: Abingdon, 1994), 8, 31–32.

2. Alexander Whyte, *Bible Characters* (New York: Fleming H. Revell, n.d.), 34.

3. Laura Merrihew Adams, *Mothers* (Philadelphia: Union Press, 1924), 14–15.

4. H.V. Morton, *Women of the Bible* (New York: Dodd, Mead & Company, 1956) 14–15.

5. Virginia Stem Owens, *Daughters of Eve: Women of the Bible Speak to Women Today* (Colorado Springs: NavPress, 1995), 11.

6. Trevor Dennis, 58–59.

7. Alexander Whyte, *Bible Characters From the Old and New Testaments* (Grand Rapids: Kregel, 1986), 107–108.

8. Dee Brestin, *And Then We Were Women* (Wheaton: Victor, 1994), 46–47.

9. Virginia Stem Owens, *Daughters of Eve: Women of the Bible Speak to Women Today* (Colorado Springs: NavPress, 1995), 11.

10. William E. Phipps, *Assertive Biblical Women* (Westport, Conn.: Greenwood Press, 1992), 63–64.

11. Eleanor Doan, *A Mother's Sourcebook of Inspiration* (Grand Rapids: Zondervan, 1969), 99.

12. Mary Bosanquet, *The Life and Death of Dietrich Bonhoeffer* (New York: Harper & Row, 1968), 32–33, 45.

13. Edith Deen, *Great Women of the Christian Faith* (New York: Harper & Row, 1959), 99.

14. Laura Merrihew Adams, 79–80.

15. Ruth Bell Graham, *Sitting By My Laughing Fire* (Waco: Word, 1977), 154.

16. Virginia Stem Owens, 7.

CHAPTER 13

1. Herbert Lockyer, *All the Women of the Bible* (Grand Rapids: Zondervan, 1985), 302.

2. Caroline W. Bynum, *Jesus as Mother: Studies in the Spirituality of the High Middle Ages* (Berkeley: University of California Press,

1982), 114, 117.

3. Herbert Lockyer, 302.

4. Gayle Kimball, *The Religious Ideas of Harriet Beecher Stowe: Her Gospel of Womanhood* (New York: Edwin Mellen, 1982), 18–19.

5. Herbert Lockyer, 303.

6. Anonymous, cited in Elisabeth Elliot, *The Shaping of a Christian Family* (Nashville: Oliver Nelson, 1992), 190.

7. Laura Merrihew Adams, *Mothers* (Philadelphia: The Union Press, 1924) 120–26.

8. William Lyon Phelps, *The Mothers' Anthology,* (New York: Doubleday, 1940), xvi–xvii.

9. Ibid., 96.

10. Henry Davidoff, *The Pocket Book of Quotations* (New York: Pocket Books, Inc., 1942), 233.

11. John B. Judis, *William F. Buckley, Jr.: Patron Saint of the Conservatives* (New York: Simon and Schuster, 1988), 23.

CHAPTER 14

1. Anna A. Gordon, *The Beautiful Life of Frances E. Willard* (Chicago: Woman's Temperance Publishing Association, 1898), 46–47.

2. J. Harold Gwynne, compiler, *In Praise of Mothers* (Grand Rapids: Eerdmans, 1939), 54.

3. A. Gregory Schneider, "Focus on the Frontier Family," *Christian History* (Issue 45), 38–39.

4. Helen Russ Stough, compiler, *A Mother's Year* (New York: Fleming H. Revell, 1905), 136.

5. L. Penning, *Genius of Geneva: A Popular Account of the Life and Times of John Calvin* (Grand Rapids: Eerdmans, 1954), 11; Thea B. Van Halsema, *This Was John Calvin* (Grand Rapids: Baker, 1981), 11–13; Louis M. Notkin, ed., *Mother: Tributes from the World's Great Literature* (New York: Samuel Curl, 1943), 229.

6. Mildred P. Harrington, ed., *Mother's Day in Poetry* (New York: H.W. Wilson, 1926), 23.

7. Howard and Geraldine Taylor, *J. Hudson Taylor* (Chicago: Moody, 1978), 6–7.

8. Mabel Francis with Gerald B. Smith, *One Shall Chase a Thousand* (Harrisburg, Penn.: Christian Publications, 1968), 14, 16, 42.

9. Kathie Lee Gifford, *I Can't Believe I Said That!* (New York: Simon & Schuster, 1992), 296–300.

10. J. Harold Gwynne, 34.

11. Kate Douglas Wiggin, compiler, *To Mother: An Anthology of Mother Verse* (Miami: Granger Books, 1917), vii–viii.

12. Eleanor Doan, *A Mother's Sourcebook of Inspiration* (Grand Rapids: Zondervan, 1969), 45.

13. Louis M. Notkin, ed., *Mother: Tributes from the World's Great Literature* (New York: Samuel Curl, 1943), 142.

14. Eleanor Doan, 99.

15. Ibid., 100.

16. Ibid., 61.

17. Minnie Pearl with Joan Dew, *Minnie Pearl: An Autobiography* (New York: Simon and Schuster, 1980), 27–30.

18. Jerry Falwell, *Strength for the Journey: An Autobiography* (New York: Simon and Schuster, 1987), 43, 50,51, 59.

19. Marian Anderson, *My Lord What a Morning* (Madison: University of Wisconsin, 1992), 92–98.

CHAPTER 15

1. Helen Russ Stough, compiler, *A Mother's Year* (New York: Fleming H. Revell, 1905), 66.

2. Robert Payne, *The Life and Death of Adolf Hitler* (New York: Praeger, 1973), 17, 57, 59.

3. Malcolm Forbes with Jeff Bloch, *Women Who Made a Difference* (New York: Simon and Schuster, 1990), 280–83.

4. Elisabeth Badinter, *Mother Love, Myth and Reality: Motherhood in Modern History* (New York: Macmillan, 1980), 208–13.

5. Eleanor Doan, *A Mother's Sourcebook of Inspiration* (Grand Rapids: Zondervan, 1969), 99.

6. William Lyon Phelps, compiler, *The Mothers' Anthology,* (New York: Doubleday, 1940), 288.

7. Mildred P. Harrington, ed., *Mother's Day in Poetry* (New York: H.W. Wilson, 1926), 30.

8. Nancy Rubin: *The Mother Mirror: How a Generation of Women Is Changing Motherhood in America* (New York: G.P. Putnam's Sons, 1984), 49–51.

9. Sidney Olson: *Young Henry Ford: A Picture History of the First Forty Years* (Detroit: Wayne State University, 1963), 17–18.

10. Joseph Frazier Wall, *Andrew Carnegie* (Pittsburgh: University of Pittsburgh, 1989), 65, 71, 86, 128, 419, 421.

11. Mabel Bartlett Peyton and Lucia Kinley, *Mothers: Makers of Men* (New York: Robert M. McBride, 1927), 136, 144.

12. Peter Collier and David Horowitz, *The Kennedys: An American Drama* (New York: Simon and Schuster, 1984), 40, 49, 68.

13. Ralph G. Martin, *Golda: Golda Meir, The Romantic Years* (New York: Charles Scribner's Sons, 1988), 150–51.

CHAPTER 16

1. Judith Walzer Leavitt, *Brought to Bed: Childbearing in America, 1750–1950* (New York: Oxford University Press, 1986), 18.

2. Jean H. Baker, *Mary Todd Lincoln: A Biography* (New York: W.W. Norton, 1987), 211.

3. William Lyon Phelps, compiler, *The Mothers' Anthology* (New York: Doubleday, 1940), 219.

4. Harriet A. Jacobs, *Incidents in the Life of a Slave Girl Written By Herself*, edited by Jean Fagan Yellin (Cambridge, Mass.: Harvard University, 1987), 16.

5. Walter Fisher, ed, *Father Henson's Story of His Own Life* (New York: Corinth Books, 1962), 11–13; in Fishel and Quarles, eds, *The Negro American*, 87.

6. Carolly Erickson, *To the Scaffold: The Life of Marie Antoinette* (New York: William Morrow, 1991), 187, 216, 344.

7. Washington Irving, *The Sketch Book* (New York: Literary Classics, 1848), 147.

8. Anne Morrow Lindbergh, *Hour of God, Hour of Lead: Diaries and Letters, 1929–1932* (New York: Harcourt Brace Jovanovich, 1973), 212–13, 247, 248.

9. Frances Bradsher, *The Preacher Had 10 Kids* (Wheaton, Ill.: Tyndale, 1980), 37–40.

10. Jason Bonderoff, *Mary Tyler Moore: A Biography* (New York: St. Martin's, 1986), 139–49.

11. Chaim Herzog, *Heroes of Israel: Profiles of Jewish Courage* (New York: Little, Brown, 1989), 148–63.

12. James E. Seaver, *The Life of Mary Jemison* (Canandaigua: J.D. Bemis, 1924).

CHAPTER 17

1. Kate Douglas Wiggin, compiler, *To Mother: An Anthology of Mother Verse* (Miami: Granger Books, 1917), xvii–xxi.

2. Malcolm Forbes, *Women Who Made a Difference* (New York: Simon and Schuster, 1990), 106–8.

3. Edith G. Neisser, *Mothers and Daughters: A Lifelong Relationship* (New York: Harper & Row, 1967), 360–63.

4. Edith Wharton, *The Mother's Recompense* (New York: Grosset & Dunlap, 1925), 3, 12, 22, 37, 83, 276.

5. John Halperin, *The Life of Jane Austen* (Baltimore: Johns Hopkins University, 1984), 63, 144–45, 229, 285.

6. Darden Asbury Pyron, *Southern Daughter: The Life of Margaret Mitchell* (New York: Oxford University, 1991), 204–7, 240, 259.

7. Monica Stirling, *The Wild Swan: The Life and Times of Hans Christian Andersen* (New York: Harcourt, Brace & World, 1965), 24, 44–45.

8. Mark Sufrin, *Stephen Crane* (New York: Atheneum, 1992), 10–11, 88.

9. Jane Swigart, *The Myth of the Bad Mother: The Emotional Realities of Mothering* (New York: Doubleday, 1991), 84–85.

10. Ibid., 136.

CHAPTER 18

1. Alice Walker, *In Search of Our Mothers' Gardens* (New York: Harcourt Brace Jovanovich, 1983), 240–41.

2. Maynard Solomon, *Mozart: A Life* (New York: HarperCollins, 1995), 7, 10, 181–86.

3. David Sweetman, *Van Gogh: His Life and His Art* (New York: Crown, 1990), 14–15.

4. Nancy Hale, *Mary Cassatt* (Garden City, N.Y.: Doubleday, 1975), 175.

5. Jane Silverman Van Buren, *The Modernist Madonna: Semiotics of the Maternal Metaphor* (Bloomington, Ind.: Indiana University Press, 1989), 124–33.

6. Lawrence Thompson, *Robert Frost: The Early Years, 1874–1915* (New York: Holt, Rinehart and Winston, 1966), 19, 20, 44, 67, 539–41.

7. Liz Smith, *The Mother Book* (Garden City, N.Y.: Doubleday, 1978), 63.

8. Mabel Bartlett Peyton and Lucia Kinley, *Mothers: Makers of Men* (New York: Robert M. McBride, 1927), 45–46.

9. Arianna Stassinopoulos Huffington, *Picasso: Creator and Destroyer* (New York: Simon and Schuster, 1980), 15, 37–38.

CHAPTER 19

1. Lady Bird Johnson and Carlton B. Lees, *Wildflowers Across America* (New York: Abbeville, 1988), 8; Betty Boyd Caroli, *First Ladies* (New York: Oxford University, 1987), 238.

2. Julie Nixon Eisenhower, *Pat Nixon: The Untold Story* (New York: Simon and Schuster, 1986), 120, 169.

3. Liz Smith, *The Mother Book* (Garden City, N.Y.: Doubleday, 1978), 66.

4. Eleanor Doan, *A Mother's Sourcebook of Inspiration* (Grand Rapids: Zondervan, 1969), 100.

5. Joseph B. Baker, *Sermons on Our Mothers* (Philadelphia: Harvey M. Shelley, 1926), 88–89.

6. Fawn M. Brodie, *Thomas Jefferson: An Intimate History* (New York: W.W. Norton, 1974), 40.

7. Ibid., 40–43.

8. Edith B. Gelles, *Portia: The World of Abigail Adams* (Bloomington: Indiana University, 1992), 137–38.

9. Betty Boyd Caroli, *First Ladies* (New York: Oxford University Press, 1987), 52–53.

10. Edith Deen, *Great Women of the Christian Faith* (New York: Harper & Row, 1959), 227.

11. Michael Burlingame, *The Inner World of Abraham Lincoln* (Chicago: University of Illinois, 1994), 137, 94.

12. Eleanor Doan, 100.

13. H. Wayne Morgan, *William McKinley and His America* (Syracuse, New York: Syracuse University, 1963), 4, 5, 12, 270.

14. Eugene Lyons, *Herbert Hoover: A Biography* (Garden City, N.Y.: Doubleday, 1964), 4.

15. Bernard Asbell, ed, *Mother and Daughter: The Letters of Eleanor and Anna Roosevelt* (New York: Coward, McCann & Geoghegan, 1982), 9–10.

16. Doris Kearns, *Lyndon Johnson and the American Dream* (New York: Harper & Row, 1976), 24–25, 88–89.

17. David Kucharsky, *The Man from Plains* (New York: Harper & Row, 1976), 31–32.

18. Ronald Reagan, *An American Life* (New York: Simon and Schuster, 1990), 19–23.

19. George Bush with Victor Gold, *Looking Forward* (New York: Doubleday, 1987), 26–27.

CHAPTER 20

1. Malcolm X as told to Alex Haley, *The Autobiography of Malcolm X* (New York: Ballantine Books, 1964), 3–25.

2. Ruth A. Tucker, *Stories of Faith* (Grand Rapids: Zondervan, 1989), 312.

3. Louis Genevie and Eva Margolies, *The Motherhood Report: How Women Feel About Being Mothers* (New York: Macmillan, 1987), 367.

4. Liz Smith, *The Mother Book* (Garden City, N.Y.: Doubleday, 1978), 447.

5. Lena Horne and Richard Schickel, *Lena* (Garden City, N.Y.: Doubleday, 1956), 178–79, 298–99.

6. Naomi Judd, *Love Can Build a Bridge* (New York: Random House, 1993), 23, 29, 168.

7. Elizabeth O. Colton, *The Jackson Phenomenon: The Man, the Power, the Message* (New York: Doubleday, 1989), 160–61.

8. Ruth A. Tucker, "Working Mothers," *Christianity Today* (July 15, 1988), 18.

CHAPTER 21

1. Robert Bernard Martin, _Tennyson: The Unquiet Heart_ (New York: Oxford University Press, 1980), 17–20.

2. Page Smith, _Daughters of the Promised Land: Women in American History_ (Boston: Little, Brown and Company, 1970), 208–09.

3. Helen Russ Stough, compiler, _A Mother's Year_ (New York: Fleming H. Revell, 1905), 25.

4. Susan Tracy Rice, compiler, _Mothers' Day: Its History and Origin_ (New York: Dodd, Mead and Company, 1927), 24, 57.

5. Catherine Drinker Bowen, _Francis Bacon: The Tempter of a Man_ (Boston: Little, Brown and Company, 1963), 28, 59.

6. Edith Deen, _Great Women of the Christian Faith_ (New York: Harper & Row, 1959), 224.

7. Sonya Friedman, _Men Are Just Desserts_ (New York: Warner Books, 1983), 145–46.

8. Aissa Wayne with Steve Delsohn, _John Wayne: My Father_ (New York: Random House, 1991), 17, 58–59.

9. Matthew Josephson, _Edison: A Biography_ (New York: McGraw–Hill, 1959), 1, 14–16, 22, 84–85, 379.

10. Alistair Horne, _Harold Macmillan, 1894–1956_, Vol. 1 (New York: Viking, 1989), 11–13, 114.

11. Burton Stevenson, ed., _The Home Book of Quotations_ (New York: Dodd, Mead & Company, 1958), 1253.

12. Mabel Bartlett Peyton and Licia Kinley, _Mothers: Makers of Men_ (New York: Robert M. McBride, 1927), 24–28.

13. Katharine Anthony, _Louisa May Alcott_ (New York: Alfred A. Knopf, 1938), 38–39.

14. Louisa May Alcott, _The Selected Letters of Louisa May Alcott_, ed. by Joel Myerson and Daniel Shealy (Boston: Little, Brown and Company, 1987), 11.

15. Benjamin Spock, M.D., and Mary Morgan, _Spock on Spock: A Memoir of Growing Up with the Century_ (New York: Pantheon Books, 1985), 3, 5, 17–18.

16. Katharine Hepburn, _Me: Stories of My Life_ (New York: Alfred A. Knopf, 1991), 18–20.

17. C. Everett Koop, _Koop: The Memoirs of America's Family Doctor_ (New York: Random House, 1991), 13–14.

18. William Manchester, _American Caesar: Douglas MacArthur, 1880–1964_ (Boston: Little, Brown and Company, 1978), 42, 93, 134.

19. E. Paul Hovey, compiler, _The Treasury of Inspirational Anecdotes, Quotations and Illustrations_ (Westwood, N.J.: Fleming H. Revell, 1959), 179.

CHAPTER 22

1. Chaim Bermant, _The Walled Garden: The Saga of Jewish Family Life and Tradition_ (New York: Macmillan, 1975), 9, 51, 141.

2. K.P. Yohannan, _The Coming Revolution in World Missions_ (Alamonte Springs, Fla.: Creation House, 1986), 23–25.

3. Mildred P. Harrington, ed., _Mother's Day in Poetry_ (New York: H.W. Wilson, 1926), 18.

4. Edna Healey, _Wives of Fame: Mary Livingstone, Jenny Marx, Emma Darwin_ (1986), 8, cited in Rosalind Miles, _Women's History of the World_, 179–80.

5. Sheila Kitzinger, _Women As Mothers_ (New York: Random House, 1978), 78.

6. Gail Sheehy, _The Man Who Changed the World: The Lives of Mikhail S. Gorbachev_ (New York: HarperCollins, 1990), 34–35.

7. Anne Morrow Lindbergh, _Hour of God, Hour of Lead: Diaries and Letters, 1929–1932_ (New York: Harcourt Brace Jovanovich, 1973), 214.

8. Fatima Meer, _Higher Than Hope: The Authorized Biography of Nelson Mandela_ (New York: Harper & Row, 1988), 3–7.

9. Mary Lou Cummings, _Surviving without Romance: African Women Tell Their Stories_ (Scottdale, Penn.: Herald Press, 1991), 9.

10. Ross Terrill, _Mao: A Biography_ (New York: Harper & Row, 1980), 5, 10–13.

11. Tariq Ali, _An Indian Dynasty: The Story of the Nehru–Gandhi Family_ (New York: G.P. Putnam's Sons, 1985), 116–17, 131.

CHAPTER 23

1. Donald Thomas, _Robert Browning: A Life Within Life_ (New York: Viking, 1982), 95, 125–26.

2. Russell Baker, *Growing Up* (New York: New American Library, 1982), 1, 4, 5, 8.

3. Billy Graham, *Facing Death and the Life After* (Waco, Texas: Word Books, 1987), 93–94.

4. Madeleine L'Engle, *The Summer of the Great-Grandmother* (San Francisco: Harper & Row, 1974), 19–20, 37–38, 43.

5. Cynthia Pearl Maus, *Christ and the Fine Arts* (New York: Harper, 1959), 576.

6. Clifford Dowdey, *Lee* (Boston: Little, Brown and Company, 1965), 38, 47.

7. Bernard Sloan, *The Best Friend You'll Ever Have* (New York: Crown Publishers, 1980), 204, 210.

8. Faye Moskowitz, *A Leak in the Heart: Tales From a Woman's Life* (Boston: David R. Godine, 1985), 22–26.

CHAPTER 24

1. Anna A. Gordon, *The Beautiful Life of Frances E. Willard* (Chicago: Woman's Temperance Publishing Association, 1898), 214–16.

2. Carl F.H. Henry, *The Pacific Garden Mission: A Doorway to Heaven* (Grand Rapids: Zondervan, 1942), 41–46.

3. Thomas Curtis Clark and Esther A. Gillespie, compilers, *1000 Quotable Poems* (Chicago: Willett, Clark & Company, n.d.), 255.

4. Paul W. Tibbets, Jr. with Clair Stebbins and Harry Franken, *The Tibbets Story* (New York: Stein and Day, 1978), 197.

5. Eleanor Doan, *A Mother's Sourcebook of Inspiration* (Grand Rapids: Zondervan, 1969), 92.

6. Arthur Ashe and Arnold Rampersad, *Days of Grace* (New York: Alfred A. Knopf, 1993), 3–4.

7. Milbourne Christopher, *Houdini: The Untold Story* (New York: Thomas Y. Crowell, 1969), 6, 17, 132, 180.

8. Carol V.R. George, *God's Salesman: Norman Vincent Peale and The Power of Positive Thinking* (New York: Oxford University Press, 1993), 28, 96.

9. Louis M. Notkin, ed., *Mother: Tributes from the World's Great Literature* (New York: Samuel Curl, 1943), 202.

10. Ronald Pollitt and Virginia Wiltse, *Helen Steiner Rice: Ambassador of Sunshine* (Grand Rapids: Fleming H. Revell, 1994), 15–16, 148–49.

INDEX